TRANSFORMING EXPERIENCE
IN ORGANISATIONS

TRANSFORMING EXPERIENCE IN ORGANISATIONS

A Framework for Organisational Research and Consultancy

edited by

Susan Long

Routledge
Taylor & Francis Group

LONDON AND NEW YORK

First published 2016 by Karnac Books Ltd.

Published 2018 by Routledge
2 Park Square, Milton Park, Abingdon, Oxon OX14 4RN
711 Third Avenue, New York, NY 10017, USA

Routledge is an imprint of the Taylor & Francis Group, an informa business

British Library Cataloguing in Publication Data

A C.I.P. for this book is available from the British Library

 ISBN 9781782203483 (pbk)

Edited, designed and produced by The Studio Publishing Services Ltd
www.publishingservicesuk.co.uk
e-mail: studio@publishingservicesuk.co.uk

CONTENTS

ACKNOWLEDGEMENTS vii

ABOUT THE EDITOR AND CONTRIBUTORS ix

PREFACE xv

INTRODUCTION xix

CHAPTER ONE
The transforming experience framework 1
 Susan Long

CHAPTER TWO
Background to the TEF 15
 Bruce Irvine

CHAPTER THREE
The transforming experience framework and 31
unconscious processes: a brief journey through the
history of the concept of the unconscious as
applied to person, system, and context with an
exploratory hypothesis of unconscious as source
 Susan Long

CHAPTER FOUR
Reframing reality in human experience: 107
the relevance of the Grubb Institute's contributions
as a Christian foundation to group relations in
the post-9/11 world
      John Bazalgette and Bruce Reed

CHAPTER FIVE
Daring to desire: ambition, competition, and   135
role transformation in "idealistic" organisations
      Vega Zagier Roberts and John Bazalgette

CHAPTER SIX
Working to improve institutional strength: 155
the challenge of taking multiple roles in
multiple systems
      Rebekah O'Rouke and John Bazalgette

CHAPTER SEVEN
Finding, making, and taking role: a case study   175
from the complexity of inter-agency dynamics
      Aarti Kapoor

CHAPTER EIGHT
Transitioning tasks in an impossible context through   189
use of drawings: a case example
      Rose Redding Mersky

CHAPTER NINE
Connectedness with source: our collective reality   195
      John Bazalgette (in conversation with Bruce Irvine)

CHAPTER TEN
The experience of connectedness with source: how does   231
one's understanding of connectedness with source
contribute to thinking about accountability in role?
      Marjoleine Hulshof

INDEX   243

ACKNOWLEDGEMENTS

We thank Jason Long for his cover design using the image of a sculpture by Luigi Galligani (www.luigigalligani.it). When I asked Luigi why he modelled mermaids, he said it was because they were both beautiful and dangerous. Just as mermaids are both beautiful and dangerous, so is the unconscious in organisations. Hence, the cover to this book.

Thanks to Maurita Harney, who read the early sections in Chapter Two and who supported my writing (Susan Long).

I am greatly indebted to Phillip Boxer for providing me with reading and modifying the section on Lacan in Chapter Two. Of course, I take full responsibility for any mistakes or misconceptions (Susan Long).

Chapter Four opens with some reflections on the significance of group relations thinking in the global context. Utilising the transcript of a paper presented by Bruce Reed to a meeting of the Great Britain and Ireland Group Relations Forum held at the Tavistock Institute of Human Relations on 21 February 2003, it outlines ways that The Grubb Institute has developed its own group relations work. Bruce Reed worked with John Bazalgette to develop the transcript of Reed's paper and together they worked on sections of this essay until Bruce's death on 4 November 2003. John Bazalgette is responsible for the final version and wishes to acknowledge the contribution of his colleagues, but to give special thanks to Professor Kathleen B. Jones for her help in reducing a very long paper, to Amy Fraher for helping to clarify the more obscure passages, and to Karen Izod for her suggestions and encouragement about the final writing. The final version of this chapter (with some minor edits) was originally printed as "Accessing reality: reframing human experience: the relevance of The Grubb Institute's contributions as a Christian foundation to group relations in the post-9/11 world" in Organisational and Social Dynamics, 5(2): 192-224), edited by Laurence J. Gould and Paul Hoggett (published by Karnac in 2005), and is reprinted with kind permission of Karnac Books.

Chapter Five was first presented as a paper at the Symposium of the International Society for the Psychoanalytic Study of Organisations in 2006: The Dark Side of Competition.

In Chapter Six, the authors say "we are indebted to Alan Flintham (2010) for the phrase 'reservoirs of hope', whose book about head-teachers is entitled *Reservoirs of Hope* (Cambridge Scholars Publishing). However, he uses the term in a significantly different way from us".

The work of the Grubb is currently being taught in The Masters Philosophy of Social Innovation, offered by Crossfields Institute in co-operation with Alanus University. It offers a pathway in organisational analysis and leadership which is designed and facilitated by the Grubb School of Organisational Analysis and Leadership (www.grubbschool.org.uk).

John Bazalgette, for over fifty years, has been exploring the kind of organisational leadership that enrols the passions of men, women, and children to serve the best purposes of the organisations that bring them together. He has learnt from children, parents, teachers, employ-ers, senior executives, clergy, probation officers, prison governors, public servants, and others that engaging people's untapped resour-ces is, at one and the same time, both simple and exceedingly difficult. His work has taken him into many different cultures and countries. He has lectured, written, and broadcast about what he has learnt. He has led the Grubb Institute's development of its higher education programmes in Leadership and Organisational Analysis over the past ten years. His current interest is in how values, beliefs, faith (or no faith) can be drawn upon as potent resources in working to purpose, wherever one is in a working organisation. He is currently a senior organisational analyst, an Honorary Fellow of the Grubb School of Organisational Analysis, and Visiting Professor at the Indian Institute of Management Ahmedabad.

Marjoleine Hulshof is an organisational analyst and programme co-director for "Leading at the Edge—Organisational Analysis in the

Now", a societal, systemic and experiential approach for organisational transformation. She is also a sailor, life-long learner, and musician. As an organisational analyst, her passion is to create spaces in which the full human experience and energy present in organisations and its leadership is released, to reveal the core purpose of why and how we do our work and co-create the way forward to unleash possibilities and performance. She works in a variety of cultures, languages, sectors, and organisations with senior leaders, leadership teams, and whole systems. Her approach integrates experiential and action learning with systems thinking and psychodynamic approaches to organisational transformation, including insights from new sciences, the arts, and spirituality. She is an experienced executive coach, certified for The Leadership Circle™, a 360° Leadership Profile, and as a facilitator she is well versed in using Appreciative Inquiry, World Cafe, Open Space, Theory U (Scharmer) and Values Centre's Culture Values Assessments. She is also Leadership Development & Learning Networks Specialist for the Caribbean Leadership Project, a seven-year integral project funded by the Canadian DFATD to strengthen public sector leadership in thirteen participating Caribbean countries through leadership development programmes, communities of practice, building an enabling environment, and strengthening governance frameworks.

Bruce Irvine (see biographical notes in the Preface).

Aarti Kapoor is the founder and Managing Director of Embode, an international consultancy on human rights, responsible business, and organisational analysis. She provides consultancy on issues ranging from child protection in the tourism industry (child safe tourism) to evaluating and eradicating child labour and slavery from global cocoa supply chains. Her clients include international businesses and intergovernmental organisations, as well as non-governmental organisations. Prior to this role, Aarti held various management and leadership posts working on issues of child exploitation and human trafficking in the UK and Southeast Asia. She is a candidate for the Masters Programme "Leading at the Edge: Organisational Analysis in the {Now}" of the Grubb School and Crossfields Institute and is undertaking her research with a UN anti human trafficking project. Aarti holds an LLB, an LLM and is a qualified member of the Bar of England and Wales (UK) and New York State (US).

Susan Long Susan Long supervises research students and conducts organisational research at a variety of universities including INSEAD in Singapore, MIECAT, University of Melbourne, University of Divinity in Melbourne, and Crossfields Institute. As an organisational consultant in private practice, she works with organisational change, executive coaching, board development, role analysis, team development, and management training. She originally trained as a clinical psychologist and psychotherapist. Her experience of working with people as individuals and in groups and organisations gives her a broad perspective on management practices. Susan's capacity as a teacher and organisational consultant/researcher has resulted in her being invited on to the boards of prestigious organisations and elected on to the committees of professional bodies. She is a member of the Board of the Judicial College of Victoria and of Comcare's advisory board for the Center of Excellence for Research into Mental Health at Work. She was the founding President of Group Relations Australia and a past president of the International Society for the Psychoanalytic Study of Organisations. Her participative action research has attracted grants through the Australian research Council and industry. She has published six books and many journal articles.

Rose Redding Mersky, MS, has been an organisational development consultant and executive coach for twenty-five years. She has taken various roles in group relations conferences internationally and offers workshops in various methodologies, such as organisational role analysis, social dream-drawing, organisational observation, social photo-matrix, and social dreaming. She is an International Honorary Trustee of the Gordon Lawrence Foundation for the Promotion of Social Dreaming. She has been a member of the International Society for the Psychoanalytic Study of Organisations (ISPSO) for twenty-five years and served as its first female president. Her publications have focused primarily on the practice of consultation. She is currently studying for her doctorate at the Centre for Psycho-Social Studies at the University of West England in Bristol. She lives and works in Germany.

Rebekah O'Rourke specialises in leadership development, organisational purpose, and the leadership of whole system transformation programmes. Working globally, she develops and directs experiential learning programmes and stimulates partnerships exploring what is called forth from leaders and organisations in a changing global economy and market. She has worked in various capacities across Africa, the USA, the UK, and South America, including senior and executive level organisational roles. Sectors include: aid and development, engineering and construction, education, telecommunications, information technology, and retail. She is a director of the Grubb Guild Masters Programne, "Leading at the Edge: Organisational Analysis in the {Now}".

Bruce Reed (2.2.1920–4.11.2003), was a cleric and organisational analyst. In 1957, he was involved in setting up the Christian Teamwork Trust. From this sprang a series of charities, many of which still exist to day: the Richmond Fellowship, supporting the mentally ill; Langley House, rehabilitating ex-prisoners; the Abbeyfield Society, providing homes in the community for the elderly. For more than thirty years, Bruce was involved in the Lyndhurst Club for disadvantaged young people in Kentish Town, north London. Bruce founded the Grubb Institute of Behavioural Studies, an applied social research institute, working for government departments, businesses, and other bodies around the world. From 1980, Bruce designed and led conferences for parish clergy which transformed the way they understood their roles as servants of whole communities, not simply their gathered congregations. In 1990, he was awarded a Lambeth degree of MLitt for his "very valuable services to the church" by Archbishop Robert Runcie.

Vega Zagier Roberts trained as a psychiatrist and psychotherapist in the USA, coming to the UK in 1984 as a Fellow of the Action Research Training Programme at the Tavistock Institute of Human Relations. From 2005–2014 she was a senior organisational analyst at The Grubb Institute. She is a faculty member of the MA "Leading and Consulting: Psychodynamic and Systemic Approaches" (Tavistock & Portman NHS Trust with the University of East London), a senior associate of the Health Service Management Centre at the University of Birmingham, a consulting associate of Tavistock Consulting (Tavistock and Portman NHS Foundation Trust), and a member of the international editorial board of *Organisational and Social Dynamics*. Vega works with executive, management and operational teams mainly in the public and voluntary sector, and supervises consultants and coaches with a special interest in developing leadership potential at all levels of an organisation. She explores how our desires, values and purpose can be aligned to enable us, personally and collectively, to find new freedom and energy to make a difference. Vega has lectured and run workshops on leadership and change in Europe and the USA, has contributed papers to books and professional journals, and is co-editor of *The Unconscious at Work: Individual and Organisational Stress in the Human Services*.

To Bruce Irvine: 1961–2015

This book is dedicated to Bruce Irvine, who was a person with a mission; not a simple mission, but a profound one. This mission was about regime change. He began that mission, as those in South Africa know, in the struggle that led up to the accession of Nelson Mandela as President, but he continued it once he arrived in the UK. In particular, drawing on his skill as a clinical psychologist working with children, he expanded his field of work from the support of seriously damaged individuals to the organisational circumstances that created the conditions which caused that damage. His approach to regime change was not about replacing one group with another who simply reproduced the ills of their predecessors under a different banner: the familiar "flip-flop" of most revolutions. Bruce was about transforming cultures so that freedom, justice, and mercy could prevail.

He arrived at the Grubb Institute while it was being led by the Reverend Bruce Reed, an Australian Anglican priest. From Reed, Irvine learnt new ways of thinking about Jesus of Nazareth and the implications of his teaching about leadership in society. This invigorated Bruce's own thinking about the kind of regime change that is called for when one pays attention to the movement of the Spirit in the immediate present. He joined the staff of the Grubb Institute in

2002 and took on the executive directorship in 2003. The Institute had a body of action research stretching back over fifty years, in which faith, belief, values, and spirituality were central to its approach to purpose. Bruce could see the rich resource that these provided to the ministry to which he was called. What he could also see was that the Institute that Bruce Reed had founded needed to expand from being known as a primarily church-based, English institution to one that was experienced as being part of a global movement addressing the major issues facing the world today.

Therefore, he opened up two initiatives.

The first was to seek to engage with the leaders of major organisations that serve human wellbeing across the world. He set out to reveal the underlying impact of the unexamined assumptions made by those in leadership positions on every continent. He engaged with leaders in business, finance, education, government, NGOs, and religious bodies to explore ways of challenging assumptions courageously and, thus, revealing untapped resources which could fulfil more effectively the true, underlying purposes of the institutions those men and women led. This approach was similar to that of which Jesus of Nazareth spoke when he told his listeners "Don't think I have come to abolish the law and the prophets: I have come to fulfil them" (Matthew 5.17). Bruce Irvine was not about toppling establishments, but about enabling those in power to see the abundant potential that was available to them to fulfil the higher purposes for which they and others yearn. His faith in the Almighty (though not a conventional one) was something he drew on profoundly and from which he derived strength in his demanding mission, even in the darkest times. He assembled a new network of men and women across the world whom he inspired to join him in this new mission of regime change. They are committed to taking forward the work that Bruce began, now galvanised by their experience of their loss of him in person.

The second initiative was to lead the Grubb Institute into becoming one whose purpose was more clearly educational. In this work, he led the Institute into becoming widely visible as an organisation with a body of understanding about human experience and ways of imparting that to those in leadership positions. This is now recognised as the discipline of organisational analysis. The move to become the Grubb School of Organisational Analysis, with its Masters' degree in Leadership and Organisational Analysis offered through the Alanus

University's School of the Philosophy of Social Innovation, is both the authentic evolution of Bruce Reed's founding vision of the Christian Teamwork Trust in 1957 (which became the Grubb Institute in 1969), and the true validity of Bruce Irvine's transformative impact on the Grubb Institute which he took over from Bruce Reed.

In Bruce Irvine's passing, we have lost a great deal personally, but he has gifted us and the world with a magnificent legacy. If you wish to understand more the nature of this legacy, read the papers in this book.

John Bazalgette, on behalf of the editor
and all contributors to this book.

Introduction

The chapters in this book expand on different aspects of the model described in the opening chapter. This is the "transforming experience into authentic action in role framework" (hereafter referred to more briefly as the transforming experience framework (TEF)). The intention of bringing this collection together is to demonstrate how the model can be used in organisational analysis, research, and consulting. The chapters have been written by practitioners and by staff and students of programmes teaching in the light of this framework and using depth psychology and socioanalytic approaches (Long, 2013a). The framework has been gradually developed over many years with evolving versions being tried and tested in organisational research and consulting, but has not been comprehensively described previously. The framework is in constant evolution and should be regarded as a living model, responsive to new ways of thinking and to changes in organisational experiences and contexts.

The chapters use the TEF for examining both theoretical and practical issues in the field of socioanalysis and systems psychodynamics.

Chapter One introduces the TEF.

Chapter Two is taken from transcriptions of two talks given by Bruce Irvine. The first is part of his presentation to the Branding

Workshop of the Grubb Guild early in 2015: "Working with the emergent: the brand of the Guild". This talk outlined the three pillars and six principles of the Grubb Guild. The second was a talk that traced some of the history of the development of the TEF, given to participants in the Grubb Guild Master's programme. "Leading at the Edge: Organisational Analysis in the {Now}" at the Crossfields Institute.

Chapter Three examines the idea of unconscious processes and utilises the TEF to explore the history of this idea. The "unconscious" or unconscious processes were described and thought about long before Sigmund Freud discovered the method of free association to access these processes. This chapter explores the unconscious as understood through the experiences of persons and how it appears as a concept in roles, systems, and contexts. The idea of unconscious as source—first appearing in the work of the philosopher Schelling—is examined.

Chapter Four is a reworked paper by John Bazalgette and the late Bruce Reed, looking at the history of the work of the Grubb Institute (now the Grubb Guild) through its group relations work. Titled "Reframing reality in human experience", it uses ideas and concepts from the TEF, focusing on the ethical accountabilities that we have as human beings. It examines the experiences of group relations conferences as here-and-now evidence of our connectedness across all human differences.

Chapters Five through to Eight provide case examples of work that can be understood through the lens of the TEF. In Chapter Five, Vega Roberts and John Bazalgette present a case study set in what they term an "idealistic organisation". This chapter demonstrates the progress that can be made when using the TEF to aid managers in changing their perspectives.

Chapter Six, by Rebekah O"Rouke and John Bazalgette, examines the complexities of working from multiple roles in multiple systems. This calls for a readiness to handle the reality that, in modern society, systems overlap one another and normal life involves prioritising the demands of differing systems. Role holders with an understanding of the forces and factors at play in relation to multiple roles and multiple systems are, therefore, better equipped to serve the purpose and contribute to institutional strength.

Chapter Seven provides a case study completed by Aarti Kapoor, one of the participants in the Grubb Masters programme: "Leading at the Edge: Organisational Analysis in the {Now}". The chapter provides a partial record of her journey as a team leader of a donor-funded, NGO child protection project, and the challenges she faced in this role. Framing her role in terms of the TEF allowed new perspectives to be opened and new solutions to be found to seemingly intractable problems.

In Chapter Eight, Rose Mersky describes a consulting intervention, only later seen, in light of the TEF theory in this book, as a way of helping a group transition itself from its original impossible task to a more reasonable and fulfilling one. Unable to find an authorised consulting role during an important meeting, the author began to draw in order to understand the situation as revealed in the discussion around the table. This personal drawing transitioned into a group drawing and, ultimately, served as a transitional object for them all to reframe their purpose and goals for a very important roll-out of a new product.

Drawing particularly on the domain of "connectedness with source" to interpret lived experience, Chapter Nine offers three vignettes to explore the theme. An approach to human development is outlined, drawing especially on the work of Winnicott and his thinking about illusion as a necessary part of human maturation. Following this, links are made with leadership and organisational analysis developed through the Grubb Institute's work over fifty years. This focuses on the way faith, belief, and spirituality provide potent resources in addressing the challenges of accountable living in today's interconnected world—and, indeed, interconnected universe. Connectedness with source is an essential part of the authentic process of finding, making, and taking roles that make a difference in today's world. From the three examples of lived experience, meaning is surfaced.

The final chapter outlines the journey of the author, Marjoleine Hulshof, as she discovers source as a powerful enabler in her work and life.

Reference

Long, S. D. (Ed.) (2013). *Socioanalytic Methods: Discovering the Hidden in Groups and Organisations*. London: Karnac.

CHAPTER ONE

The transforming experience framework

Susan Long

Introduction

Decisions, conscious or not, are at the basis of social interactions. It could be said that a work organisation is made up
of a network of decisions: people deciding policies; how to
approach work tasks; what processes to engage; strategies; answers to
give others; managing resources; deciding budgets. Organisation is a
social structure of interacting roles making decisions and taking
action from those decisions.

We all make decisions constantly throughout our daily lives, at
work, at home, and in our leisure times. Sometimes, decisions are
made consciously with a great deal of thought and consultation with
others. Many everyday decisions are made out of habit and we are
barely conscious that we have been making a decision. Other decisions are driven by influences outside our awareness.

This book will look at a model for examining those influences that
are largely out of our awareness. We tend, at least in western cultures
to think of ourselves as autonomous, independent individuals. We
pride ourselves on being "self-made". Yet, our behaviours, the decisions we make, and actions we take are strongly influenced, if not

largely determined, by influences, both internal and external to ourselves, of which we do not hold an ongoing awareness. The model aids in identifying and bringing to awareness these influences. It enables us to see our organisations and social systems from a multi-layered perspective. Through the lens provided, it enables us to discern the influences from within our complex psyches, from the roles we take up, the systems we are embedded in, the wider contexts of life, and from the sources behind our purposes that sustain and direct us.

The transforming experience framework

The transforming experience framework (TEF) explores how people can take authentic action through taking up role: the full name of the model being "The transforming experience into authentic action through role". Although the idea of role evokes the notion of "acting" in a theatrical context, it is used here to describe a social "position". Role is, then, a systemic concept, defined in terms of the other roles with which it interacts. Its origin as an idea in the theatre does give us some clues, however. "Role" can be distinguished from "person" in so far as different people may take up particular roles in a group, just as different actors might play the role of Hamlet in Shakespeare's play. The roles available in a group are circumscribed by their positional relation to other roles, just as the actor is circumscribed by his written lines in relation to the lines of other actors. Just as any actor gives his own imprint to the role of Hamlet, so do people enact group roles in their own ways.

None the less, the situation is more complex than a simple distinction would have it. Without an incumbent, a role is nothing but an empty description. With a person in the role, it becomes alive and real. The role incumbent might only be in the imagination of the reader of a play or novel. This is enough. The character becomes alive. To demonstrate this point, one only needs remember the times when, after reading a book and on seeing a film adaptation, the film actor seems quite different to the character you imagined. It is the person-in-role that has an impact. Can we think of Scarlett O'Hara without thinking of Vivienne Leigh, or Mr Bean without Rowan Atkinson?

To add to the complexity of the idea of role, it might not be sharply defined as a character. A role could be a particular emotional role in a group, or a task or political role in an organisation. Again, such emotional, task, or political roles both affect and are affected by the people who are in those roles. When we think of pacifism, do we also think of Ghandi? When we think of the role of dictator, might we think of Stalin? And, indeed, the reciprocal effect is fundamental: the positional roles that people take up in social or work systems themselves have an effect on behaviours and, in turn, influence how personalities develop. Many people adopt the character traits of their trades or professions in their personal lives.

The idea of systemic processes means that roles are interrelated. Each role has an influence on other roles. Take a family system, for instance. The parental roles have an effect on how children take up their roles in the family: who does what, when, and where, for example. The nature of the child affects the way that the parent takes on his or her parenting. Birth order also gives rise to different roles—the older, middle, or younger children having different influences on each other and on the parents. Parents form a subsystem as a couple; siblings also have a subsystem, and other subsystems emerge at different times, perhaps based on gender, or interests, or power struggles.

Role in work systems is not a simple position description or set of instructions. It is more dynamic and complex. The task system is made up of particular roles that are taken up in relation to tasks and those tasks in turn are related to organisational purpose. The task system has many roles that influence each other. Moreover, there is a continual process of negotiation between roles as the role holders go about engaging tasks together. An example might be a school staff. While each teacher has his or her subject realm, the curriculum must be integrated overall and some subject matter will overlap. How lessons are designed and how the school as a whole operates involves a process of negotiation in conjunction with leadership roles.

The domains of experience

Roles taken up at work, at home, or in social contexts are situated at the intersection of four domains of experience: the experience of being a person (psychological), the experience of being in a system (e.g., organisations, institutions), the experience of being in a context (social, economic, political, global), and the experience of connectedness with source, that is, the spiritual domain that perhaps might be understood as the domain of deeply held values. Alternatively, source may be seen as that domain that links us to the whole of humankind in its connectedness to the natural and physical worlds. Each of these can be explored and explained using many conceptual models drawn from a range of disciplines. Because these domains of experience are located in, and intrinsically linked to, social systems and contexts, action through role means action on behalf of a broader system. The action is taken by a person in a particular role at a particular moment in the history of that system (i.e., the context) in the light of an overall purpose (link with source). This might or might not be consciously apprehended by those making the actions.

Over the past thirty years working with whole of system interventions, Grubb Institute consultants have discovered the importance of working across these four dimensions and developed the TEF in their work with organisations and social systems. The Institute has now been transformed into a Guild—"a global network of consultants and like-minded organisations that are committed to making an active and sustainable difference to individuals, organisations and societies in the World which we have all co-created" (www.grubb.org.uk/about-us/33 9/03/2014). The TEF provides a framework for a broad range of professionals from different disciplinary backgrounds who embrace a broad range of beliefs, purposes, and theories.

As a framework, rather than a specific theory, the TEF offers a dynamic, facilitative tool. Workplace situations can be seen through a systemic lens and dilemmas and problems can be approached in ways that avoid "personalisation" of issues.

The framework focuses on experience, with the idea that experiences are filtered through different lenses. In exploring the system experience of a new Master of Science degree conducted by the Guild, the programme directors make it clear that these different lenses are part of a whole.

This exploration suggests an assumption that the experience of *person* and the experience of *system* are being understood as if they were necessarily incompatible and that there is a perspective in parts of the programme system that person or feelings are ignored when working systemically: that this is almost the "cost" of working systemically. However, the reality, in our experience, is that personhood is essential to a system and the system is essential to the person.

Integrally, our experience is always composed of both—and of context and connectedness with source. The framework's full title is the "Framework for transforming experience into authentic action through role". Our experience is an integrated whole, which can be viewed through different lenses in order to enable us to work out how to take action in role. It enables brain and heart to be brought into energetic alignment and the resulting energy to be put to work (internet post to the programme members—staff and students, March 2014).

The framework

The TEF framework (Figure 1.1) centres round role because it is within roles that decisions can be made and actions taken. Persons take up roles and act from within their constraints—both explicit and tacit or implicit. However, the traditional egocentric way of seeing persons at the centre of all things can be challenged through the framework. The challenge comes from looking not from the "inside out" (person to group), but from the "outside in" (seeing the group and context first).

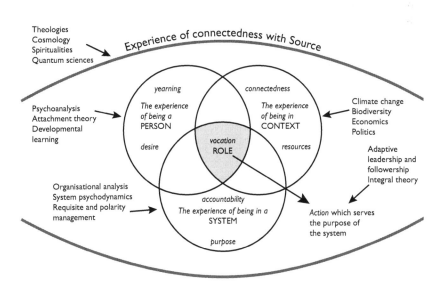

Figure 1.1. Transforming experience into authentic action through role (TEF).

This enables us to see the many influences around us, to take on different perspectives, and to understand diversity. It enables us to see the "bigger picture" and to contemplate issues beyond ourselves.

Persons in roles are subject to the pushes and pulls of forces well beyond them, forces that originate in systems and contexts. For example, in the context of country, there are expectations put upon people's actions through the laws of the land. In an organisation or company, authority is conferred on roles and accountabilities exist for performance in the light of that authority. In an office or a family, there are many overt rules of behaviour, but also covert, unspoken rules of relationship. All these influence how we behave in role. This can be understood if we distinguish the person from the office they hold. The office or role demands certain behaviours, certain responsibilities and value stances, even if the person is challenged by such demands.

The following briefly outlines each of the domains of experience indicated in the framework. It should be noted that the framework is not a particular theory, but a way of integrating several theories within an overall framework.

Person

Practically everyone intuitively understands the idea of being a person. The person is the locus of subjectivity and conscious experience. Yet personhood is achieved through a complex process of psychological and physical development. Winnicott (1958), for example, demonstrates how infants go through a process of integration, personalisation, and reality testing in order to achieve a sense of self. Indeed, the whole of the discipline of developmental psychology shows that the continuous development of personhood—emotionally, intellectually, physically, and in terms of relationships—is a continuous journey. The experience of being a person includes developing and transforming an identity through the different ages and contexts of life. It also involves the development of intellect, skills, and what Bion (1970) calls the apparatus for thinking the thoughts that exist in the social context around us. It involves the construction of a personality, the adoption of values and purposes, and the creation of personal strategies for managing emotional and relational life. All of these developments occur through genetic and environmental influences largely outside our personal volition. Our capacities consciously to steer our own destinies are hard won through increasing experiences of ourselves in our world and our capacity to learn from those experiences and adapt our learning in new situations. Even then, such capacities are necessarily constrained by context and physical and social factors: social inequalities and availability of resources and technologies, for example.

In the TEF model, the experience of being a person is impelled by both desire and yearning. Psychoanalysis has extensively demonstrated the power that conscious and unconscious desires have on our behaviour and our conscious experience. The changing vicissitudes of desires form the central dynamics of personhood and infiltrate the way we take up roles and experience their effects. Less discussed in psychoanalytic and psychological literature is the idea of yearning. Yearning is the experience of deep and extensive longing. Although it might be regarded as deep desire, the meaning given here differentiates it from the desires stemming directly from bodily needs and egoistic concerns. Yearning, in psychological terms, is established through the process of sublimation, where desire becomes linked to a purpose beyond the ego. In spiritual terms, yearning is the link between person and source. It is the longing of the spirit or soul and impels the person towards finding meaning and identity within a purpose beyond the self.

System

We are all born into social systems: our family, our local community, and our country are some that come immediately to mind. These systems have their own cultures, languages, and rules and they generally have a place for us to fit into, and expectations about us. These systems influence and constrain us in our personal development. As we grow, we become part of an increasing network of systems: school, work organisations, social and sporting groups, perhaps religious or political groups. The rules and cultural patterns, both conscious and unconscious, of these systems figure greatly in the pushes and pulls to which persons in roles are subject.

If we are to take the "outside in" perspective, then the system claims a priority in our thinking. The family, for instance, has a place, a name (at least, the family name), and even a fantasised identity for a new child before he or she is born. This becomes cemented with the birth of a new child, who might be seen to have her mother's eyes and her father's nose, and even personality characteristics that, as she grows, she will come to take into her identity. In this way, the system has a great influence on the person and the roles that are played by that person. The organisation, as another example, has a position description and perhaps a history for the role that a new employee is to take up.

People come together in systems in order to fulfil their needs and desires: in work systems, this includes the need to produce products and services. That is, systems have a purpose. The experience of being in a system brings forward the tension between personal needs and desires and the needs and desires of others. Sociology has studied in depth the nature of social systems and how they are formed and operate. Theories range from ideas about social contracts, both conscious and unconscious, through to social and biological ideas of the basis of social connectedness. In the TEF model, attention to the purpose of the system and accountability for one's role within the system enables the tensions between individual and group to be managed. This does not mean that these tensions disappear. On the contrary, good management (by self or others) has to constantly work at the boundary of person and system, allowing the experience of person, in role, in the system to be effective and purposeful while also being nurturing and supportive of the health and wellbeing of persons.

Systems can take on a life of their own, often referred to as the "culture" of the group, organisation, or society. Bion (1961) has described how group cultures become established at a deeply unconscious level and affect the dynamics of the group, especially in relation to leadership. Menzies (1970) introduced the idea of organisational defences against anxiety where group and organisational structures and processes are organised at an unconscious level to protect their members from anxieties inherent in the tasks undertaken. These defences may, in turn, create new anxieties and present as symptoms of complex organisational problems (Armstrong & Rustin, 2015). Neurotic, psychotic, and perverse organisational cultures have each been described (Kets de Vries & Miller, 1984; Long, 2008; Sievers, 2006) all structured by dynamics at the systemic level. The literature in this area is vast. It demonstrates the effect of systemic dynamics, beyond the ken or control of any one individual, on behaviour.

It should also be noted that organisations are made up of many systems of roles and decision-making from roles. These may be work or task sub-systems, but also social, political, emotional, linguistic, etc. systems within which people take up roles.

Context

The idea of context speaks for itself. It is the environment within which a social system occurs. That environment includes the physical, political, economic, social, historical, international, and emotional context for the system. What is currently occurring in the context will have an effect on persons, organisations, and social systems.

Sometimes, we might not be aware of contextual issues, but they still affect us. For instance, climate change and its effects on species survival might not seem to affect us directly, but loss of some insect species could affect food production and the direct effect on us might be in prices. Similarly, we might be unaware of the way we perceive different groups of people due to political or economic contextual issues and their presentation in the media and, hence, the effects this has on our judgements and decisions about them.

Awareness of context allows us to discern the resources and connections that may be found there. The experience of connectedness to context enables the use of resources in a sustainable, rather than an exploitative, manner.

Source

The *Oxford Dictionary* gives the following meanings for source: "1. A place, person, or thing from which something originates or can be obtained; and 2. A body or process by which energy or a particular component enters a system".

In terms of a spiritual source, God, a deity, or even natural forces (e.g., Gaia) may be the source. In more secular terms, source may come from an overall purpose beyond individual egos—a communal purpose or a historical, cultural dynamic.

In the TEF framework, we can look at how person, role, system, and context are connected with their source. Often, the source must be discovered through a process of enquiry and connection: for instance, prayer, meditation, body awareness, the arts, cultural ritual, or socio-analytic practice. Source is not always self-evident and might be deeply unconscious, requiring reflective methods, both individual and group, in order to gain access.

The idea in the framework of connectedness with source was arrived at after much thought and discussion. Initially, this part of the framework looked at connectedness with the other and with all others. The moral philosopher John Macmurray (1935) makes the point that, to be truly responsible human beings, we need to include bearing in our minds the difference we are contributing to the unfolding history of human kind. Ideas such as this led to the notion that the connectedness to others was via the nature of source—that which connects us through our origins and their energies, whether these are divine or cosmic, or both. This opens up the exploration of connections within the physical and biological sciences.

Role

Role is at the centre of the framework. It becomes the public expression of the way someone integrates the inner processes of the four domains (Bazalgette, 2014). Role lies at the intersection of the person, system, and context. When a person joins a group or organisation, she enters a particular system and its context. The person brings her personality, skills, capacities, interests, motivations, emotional propensities, and personal history. These characteristics may fill the roles that she takes up. However, because roles belong to, and are also shaped by, the system and its context, the person does not so much as create the role as fill it. It is as if the person "colours" the role with her own way of doing things and with the valencies (Bion 1961) that drive her. Different people will take up the same roles in different ways. None the less, the basic position of the role in the system remains the same (Long, 1991). This can be explored through role biography (Long 2013), a process that explores patterns in the various roles taken up over the course of a person's life and how these roles influence current role taking.

Critical to the idea of role is that it is from role that action occurs in a system. The person never acts in isolation. We are social animals and always part of a group—of many groups. So, our actions are always from a role in relation to other roles. This might be the role of mother in a family system, the role of manager in a work system, the role of friend in a friendship relation. Imagine being outside of role. Is this possible? Even in isolation, individuals are part of social systems; they use language or money or thought or art that are all social products. Even the role of isolate or hermit is *in relation* to others.

This idea of "in relation to" is different from being in "relationship with". A relationship is a personal thing where the parties know each other in face-to-face or, at least, closely linked communication. Being in "relation to" means taking up a role that is linked to other roles even when you do not know the role holder personally. For instance, I am in relation to the Australian Prime Minister even though I do not know him and have never met him personally. My relation is systemic. I am a citizen and he is the leader. There is accountability and authority in that relation even if I am unable to recognise or understand it, or if I refuse to acknowledge it, or, importantly, if I cannot act within the relation for a variety of systemic reasons that might frustrate my giving power to the role of citizen.

To take this a little further, the concept of the "institution-in-the-mind" can be invoked (Armstrong, 1997). This is a mental image of the organisation that is connected to the role in the mind of the role holder. It is more or less conscious and is evident in the behaviour of the role holder. For instance, a social worker might take up her role as a kind of saviour of her clients by providing them with services, or even provisions, that they need. Alternatively, she might see herself as an enabler through aiding her clients to develop the capacities needed to help themselves. Taking the role in either of these ways depends on her social work system-in-the-mind. Moreover, her role taking will also be linked to the pushes and pulls from the system-in-the-mind of her clients.

Role may also be thought about in terms of the perspective from the person and the perspective from the social context. The psychological role is the role idea in the mind of the person. It includes the expectations we have of ourselves in role. The sociological role is the role idea in the minds of others. It includes the expectations that others have of us in role. These two—the psychological and the sociological roles—might or might not coincide.

This conceptualisation links with Goffman's (1969) essay "Where the action is". In this, Goffman differentiates "Commitment", from "Attachment" and "Embracement". Commitment is where the circumstances give the actor no choice about engaging (the police officer at an accident when in uniform): that is, the sociological role. Attachment is where the actor does what they believe needs to be done: that is, the psychological role. Embracement adds to both of those and integrates them (Bazalgette, 2014).

In considering how the domains relate to one another, it can be seen that dynamics in the person, system, or context can, as it were, call us into role. A context can call for a particular system: the country's need for economic management, for example. A person can call for a system and context: an asylum seeker in need of a new home, for instance. Most importantly, source can call us into role in a way that enables us to act authentically with purpose.

Using the framework

The domains of experience: person, system, context, source, and role and their theoretical interconnections have been introduced in this chapter. The framework, however, is not ethically neutral. It has implicit values and directives for approaching the study of organisations and their roles and contexts.

1. The systemic approach considers all experience as interconnected and understands the responsibilities and accountabilities of players in an interconnected world. The demonstration of interconnectedness can be associated to Goffman's idea of embracement (see above), indicating the responsibilities we have to integrate our understandings of our roles with the understandings of others.
2. Organisational purpose as a basis for tasks and roles provides an ethic for collaborative work beyond individual egos and desires. The framework also allows a focus on where and how purpose is perverted, corrupted, or avoided through unconscious defences and/or improper political process.
3. The importance of contextual experience emphasises the need to look beyond current experience whether this is toward an

awareness of multiple cultures, political dynamics, or possibilities into the future. Contextual awareness in a complex society also means an encouragement of interdisciplinary approaches to "wicked problems", so called because they are unable to be solved through the efforts of individual disciplines alone.

4. The interconnections in actual experience may appear both conscious and immediately discernible but beneath this appearance are implicit and still unconscious connections. For example, how might the desires of persons within particular personal contexts influence their take-up of roles in a hospital system or a bank? How might the experience of context affect the way resources are distributed, including intellectual resources, in a global organisation? How might the purpose of a system conflict with its political context? The framework can assist with identifying which aspects of experience might be fruitfully investigated.

While the diagram (Figure 1.1) and descriptions of the different domains of experience may appear to be two-dimensional and static, this is not the case. They exist in four dimensions, including the dimension of time. Persons, roles, systems, contexts, and even connectedness to source, change over time. Roles are constantly in need of renegotiation given changing persons, systems and contexts. These are dynamic, not static, concepts.

References

Armstrong, D. (1997). The institution-in-the-mind: reflections on the relation of psychoanalysis to work with institutions. *Free Associations*, 7(41): 1–14.

Armstrong, D., & Rustin, M. (Eds.) (2015). *Social Defences Against Anxiety: Explorations in a Paradigm*. London: Karnac.

Bazalgette, J. (2014). Personal communication.

Bion, W. R. (1961). *Experiences in Groups*. London: Tavistock.

Bion, W. R. (1970). *Attention and Interpretation*. London: Tavistock.

Goffman, E. (1969). *Where the Action Is: Three Essays*. London: Allan Lane.

Kets de Vries, M., & Miller, D. (1984). *The Neurotic Organisation: Diagnosing and Changing Counterproductivestyles of Management*. New York: Jossey-Bass.

Long, S. D. (1991). The signifier and the group. *Human Relations*, 44(4): 389–401.

Long, S. D. (2008). *The Perverse Organisation and Its Deadly Sins*. London: Karnac.

Long, S. D. (2013). Role biography, role history and the reflection group. In: S. D. Long (Ed.), *Socioanalytic Methods* (pp. 227–236). London: Karnac.

Macmurray, J. (1935). *Reason and Emotion*. London: Faber and Faber.

Menzies, I. E. P. (1970). *The Functioning of Social Systems as a Defence against Anxiety: A Report of a Study of a Nursing Service in a General Hospital*. London: Tavistock.

Sievers, B. (2006). Psychotic organization: a socio-analytic perspective. *Ephemera*, 6(2): 104–120.

Winnicott, D. W. (1958). *Collected Papers: Through Paediatrics to Psycho-analysis*. London: Tavistock.

CHAPTER TWO

Background to the TEF

Bruce Irvine

T his chapter has been edited from two talks given by Bruce Irvine. The first is part of his presentation to the Branding Workshop of the Grubb Guild early in 2015: "Working with the emergent: the brand of the Guild". This talk outlined the three pillars and six principles of the Grubb Guild. The second was a talk given to participants in the Grubb Guild Master's programme. This talk traced some of the history of the development of the transforming experience framework. Bruce rarely wrote about his ideas or the TEF, but he did give many talks. This chapter attempts to capture some of what he said.

Pillars of the Guild's brand and six principles

The three pillars of the Guild are:

- challenge everything;
- reveal resources;
- unleash potential.

First, there is the pillar "challenge everything". As conditional beings, we humans base our behaviour and thinking upon assumptions; things we take for granted. We then base our rationalisations on those assumptions. This first pillar of the brand invites us to search out those assumptions and put them to the test. This is what lies at the heart of true scientific method. Richard Feynman, one of the great physicists of the twentieth century put it nicely: "Science is the belief in the ignorance of the experts" (Feynman, 1966, 1969).

The second pillar calls for resources to be revealed. A starting point in the work of the Guild is that untested assumptions effectively conceal resources that are available for the work in hand. The blinkers that blind us to those resources are assumptions about where boundaries are located, who controls them, and for what purpose. Often, our assumptions interpret things as threats or burdens which, if thought about differently, might be resources. A major example in the Guild's work through "Ubuntu4Schools" is the assumption about schools: that pupils are potential products of the system on which its public reputation depends. Rather, they are co-creators of all the processes of that system, of which they become the principal beneficiaries.

The third pillar is about unleashing potential. Once existing but untapped resources are revealed, new energy becomes available to bring about more effective work at every level. In the Guild's Masters' Programmes, especially the one now running in Australia, this is demonstrated through the programme's virtual learning environment, where stunning levels of engagement and mutual support, challenge, and action occur.

These three pillars are built on a recognition that the pace of human capacity to learn is speeding up and, along with our expanding consciousness, we are called on to use new tools for thinking and working. The following principles open that up to us.

The six principles

Principle 1: The Principle of Working with Experience. In reality, we work with experience all the time. We might not be aware of how we do it, but our behaviour is always intentional, both consciously and unconsciously, in relation to the sense we make of our experience.

Principle 2: We create the experience we need in order to develop and learn. Every experience we have is our co-creation and we create it as part of our evolution as human beings. We have the experience that we need, both consciously and unconsciously, which holds us at our developmental edge until we have the new insight or under-standing that enables us to move on. Each experience is an opportu-nity to exercise freedom and choice, an opportunity to learn.

Principle 3: The Principle of Connectedness. We are connected with everything that is. Therefore, we need to learn to see what is happen-ing in the *now*. In reality, this is the only thing that is. So, the questions we need to ask at any one time are, "What takes me away from the *now*?" and "What do I avoid in connection *now*?"

Principle 4: The Principle of Abundance. The context is full of resources, always present and always available. Our struggle to see them is tied to our fear of scarcity. The fear of scarcity—including scarcity of time as well as money or food—results in feeling that we are victims and leads to a mind-set of "tunnel vision" which limits our awareness of what is available, leading to poor decision making which reinforces rather than relieves us (Mullainathan & Shafir, 2013). The Cartesian split of either/or is replaced in the Guild's work by both–and, which, in turn, leads to both–and–and also. It challenges the Freudian human development theory based on learning to divide the world into "me" and "not-me", replacing it with "me" and "more-of-me-but-different". This follows the ideas presented in ecopsychology (Roszak et al., 1995). Thus, perceived threats can be transformed into resources.

Principle 5: The Principle of Co-creation and Self-authorisation (see, for example, Long, 2010). Because we are always connected, all that is is co-created by the authors of our different realities. Like the shape of a balloon, the internal and external forces and factors at work around us balance each other out to produce the "shape" we co-create through the choices made by all those involved. Consciously owning our co-creations is the first step to self-authorisation, personal respon-sibility, and systemic accountability.

Principle 6: This is the Principle of Working to Purpose, of respond-ing to what is being "called forth". A central concept in the work of the Guild is that of purpose, that which is called forth from the context, but even more important through being attentive to one's connectedness with source. This involves drawing on images, music, and movement which surface spirit. At the heart of intentionality in Guild members is the awareness that one has a sense of "vocation": the call to contribute to the healing, repair, transformation, and well-being of society through the mobilisation of values, beliefs, spirituality, and religion as resources through leadership and organisations.

Development of the Grubb Institute and the Guild

There were four key archetypes that were created wherever you looked. It was either the creation of the family system, the creation of an education system, the creation of the military system, or the creation of the institution of the church. These were the four critical issues. The data for that was the number of times you asked people to draw a picture of themselves in their organisation and what you ended up with was one of those four pictures. So, in our histories, we have developed these types of archetypes. The presence of the military and the church is slightly less these days but it is still present. The main one that comes up is the archetype of family. This is not surprising in many senses, because in the late 1940s and early 1950s most organisations were family businesses. So, what was being played out in these businesses was the big dynamic of family. Employment was not on the basis of capacity and skill but was on the basis of your place in the particular family. For instance, within the culture that I currently live in, not the culture I come from, if you had three or four sons, one became a doctor, one became a lawyer, and the stupid one went to the church and that became the general rule. So, the professions were developed out of those senses of moving but always using the psychological role rather than the sociological role. The sociological role and understanding emerged out of thinking, well, instead of seeing an organisation of the family, one was going to see an organisation as a set of representations of what was happening in the broader world. How might an organisation be different if, instead of seeing the managing director as a father, we saw him as a managing director with all the pieces that came with it?

At the same time, there was an exploration—for the first time, really—of work that began in the 1930s and 1940s, which was the idea of the T-group. The T-group was the group where you sat in the here and now to engage each other. In the late 1950s and 1960s, the tea group became infused with the use of LSD and all of those kinds of substances to increase people's capacities to shed the limitations and boundaries that were preventing them from true engagement. From that moment on, that movement went in a very strange direction.

Bruce Reed was invited at the time by the Billy Graham Association to do something with all the people who had come forward at rallies in London in 1956, because the Billy Graham Association saw Britain as the place of the "great unwashed". So, then, they were coming over to evangelise to the great unwashed. Many people came forward at these rallies, where they found new forms of faith, were living in cities, civil servants, and they did not know what to do with them. It was easier to slot the unwashed into local churches than it was to do anything else. So Bruce was invited to try to find a way of helping people with these new-found faiths to engage. He came up with the idea of the first real multi-disciplinary think tanks. What he would do was to pull together a diverse group of eight people from different sectors of society and say, "OK, let's get together and think about some of the problems that society faces." Mental health was one, and out of the think tanks for mental health came the Richmond Fellowship, which is now an international organisation providing residential care for people with severe mental illness. From that came the housing association within the UK, and beyond that the Elfrida Rathbone Society, which was an organisation dedicated to working with disability. So this was the early work, but what was then being challenged was the function of the church. It seemed that as soon as someone joined a church, without any particular skill, they were put on the parish council, made to be a treasurer, and the whole objective of church seemed to be to create a very strong boundary between "us" and "them". That is when Bruce's work began to analyse religion. His hypothesis was that church was a way of re-energising the leaders to go out into the world, so you entered church in some form of "discombobulation". After a heavy week and if the liturgy was good, what you experienced in the liturgy was a move to dependence and then a move out of the liturgy to extra dependence, which meant that you were free, imbued, to go back into the world. Now, a lot of our churches still struggle with that. It actually becomes kind of an imposed groupthink and it could refer to any other institution as to how the religious institutions become wholes in themselves.

So, it then started to ask itself the question, where do you find God? It came to the conclusion that the only place to find God was in the here and now. Any other attempts were rarely finding the question. If God could be found in the here and now, the question arose: what if God was not something that one could be certain existed; that was God not a hypothesis that you were constantly testing and that you were gathering data which supported that hypothesis or disproved that hypothesis? So all the debates and discussions around why suffering exists, and all those things, may be perceived as moments of disproof.

To cut a long story short, you have, in 1962–1963, Pierre Turquet and Ken Rice, who started to work on the idea of socio-analytic systems. You have all seen those papers on socio-analytic existence and that was found really in the services sections and resource sections and the interaction between those. That is where the first demarcation of the double boundary came out, which put management and leadership on that boundary. So, the hypothesis at that point was that the role of the leader was to regulate what came into the system and to interpret what was coming into the system in order that something would happen inside the system that could produce a product. So, wool comes in, knitting machines happen, and jerseys go out. That was the first input–output–transform idea.

After a while, what started to be explored was the development of group relations conferences by Ken Rice and Pierre Turquet of the Tavistock Institute, and Bruce Reed and Barry Palmer of the Grubb Institute, lasting many years. Over time, the faith base of the Grubb foundation became increasingly into consideration, leading in due course to the Being, Meaning, Engaging conferences which led in turn to the design of the Passion, Purpose and Potency (PPP) conference which is now a required part of the MA. Because what was discovered initially was that people would have this amazing experiential experience but there was no way of living it out. And this movement came out of the shift after the Second World War in terms of improved life. So one of the issues happening in organisations at that point was the real struggle to take up authority. Those of you who were in the online seminar in leadership would have remembered the graph that I put up depicting the different states of leadership. This was the bottom end—the person who followed rules, the great follower, did not do anything that he was not told to do. In the old days, we might have called that person "jobsworth". "It's not worth my job to do that", because it is out of the structure. So, what started to emerge was the first Venn diagram described in the TEF. Because what Bruce Reed was starting to look at was the relationship between person, system, and role. So this was beginning the exploration of what it meant to take up a role. At that point, the dominant theory base was Bion and the basic assumptions of behaviour. The idea that all groups move to a basic assumption for survival: pairing, dependency, and flight or fight. Since then, other theories have been developed, other basic assumptions. The challenge of that was that there was a sense that there was always something wrong. The reality was that many organisations, yes, had basic assumption functioning, but also managed to achieve a task. So how can we understand that even if your grouping was organised around flight or fight, there was still possibility that the work group could be established? And Bion talked about the work group as that group able to tolerate the anxiety of survival long enough to achieve a task.

So began the whole process of thinking about aim and task: what is the aim of the organisation? What is the task of the organisation? What is the unconscious task that is worked at to achieve survival? Isabel Menzies Lyth was one of the first people to write about social defences against anxiety. In her study of a hospital, she looked at the impact of white coats as a way of defending against the suffering and death that staffs were exposed to. So, the white coat was put on and it was like a jacket that protected you from the realities. There was the whole idea that it was a very good idea for patients to be woken up at five o'clock in the morning and given a bath. It was talked about as if it was in the patient's best interest. It was also decided that visitors should come for only short periods of time. But what she started to understand was that all of those things were ways of enabling the staff in those organisations to survive, and that was basic assumption behaviour. The only reason that people were woken up at five o'clock in the morning for a bath was so that the night staff had something to do and release the day staff from having to do the bathing and get on with the day. So there was a lot of really powerful work being done in those early stages and this framework of understanding the person–system–world continued for a long, long time.

Then came postmodernism and, suddenly, everything was being deconstructed. As part of the context in which that was happening, this framework started being deconstructed. And what Bruce was starting to discover was that deconstructing this model did not actually change it. What it did was deepen the understanding of each of these sections. But it still was clunky and there was something that just did not work. It was only twelve years ago that we started to look at the difficulty of looking at the socio-analytic model of an organisation when the inputs did not take into account the context in which that organisation was operating. So it was at that point that we changed and introduced context into the TEF diagram and started to see role as the mobilisation of the experience of being in system, being in context, and being the person that you are. The role was a choice about what you meant to mobilise in that moment, to take action to serve the purpose of the organisation. This also grew the whole idea that leadership is linked to position. So, what we were arguing is that leadership can come from anywhere in the organisation. The evidence of a leadership act is something that purposefully fulfils what the organisation exists for.

Then we started to work significantly with the ideas of pre and post-conventional thinking. What would happen if we started to read Bion from a post-conventional mind-set as opposed to a pre-conventional mind-set? Up until that point, most people working from Bion in any kind of group setting would say that faith, belief, and religion should not be talked about. Reading Bion post-conventionally, however, we started to see what he had been trying to do was write into a context. And actually, if you read him in a context where spirituality was an acceptable thing to talk about, suddenly you came to have a greater understanding of Bion's thought, which was beyond oneness and what that oneness meant. That started to challenge us enormously because we had always started from the point of "What is your desire?" Suddenly we had to reverse that question and ask, "What is the desire that is being called forth from you at this point?" Because we were looking at the history of organisations and organisations that survive and organisations that do not. One of the characteristics of organisations that survive was their being nimble enough to meet a changing context. So, the really successful organisations were not the ones that were saying, "We have this nice, special thing" and they need to persuade the world to have it, but they were organisations that were innovating on the basis of the need established in the context. That was quite a shift that was taking place in the 1960s, 1970s and 1980s in thinking about organisational life.

It still did not feel as if the framework was providing us with enough of an understanding of the multiplicity in which people were taking up roles. At the same time, we had—in my view—the most tragic view in all of the many tragedies in organisational structuring and functioning, the demise of personnel departments and the creation of human resource departments (HR). Frankly, I think human resource departments are the incarnation of all evil because what they have done is to commodify human beings and turn the function of people management and development into a set of methods and rules, rules to prevent people engaging with each other in any kind of sense. I have exaggerated: there are certainly some functions that do work. But my own experience of being a manager for many years was that my job was to find ways around HR. Because the plethora of ways and rules and regulations meant that I was not able to do what I needed to do. I could not appoint people if I used their procedures. If I used the HR procedures, I always got the lowest common denominator. I could not actually engage with the people I needed.

At the same time, we were starting to look at what it meant to look like an organisation that was established from a Christian basis and to be working in a world that had people who had all faith or none. And how did we understand that any particular religion did not have priority on meaning? There was a wonderful little book written in the late 1980s titled *Codename God*, which was by a Hindu physicist and was on the *Los Angeles Times* bestselling list for nearly fifteen years. Essentially, this is the man in a village in India who was incredibly bright and won a scholarship to the University of California, and the only way to take up a scholarship was to travel there. Once he got there he would have everything. His father was a schoolteacher who said, "We can't afford this—this is never going to happen." But in two and a half weeks, from all over the hillsides of India, came people with three rupees here, eight rupees there, and nine rupees there. And actually, he got the message from his community that he was going there on their behalf. They were paying for him to go there, and he managed to get enough together to go. He gets there; he meets movie stars; he is this incredibly young, attractive, and exotic man in this new setting. In the daytime, he invents laser eye surgery. In the night time, he's the beau of the ball. And then, twenty years later, he finds paucity in his life and recovers some of his Hindu spiritual practices and starts using scientific knowledge to say that the evidence that scientific knowledge shows us is that every story that is told about humanity is a story which is trying to understand what it means to be human and what it means to be connected. And that every human being who lives has a desire to be part of something bigger than themselves. We then have to bring into the whole picture spiral dynamics and adult development.

In those two streams of work, we were starting to see that there is meaning. Spiral dynamics is a pattern of behaviour that is largely about where you put your boundary. So, if your boundary is family, then you tend to be down as tribal. What we have a lot of in the world now is the lean, green me. That is the me that wants a solution to absolutely everything and is overwhelmed by their individuality. This is the core thing. I will put money on the belief that, in fifty years time, the psychological diagnostic manual for mental illness will take individuality as a mental illness. There is no evidence to support it—it is a delusional state to believe that I am an insular person who is not affected by what happens around me. We have all of these wonderful books about self-made men. We have not seen any books about self-made women yet. But self-made men are wonderful at blocking out everything that they are interconnected with that has enabled them to achieve. So, I am a self-made man but it does not matter that I have travelled on roads built by the state, that I have gone to public libraries, that I was in a public school? All of these are part of our connected experience. So, then, we start to say, all right, if meaning is one of the critical factors that human beings are engaged with, why do most organisations make believe you are leaving human meaning behind and give credibility only to financial and commercial meaning?

Something was going on where we were also at the point of beginning to develop the work–life balance. So you end up working in order to have life, which seems to suggest that work was not life. And there was a whole interesting dialogue going on where work was a necessary evil in order to achieve what you wanted for your life. That was the point that you started preparing for your retirement—doing everything you can for when you are retiring and then dropping dead within three months! There was something that was not being understood in the relationship to work. This was where we at the Grubb started looking at each of these components in the new framework with the idea of what did it mean if we worked from the hypothesis that we are connected irrespective of whether we like it, that there's nothing we can do about it, and it just is!

So what if everything in the world is connected? This, then, takes you particularly into the newer territories of cosmic theologies because the whole shift was a suggestion that the current origins of stories and the ways in which we understand our different faiths and beliefs were really narratives of telling what it was. And it was at that point, which was nearly eight years ago, that I stopped calling myself a Christian and started calling myself a follower of the Jewish prophet, Jesus Christ. Now, that may sound like a convolution, but what I could not cope with was all the assumptions that would come with the label Christian. What I also could not cope with was the denial was that this man was born within a context, and was born as a Jew and that the biggest mistake that Paul made was naming the people who followed him Christians. Because the message of the early church and Jesus was how to deal with the corruption that was happening within the Jewish state in relation to power and how synagogues and the rabbis and the Pharisees and whoever were actually manipulating the people by using the law as a way of dominating rather than enabling each person to find their experience in relation to the meaning of the lord.

At that point, we were saying that in each of these domains there is an aspect which is calling for meaning. What is the meaning of the world? What is the meaning of a country? Of a nation? What is the meaning of a system? Why do systems exist? Why do people exist? Why do I exist? Using the post-conventional questions, we then started to say, all right, if we are starting from the outside in, which is the post-conventional frame and we are working from the inside out, which was the pre-conventional, where do these meet? And how do we work between those two places as a way of illuminating something about what it is to be engaged with one's living experience. The cosmic theologists and particularly people like Dermot Murtagh started to bring forth the notion that everything was connected and that you could see God in another human being and in a tree. That was very quickly corroborated by the new sciences which then essentially said we are not anything but reverberating molecules which are going so fast that you think you have got a skin but actually that is illusionary and that no physical form is anything else than a reverberating set of molecules.

So then you have got the whole debate which was raging at that point, which was the nature of spirituality and at the end of the 1970s, early 1980s was when spirituality, seen from the inside out perspective, was seen as an incredibly selfish and indulgent activity. What was your priority and what was your post re-enlightenment? It did not seem to matter what was going on around you. And yes, it served some people to go to the top of a mountain and never talk to another human being again, but not everybody, and what would happen if we all did? So there was the question in our minds at the Grubb, what if we bring spirituality back into the workplace rather than sequestering it in that other time called life? Whether we like it or not, every single human being comes to work with all their baggage of belief and because it is unspeakable, it then means that it is not used (or unconsciously enacted). That was the point at which we started to look at what is our connectedness with source and with God. We specifically put it up there as our outer boundary although, as opposed to the Venn diagram, we do not know where that boundary is, but saying absolutely everything that takes place is within the context of a search for meaning and an acknowledgement that what keeps everything going is the field of energy. And the field of energy is what I might call one thing and someone else might call another, and then, when we go back to those origin stories, it is all about vibrations, you know? Brown issued into the void—that was the start of big bang in that particular framework—and at every point we could see the sense of the energy coming forth. So that kind of completely transformed our understanding of what person–system–context meant. Thus, context became anywhere you want to put the boundary. So, depending on what your meme was, your boundary would be smaller or bigger. If you are at a red meme, your boundary will be family. If you are at another meme, your boundary might be country. It might be a geographic region; it might be the world or the cosmos. It did not really matter where you put that boundary as long as you started to understand what was connected, what was present in that boundary and that was when we came up with the idea that context is what demonstrates our connectedness. Now, a lot of people challenged that initially. They just demonstrated endless evidence to show that it was true.

The financial crisis of eight years ago was the most beautiful gift to the world because it showed us beyond a shadow of a doubt that we are connected and we cannot avoid it. Five years ago, if you asked most people in the world walking down the street what was fair trade, no one would be able to tell you. Now, you go down any street in the world, virtually in the world, and people are able to tell you. So, what we're seeing is a shift in the way the world thinks about itself, paradigms changing, evolutions speeding up in terms of releasing and exposing new human capacity. As quantum mathematicians, if this is a Venn diagram, the context is made up of billions of millions of systems. Thus, for the transforming framework, all we are doing is pulling out one of those at any one time.

For the purpose of this, it is the Masters' programme. If we then have to start thinking about systems, we have to understand why most systems live. And we came to the conclusion that systems only live when there is a need in a context. This was shown to us by asking very simple questions. You ask a headteacher, "What do your people do", and if your headteacher says to you, "There are 100 Cs", or whatever your category is, you have got a real inkling that school is not working in context. If you ask the headteacher, "What does your school do?" and they answer, "Our students go on to leading universities or the US Senate," fifty per cent of women in the US senate were educated in college. These are the kinds of things that show outcome and that was the point that we started to look at the difference between an output and an outcome. An outcome is an output judged in context. Organisations that were surviving had outputs that were put into the context and were agreed with, accepted, and appreciated and that is what provided the feedback loop back into the organisation. So, to understand the system, we had to move beyond a task, because the aim and task language was all about deficit and difficulties of basic assumption behaviour. That is when, six years ago, we came up with the idea I am talking about: context in an organisational purpose. And purpose was supposed to be a way of an organisation understanding its response to a context. Organisations exist to do this in order to do that. The classic purpose statement has unfortunately been bastardised because I constantly hear people using it as a kind of quick phrase. You ask those people what is the purpose and they cannot tell you. It is a bit like a mission statement. How many times do you go into an organisation and ask them what it is and they say, "Hold on a minute, it's in the filing cabinet—I'm just not sure which document it's in." The purpose is something that we should be able to experience and live because if we are not able to do that, we cannot find the boundary of our system.

So, part of the purpose of our work yesterday on boundaries was to establish that boundaries are just a way of establishing one thing from another thing. The critical illustration of a boundary is knowing what its purpose is. When you know what the purpose of your system is, finding your role is easy—it is really simple. If you do not know and you confuse the system that you are in for another system and end up taking another type of role, you are going to end up in a lot of bother. My big lesson was when I was delayed in an airport. Do I go stamping up to the desk as if, because I am the executive director of an organisation, I should get some preferential treatment? I get nowhere, but actually, when I find the role of passenger, my life changed. Because then my purpose had changed—I was in the appropriate role. Then I discovered the role of educated passenger: the passenger who knows better than the staff that there is no plane from Houston to Heathrow—"OK, why don't you divert me through Buffalo . . ." So there is something about finding a role and then mobilising the experiences.

But then I have noticed an issue around post-conventionalism. Because, although we had pioneered the idea of talking about post rather than the individual as a way of engaging with the idea that post is a live, interactive, vibrant interconnected force, we were trapped in the old ways of thinking about person, which was essentially about the person in deficit and that the unconscious was somehow the reservoir of all bad. We were asking ourselves the question, "Why would anyone want to work with the unconscious if they had worked so hard to bury all of this shit? Why would you want to bring it up again?" And you would want to bring it up again only if there was a possibility that bringing it to the surface was going to be something useful and serve a purpose and that bringing it up would help you in what was happening in the role. So, then, it did not become "You are a terrible person with all this trauma!" but, rather, "What are the resources of your trauma and your story that you are mobilising in this that is getting in the way of you achieving what you want to achieve?" Then it became possible for the unconscious to have some kind of rehabilitation. And that is where we started working with the difference of desire and yearning. I am not going to get into all that. You know that. Desire is the function from within us. Yearning is the sense of desire for that connection. In working with this framework, it is so tempting to treat the domains as if they were separate. And yes, we encourage that separation on one level by training you to work on hypotheses in all of the different domains. But none of the hypotheses makes any sense unless you see an end system in its context. An end system is the person and that is where you are and, more importantly, the question that goes through all of this is: What is our sense of interconnectedness? No matter what we want to call it. Getting into debates about whether its source or energy is a real defence against an understanding of the basic reality of the current connectedness of the world that we live in. So, how about us changing the way we ask the questions. Not, "What do I want to do?" in what is called cultural meaning. Not about being surprised about a moment of synchronicity, but the surprise when it does not happen because synchronicity is the norm. If everything is connected, and everything is feeding off everything else, and each is engaging off each other, when things jar, that should be the exception, the way we look at it. In all of that, we then had to face the fact that Vatican II happened. And Vatican II was ignored by a lot of people and essentially one of its messages was that there was not a hierarchy in relation to God, that being a priest did not make you closer to God, and that the traditional sense of vocation meant that you were either called to the priesthood or became a sister or became married or remained single and these were vocations.

Professionalisation opened another dimension to vocation. What we started to work with was that any role is about a call. It is a call from a context which is imbued with interconnected energy to take part in a system with a clear purpose and offers you an opportunity of becoming more of what you want to be. And that the clearer we are about the differentiation of the roles within the system, the more able we are to expand to be the people we were created to be.

Our hypothesis in that setting is that in seeing the people we have created to be, we have only touched the tip of the iceberg and that the speeding up of the evolution of human potential has demonstrated that to us on a day-to-day basis. The lesson for today was partly that we can turn a formal solution into a technical solution. But actually, it is a living, emerging, evolving framework, which is why we do not call it a model. Because within this is a way of hanging our different thoughts, conflicting ideas, conflicting beliefs; because if we turn it into a model, we technicalise the process and we lose our capacity to actually think about the adaptive challenge that exists in every role that we take up every day.

Why is this role about leadership?

Any action that takes up the purpose of the system is called leader. I want, in my organisation, everybody to take an action that serves its purpose. The question then becomes leadership and followership. So, how do I follow other people in my organisation? I should not believe because I am the head of the organisation that I am the one who has to lead everything. I think we are trying to transform the idea that leadership is connected to position. My best example is four hundred people interviewed in a healthcare organisation. I found one leader— the cleaner, whose job was to make the place cleaner to make everyone feel better. No one in the organisation solely leads healthcare to health improvement. So I really do believe we need to be thinking about it. The leadership literature is taking us in a whole new direction in terms of categorisation of leadership; there is a mutuality and consistent dance of followership and leadership. Do we notice when we are doing the different parts? It also takes leadership away from the idea that it is just about big jobs. How do you use this model when you think about your family and the roles you take up in that? How do you think about it at any level, because any group of human beings is a system which is interacting and this takes us away from the idea of organisational systems as a mechanical thing where if you just do X, Y, and Z, that always works.

References

Feynman, R. (1966). The Fifteenth Annual Meeting of the National Science Teachers Association, New York City.

Feynman, R. (1969). *The Physics Teacher, 7*(6): 313–320.

Long, S. D. (2010). Brochure for the conference: "Leadership for the Future: Dignity, Hope and Spirit in Organisations". Melbourne: Group Relations Australia.

Mullainathan, S., & Shafir, E. (2013). *Scarcity: Why Having too Little Means so Much.* London: Allan Lane.

Roszak, T., Gomes, M. E., & Kanner, A. D. (Eds.) (1995). *Ecopsychology: Restoring the Earth: Healing the Mind.* San Francisco, CA: Sierra Club.

CHAPTER THREE

The transforming experience framework and unconscious processes: a brief journey through the history of the concept of the unconscious as applied to person, system, and context with an exploratory hypothesis of unconscious as source

Susan Long

"Here then is a formulation of the unconscious as a mental network of thoughts, signs, and symbols or signifiers, able to give rise to many feelings, impulses and images ... The associative unconscious as a system holds a set of processes of symbolisation constrained only by current expressions"

(Long & Harney, 2013, p. 8)

I n this chapter, I will trace a little of the history of the concept of the unconscious. I do this because the idea of the unconscious is central to psychoanalytic and socio-analytic theories and yet is an idea about processes that are elusive and can only be observed through their effects or inferred from the gaps in our direct experience, and, hence, is constantly hypothetical and open to challenge.

This is really the way of all scientific ideas. Such ideas attempt to explain complex phenomena and as our observation and understanding of those phenomena change, either through the use of new technologies or methods of observation, so must the hypothesis. Our ideas for explaining the world are no more static than the processes and phenomena that they attempt to explain. So we may expect the idea of the unconscious to be in constant evolution.

We tend to say such things as "ideas or thoughts come to us". We "entertain" them. We "develop and nurture" them. Sometimes, they "strike us". Other times, they creep up on us surreptitiously and hide "at the back of our minds". We have good ideas and bad ideas. Some thoughts are unbearable, some wicked, and some creative. Embedded in this language is the sense that ideas and thoughts have a life somewhat independent of us. We relate to them, and they to us. In our groups and societies, they are born, come of age, are popular or hated, and they fade out and die.

The idea of the unconscious is a thought about thoughts, an idea about ideas. It is an idea about how thoughts influence us even though we might not be aware of them. It is an idea about what we do with unwanted thoughts or thoughts that we are not ready to entertain. It is an idea about how thoughts shape and are shaped by our experience. It is an idea that responds to the question: what lies beneath consciousness? Or, put another way, what prevents our consciously thinking thoughts? Following Freud's (1915e) thinking in his paper on the unconscious, I focus on unconscious thoughts, tending to see emotions as being at times unrecognised because they are suppressed rather than repressed.

We tend to think and speak of *the* unconscious: a mysterious, unknown terrain that influences us from inside. Yet, it is not so much a hypothetical place as it is a function or a state of mind: unconsciousness. I prefer to think in terms of unconscious processes and unconsciousness rather than *the* unconscious as a static container or object, and the reason for this will become evident as I trace the history of the idea. None the less, from time to time, I might simply say "the unconscious" because that is how usage has prevailed and I want to explore the usage of the idea in the various theories that refer to it. Also, at times, it seems as if it is a container as well as a process, just as in physics light may behave both as waves and particles.

I want to look at the concept of the unconscious because it is through our changing usage of the term that we come more fully to understand the phenomena that it points to: the phenomena that we often take for granted or endow with other explanations. It is through our action of usage that we create meaning.

I neither hope nor wish to be comprehensive in my exploration of the concept. For one, there would be too many theories to approach in too much complexity and, if I wish to push my previous point to its logical extension, there are as many ideas of the unconscious as there are thinkers or actors who have such ideas. Also, I will be pursuing the idea of the unconscious from within the tradition provided through the transforming experience framework as described in this book. This might loosely be called the "Tavistock tradition" because many of the perspectives that I consider originated at the Tavistock Institute in the latter half of the past century. However, scholars and practitioners outside this tradition have also influenced my thinking. Many social scientists have used psychoanalytic ideas, including the unconscious, in their thinking about large-scale social and political processes.

An idea is a social construction built through a process of interacting thinkers. While each thinker may hold a similar meaning, there will be as much diversity within even the same theoretical school for the idea to evolve and change in its usage. This holds even within strict definitions of concepts: the stricter the definition, the longer a concept will hold to a particular meaning, but, eventually, meanings change because contexts also change. I quote here Schelling (1942) because he holds an important place in the history of the idea of the unconscious as will be discussed in this chapter: "Propositions that are unconditioned, that is, valid once for all, are antagonistic to the nature of true science, which consists in progress" (Schelling, 1942 [1814–1815], p. 94).

Moreover, the more confidence we have in the definition of the term, the less fruitful as a concept it might be, as we understand Pierce puts it when referring to the logic behind scientific hypotheses:

> Across the three forms of abduction, induction and deduction, *uberty* decreases as *security* increases: "uberty" means "fruitfulness, productiveness", also rich growth, fertility, copiousness, abundance; security means the degree of confidence we can have that our hypothesis is true. (Long & Harney, 2013, p. 12)

I shall describe just a small selection of fairly well known theories, and then examine only some of the ideas about the unconscious in these theories. The reader will identify much that I have left out in this brief story. My focus is not so much the details of each theory as my desire to look at some of the different ways that unconscious processes have been, and might be, conceptualised. It is not my purpose to evaluate these ideas or to test the veracity of unconscious processes. Those tasks are for a different composition. I want here to trace just something of the concept.

The possibilities for exploration are so extensive that I would not attempt this task without a framework for doing so: a framework that helps me order my own understanding of the different theories about the unconscious in a manageable way. The TEF provides this for me, although not perfectly. In considering unconscious processes, the TEF offers a perspective about how the idea has been applied to persons, roles, systems, and contexts. Indeed, it was on being exposed to this framework and being asked to provide a seminar on unconscious processes that I found it necessary to think in terms of an evolving concept of the unconscious. I could not understand unconscious processes without thinking in terms of the dynamic nature of them as ideas developed through time.

The TEF in its simplest form is reproduced here in Figure 3.1 and explained more fully in Chapter One, where a fuller diagram is presented.

This chapter is organised to look at the idea of the unconscious as applied or enacted in the following ways.

- The unconscious prior to psychoanalysis.
- The unconscious as applied to persons.
- The unconscious in roles and systems.
- The unconscious in contexts.
- The unconscious as source.

Although I use the TEF as an exploratory tool, I recognise that the concept of the unconscious has not been developed and expounded specifically to fit this framework. Unconscious processes can be identified in persons, roles, systems, and contexts through a variety of methods, but the unconscious is not bound into those forms. While its effects may be described and enacted within these different forms, the

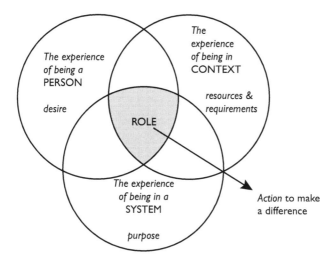

Figure 3.1. The transforming experience framework: basic version.

unconscious belongs across them. I say that the TEF does not provide perfectly and comprehensively a framework for thinking about unconscious processes because many of the theories about the unconscious see its operation across persons, systems, and contexts not just in any one of these. It is not easy to systematise the vast literature that exists about the unconscious and unconscious processes. In some ways, I will have to wander back and forth. Within specific theories, there is sometimes a focus on the individual, sometimes on the group, and sometimes on the context.

So, when one sees the operation of a symptom in the person, unconscious processes, say, in the family or work system, are present in the shadows, and when an unconscious process occurs in a larger context, such as a global financial system (Long & Sievers, 2013), we know that it may be represented and have effects in various groups, roles, or persons.

The TEF helps by putting an initial focus on the effects of the unconscious within persons, roles, systems, and contexts and on its relation to source. This focus may then widen or narrow according to where we might usefully intervene or further study—because what are ideas for if not to aid at least our survival and ideally our growth and prosperity?

The unconscious prior to psychoanalysis

From where does the idea of the unconscious come? Prior to any thinking about psychology, philosophers, religious thinkers, and scholars tended to refer primarily to the soul as the one immaterial essence of human beings. For Aristotle, the soul was the essential form of life. Soul was immortal, yet embodied. Moreover, religious mystics, such as Ignatius of Loyola, engaged in long-term and deep exploration of processes within themselves, initially hidden from awareness, in what might be seen as self-analysis long before Freud developed the method of psychoanalysis and the theory of repression.

The seventeenth-century enlightenment, following the foundations of scientific thinking formally established the idea of a mind that was different from the body. Descartes (1596–1650) placed an emphasis on the mind and our capacity to think rationally. His thinking founded what is known as Cartesian dualism: in very rough terms, this regards the body as a kind of machine animated by the mind. The thinking mind was the essence: "I think, therefore I am". However, Descartes also argued that body could influence mind and rationality through the passions. This dualism has been influential in western philosophy where the soul or mind and body distinction has become part of general parlance. It is at the basis of much of psychology and popular thinking into the twenty-first century. The mind and rational thought have become regarded as the centre of consciousness, apart from the illogical processes of the body and its emotions, albeit sometimes influenced by that irrationality. The subject, that is, the thinker, is regarded as different from the object: that is, that which can be thought about.

This position has been challenged by many philosophers, especially Heidegger and other existentialists. The challenge is also from many of the nature philosophers and an allied tradition that has held the mind and body as a unity with consciousness arising from an unconscious unity.

What, then, of unconsciousness? The influential philosopher Immanuel Kant (1724–1804) implicitly wrote of unconscious processes when introducing the idea of a "noumenal self" "that fits the theory of the system unconscious; an inner self that was unknown to the conscious self, but profoundly influenced the sense of self experienced" (Chessick, 1992, cited in Rabstejnek, 2011, p. 4).

The term unconscious, or unconsciousness, was, however, first used in a systematic way by the late eighteenth-century, early nineteenth-century German Romantic philosopher Friedrich Schelling and was understood as a source of creative power (Ffytche, 2011; McGrath, 2013). Despite a wane in Schelling's popularity as a significant philosopher during the late nineteenth and the twentieth century at a time when psychoanalysis was being formulated and extended, his influence is apparent. Perhaps this is due more to his ideas infiltrating the discourse about the unconscious through his lectures rather than any direct reading of him by Freud and his followers. Schelling's concern with the rise of self-consciousness led him to argue that consciousness itself could not be aware of its own origins. Hence, he postulated the existence of an unconscious as a substrate prior to consciousness. This unconsciousness is ground to self-consciousness, ground to existence, and a necessary substrate.

Unconsciousness was to be found in nature before any split into a subject that knows and an object that is known—a split conceptualised by Descartes but not accepted as fundamental by Schelling. The early Schelling attempts to find intuitive forms of thought in nature and links nature to spirit through this unconscious ground (McGrath, 2013). "Schelling proposed nature as unconscious spirit, and spirit as nature become conscious of itself" (Matthews, 2012). This was an idea of God as revealed through nature: "The universe or totality is the self-revelation of the absolute" (Schelling, 1942[1815], p. 17).

The ideal of nature as unconscious was linked to the development of consciousness and self-consciousness in a way that anticipates some aspects of the psychoanalytic focus on biography, denial, and repression. Schelling says,

> Certainly one who could write completely the history of their own life would also have, in a small epitome, concurrently grasped the history of the cosmos. Most people turn away from what is concealed within themselves just as they turn away from the depthsof the great life and shy away from the glance into the abysses of that past which are still in one just as much as the present. (Schelling, 1942[1815], pp. 93–94)

Following his early ideas on nature as unconscious spirit, and yet in moving away from his early idealism and criticisms that his writing was pantheist, Schelling developed a historical view about the rise of consciousness from unconscious ground (see Schelling, 2006). In describing this, Das (2014) says,

> It now appears that the condition of possibility of consciousness as such remains irreducible to consciousness itself. This is the problem that has become decisive, not only for Schelling's subsequent philosophical career, but for the fate of Idealism as such. It now appears as if our self-consciousness is driven or constituted by an unconscious ground, forever inaccessible to consciousness, which can never be grounded in consciousness itself.

In this construction, the infinite one—God—gave rise to consciousness as "other". This was the process by which God could emerge from infinite into existence (Love & Schmidt, 2006). For Schelling, the emergence of creation is a paradox because, he asks, what is needed other than infinity? Yet, without other the one cannot know itself; apart from its own infinity, it cannot be revealed. With other there is the possibility of actuality, communion, and of love. Schelling addresses this paradox through reference to the notion that the infinite can find in itself that which is finite but must make this finite part "other". "God is what is in itself and is understood only from itself; what is finite, however, is necessarily in another and can only be understood from this other" (Schelling, 1942[1815], p. 12).

McGrath (2012) traces some of the roots of this thinking to Boheme, a seventeenth-century theosopher (theosophy being a combination of theology and philosophy).

> Boheme's unground is the ineffable, non-dual, and incomprehensible darkness of the Godhead out of which the light of self-consciousness emerges through a dialectic interplay of opposites. The unground in itself "lacks" the duality necessary to revelation; Boheme repeats, like a mantra, that without distinction and duality there can be no manifestation . . . Duality emerges out of the non-duality of the unground in the form of hunger . . . nothingness as a lack and a hunger for something, ultimately for a revelation of itself. (McGrath, 2012)

For Boheme, the unground of the Godhead cannot be reduced, but it contains a drive to reveal itself. This is not a perfect actualisation, or a need, but an act of free will. An "other" is freely created in order that the one can know itself. The unground creates a ground for itself.

None the less, Boheme argues, the desire for revelation creates a "dark fire" of "pain, unappeased desire and anxiety . . . the corporeality of God" turned in on itself that hungers only for itself (McGrath, 2012). Its opposite is a "light hot fire" turned toward the other with love and the potential of revelation. The difference is crucial; that they are always together is part of their essence, just as self or ego and other are always in opposition but together.

Schelling takes Boheme's descriptions and creates a philosophical argument for the paradoxical presence of dual and opposing drives within the unity of the primordial infinite (God). The history of the world is predicated upon this and it is played out in the development of human personality—a necessary reflection of the creator. The opposing drives are an inward turning potency toward "self" and an outward turning potency toward "other". The inward turning is a negation of the totality and in this negation it is an actualisation of the ego—the ego that wants to be without other, just desirous of self (similar to Freud's primary narcissism). But it is this very turning into the darkness of self through negation (what Schelling calls the first potency) that allows for the second potency of turning outwards and the encounter of other, with the possibility of love. "An essence cannot negate itself as actual without positing itself at the same time as the actualizing, generating potency of itself" (Schelling, 1942[1815], p. 112).

This view predates Freud's (1925g) idea that cognisance of a thought, although negated, is, none the less, evidence of the vitality of that thought. The negation cannot occur unless the "essence" is at first posited.

The third potency unites these opposing drives and all three exist together in the one. Important in this argument is Schelling's view that the initial state of God is unconsciousness and that consciousness could only arise once "other" was actualised and in that process difference, otherness, narcissism, and free will are revealed. All were there in potential but the initial negation was the actualising force. Hence, the unconscious is ground to, and prior to, consciousness.

Schelling's philosophy naturally developed and changed several times throughout his life, but rather than criticise his changes of direction, we can appreciate that his thinking was always a struggle in following his belief that philosophy should consist of the pursuit of knowledge. Moreover, his epistemological development can be read as containing many of the different threads emanating from his insistence on linking philosophy to the real world (McGrath, 2013; White, 1983). Despite the differences from Schelling developed in psychoanalysis, in particular its rejection of his theological teleology, there is much in Schelling that anticipates later psychoanalytic formulations (although Schelling should not be read entirely from the psychoanalytic perspective: see Woodard, 2012).

For example, the inextinguishable nature of desire for being that is central to spirit can be found in Freud's instinctual id and the importance of negation to create otherness; the realisation of ego and desire as founded on a lack—integral to finiteness and established within difference—anticipates Lacan's (1977) reading of Freud. Bion is heir to the notion of the unconscious as infinite. For instance, take his idea of "O", described by Grotstein:

> "O" is perhaps Bion's most far-reaching conception. It designates an ineffable, inscrutable, and constantly evolving domain that intimates an aesthetic completeness and coherence. He refers to it by different terms, "Absolute Truth," "Ultimate Reality," or "reverence and awe." When preternaturally personified, it is called "God." The "Keter-Ayn-Sof" of the Zohar Kabbalah translated it as "Nothing" (Scholem, 1960; Bloom, 1983), a designation Bion (1962, 1963, 1965) focused on as the "no-thing." (Grotstein, 1997)

"O" echoes Schelling's ideas of the unconscious as infinite and ground to an aesthetic completeness (see Aurelio, 2012; Glover, 2009; Pistiner de Cortinas, 2009). Both Bion and Schelling acknowledge the influence of the Kabbalah.

Schelling's later work on myth is a forerunner to Jung.

> The last theme that came to preoccupy Schelling in the more religious period of his later years was that of mythology and revelation. Schelling saw mythological themes as the empirical verification of his metaphysical theory of the absolute and its genesis in the unconscious. For him, myths were an early, still unconscious historical manifestation of the absolute, while Christian revelation represented the free, intentional expression of a later stage. In his *The Deities of Samothrace* (1815), Schelling interprets the function of ancient Greek deities as that of precursors to the full manifestation of God. . . . Schelling's notion that myths are not the product of a rational mind but that of a much

earlier unconscious activity can be seen as a precursor to Carl Gustav Jung's archetypes. (*New World Encyclopedia*, 2014)

Schelling's ideas about unconscious process may be discerned repeatedly in the two centuries following his work. Even where there is no direct reference to him, it seems that his formulations permeate the concept as it has been developed. This perhaps indicates its strength as an idea and its complexity, in so far as its implications are constantly being realised in new ways.

The unfolding of this complexity through a variety of philosophical theories, each with different emphases, has been concentrated around major dimensions of joy and pain, creativity and destructivity, dimensions that Freud later came to designate within his idea of the pleasure principle. Throughout the history of the idea of the unconscious, the two qualities of unconscious processes—both its creativity and its angst—have been emphasised, sometimes in tandem and at other times independently.

In the nineteenth century, a major focus of ideas surrounding the unconscious was in relation to mental illnesses, as the perspective of mental illness rather than demonic possession of persons became normative. Boheme's dark fire of pain, unappeased desire and anxiety became more prominent. Gardiner comments,

> The vast nineteenth-century literature on the unconscious, and its dynamic role in dreaming, art, and mental illness, is amply documented in Lancelot Whyte's *The Unconscious Before Freud*. Eduard von Hartmann's *Philosophy of the Unconscious*, enormously popular in Germany, was published when Freud was twelve. William James, in his pre-Freudian *Principles of Psychology*, devotes many pages ... to discussing the role of the unconscious in such disorders as psychosomatic blindness. "The curative indication is evident:" he writes, "to get at the secondary personage [the unconscious], by hypnotization or in whatever other way, and make her *give up* the eye, the skin, the arm, or whatever the affected part may be." Indeed, the use of hypnosis to uncover repressed motivations was widely practiced by European and British psychiatrists before Freud and by Freud himself until he abandoned it for what he considered better methods. (Gardner, 1975, p. 1)

Freud's first explorations were into hysteria and hysterical conversion symptoms. Such a focus on how mind has its effects in the body reveals a central problematic in western philosophy since Descartes—that is, the distinction or not between mind and body and the relationship between the two.

In the history of pre-psychoanalytic thinking, two relevant streams of thought can be discerned. Knowing that the history of philosophical ideas might be segmented and classified in numerous, if not infinite, ways, the following all too brief dichotomy I recognise to be limited. None the less, among the many precursors to psychoanalytic thinking, following the arguments proposed by Whyte (1962), I wish to draw a distinction between two differing perspectives.

The first stream of thought follows the Cartesian mind–body or subject–object distinction. As noted previously, for Descartes it is the subject, the "I" that thinks and it is the object that is thought about. This distinction revolutionised our thinking about ourselves. It enabled a new way of looking at the subject, allowing for a "stepping back" such that we (subjects) could now see ourselves as objects to be studied as well as beings that experience and cognise. It brings the scientific perspective, previously developed to examine the natural world, clearly into the ambit of the study of the human mind, now seen as separate. Such a distinction, moreover, is critical for the discourse of a philosophy extracting itself from magical or theological explanations. This perspective was highly influential up until, and within, the late seventeenth- and eighteenth-century age of enlightenment, the culture of which emphasised reason and scientific investigation as an instrument to question ideas held simply through tradition and belief. We might say that Cartisian dualism was an important step in the history of thinking alongside the enlightenment development of the physical sciences, because it did aid in removing much reliance on magical explanations and their associated cultural discriminations. Notwithstanding, it provided a form of dualism that has captured and distorted thinking in the psychological and sociological domains through its separation of the integrity of organism with nature.

Michel Foucault chronicles the upheavals in thinking, perception, and language that followed the enlightenment. He describes massive changes in what he terms the structure of human discourses that began to articulate the subject in new ways. In terms of the new perspectives of science, this might be summed up where he says, "The object of discourse may equally well be a *subject* without the figures of objectivity being in any way altered" (Foucault, 1970, p. xiv).

Foucault's (1970) argument is that human subjectivity has emerged in the last two centuries, at least in western civilisation, as an episte-mological object. Humans have always had thoughts, emotions, and motives, but human subjectivity as an object of knowledge, Foucault argues, had not previously been formulated. In the classical era, human subjectivity was not, as in the modern era, a central focus for human institutions.

In his books *Madness and Civilization* and *The Birth of the Clinic*, Foucault examines the new ways of looking literally at the human body and mind that followed this enlightenment, and the concomitant changes in those social institutions that dealt with these new ways of thinking and were, hence, transformed in themselves. The changes moved ideas about causality away from devilry and superstition towards material and efficient causes.

But Foucault's analysis runs deeper. He argues that a new focus on a differently organised view was evident, where what was closely observed (the evidence) was now regarded as a surface symptom of a deeper cause. For example, the development of germ theory looked for underlying causes of bodily illnesses evidenced in symptom pat-terns. Psychological complexes began to be conceptualised "beneath" the expressions of madness. Although such ideas are found much ear-lier than enlightenment times, for example, as evidenced in Shake-speare and in literature more generally (Culler, 2002; Elam, 1986), the enlightenment, according to Foucault, brought them into science, dis-entangling them from other aspects of folklore. In this, Foucault's analysis links in with a second stream of thinking.

This second stream holds to the view that mind and body, subject and object are the same but in different forms. The eighteenth-century philosopher Herder exemplifies the position:

> The "object" is not so different from the "subject" insofar[sic] as the object is an external representation of the inner subjective: object and subject are two sides of the same coin. Will and representation are two forms of the one. That mind and body are one and not qualitatively different, was emphasised by Herder (1774) who saw them as having "different degrees of organization and development of a single 'power'". (European Graduate School (EGS), 2014)

This seamlessness between mind and body stands against the Cartisian distinction. Schelling held such a view. It states that life is a flow of experience of which consciousness is a fleeting and ephemeral part. The issue of emergence is more to do with the question of consciousness—how and why it might arise—than with the question of unconsciousness, which was understood as primordial and ground. Such a perspective could be regarded as a precursor to the thinking of much of psychoanalysis, and especially the object relations school, where concepts of projection (of inner to outer) and introjection (of outer to inner) predominate. In this view, the inner "will" is seen to hold sway over perception and representation of the outer world: an idea previously put forward by Kant, whose ideas were familiar to Freud and is referenced in his paper on the unconscious (Freud, 1915e).

Herder influenced Schopenhauer (1788–1860) who characterised "will" as a "mindless, aimless, non-rational urge at the foundation of our instinctual drives and at the foundation being of everything ... as being devoid of rationality or intellect" (Wicks, 2011), a description not too far from Freud's description of the special characteristics of the system unconscious.

> The nucleus of the ucs consists of instinctual representations ... to sum up *the characteristics of the system uncs*: exemption from mutual contradiction, primary process ... timelessness and replacement of external by psychical reality. (Freud, 1915e, p. 186, my italics)

The division of will and reason had been present in European philosophy since its beginnings. For instance, Plato discusses a tripartite organisation of the soul into reason, spirit, and appetite. Here, appetite refers to the push toward gratification and will refers (in part) to attempts to master appetite. The struggle of "will" against personal indulgence—gluttony, avarice, lust—features throughout human history and appears in our modern language as "willpower". But the notion of "will" is complex; it also takes on the notion of wilfulness. In Schopenhauer's thought, will is linked specifically to subjective experience. This idea of "will" is a precursor of Freud's idea of the drives and to Lacan's notion of desire, seen as only temporarily satisfied and displaced from one object to another.

> For Schopenhauer ... the tragedy of life arises from the nature of the will, which constantly urges the individual toward the satisfaction of

successive goals, none of which can provide permanent satisfaction for the infinite activity of the life force, or will. (Age of the Sage.com 2014)

For Schopenhauer, will is contrasted to intellect: the former state being "only there to lighten the way to the object of its desires", while the latter state

is the result of the intellect having gained ascendency over conscious-ness, where, freed from the mere service of the will, it grasps the phenomena of life objectively, and so cannot fail to see clearly the emptiness and futility of it. (Schopenhauer, 1893)

Despite the bleakness of such a view (not perhaps so different to the later Freud), Schopenhauer believed that a balance of will and intel-lect is needed for survival.

This second stream of thinking is linked to the Romantic movement of the eighteenth century and, hence, to Schelling and the German romantic philosophers. Romanticism held that the enlightenment base in reason alone was, through a rationalisation of nature, in danger of losing a more direct connection through emotional experience and subjectivity.

Criticisms of the idea of mind have been numerous. For example, referring to the idea of mind as an unnecessary "ghost in the machine" Ryle's (1949) critique of Cartesian dualism argues that the workings of mind are really no different from actions and it is, thus, unnecessary to postulate a hidden device behind action, a perspective adopted particularly by twentieth century behaviourist psychology, which, none the less, did not so much regard body and mind as one, as it dispelled both and replaced them with an automaton. The study of linguistics, semiology, epistemology, and modern neuropsychology continue to rest on the necessity of concept of mind, albeit in quite a transformed way, together with those of subjectivity and conscious-ness. Less focused on a duality of mind and body, current ideas on mind in persons, groups, and society have gained traction over the past century, leading to ideas of a collective mind. Moreover, contem-porary biosemiotics sees meaning and reasoning as embodied in nature, a logic of the sensible world (Harney, 2014) rather than in a separate human mind. This echoes Schelling's philosophy and his seminal ideas about the unconscious.

The two streams of thought outlined above infiltrate the many different theories found within psychoanalysis and socio-analysis. The idea of unconscious processes that can be studied through close observation of their effects—dreams, symptoms, slips of the tongue, and jokes—delineates an objective study of a mind–body interface. Psychoanalysis attempts the study of subjectivity as an objective endeavour, yet, at the same time, it does this through a subjective methodology: an exploration of the subjectivities of the analyst and analysand as they come together in the psychoanalytic encounter. Socio-analysis attempts this with the subject being society, the organisation, the system, and its context.

As we trace some of the ways in which the unconscious has been conceptualised within psychoanalysis and socioanalysis, it might be recognised that the pre-psychoanalytic distinctions and continuities of mind–body and subject–object are still present and influence thinking about unconscious processes. Psychoanalysis, since its inception, has been troubled by its status as a science, or lack thereof. Much positivist science tends to be based on the distinction between subject and object, notwithstanding the findings of quantum physics, while psychoanalysis and its heirs waver, unsure of their place (Long, 1996). For a fuller discussion of the unconscious before Freud, see Whyte (1962), McGrath (2012), and Ffytche (2014).

The next section will focus on unconscious processes in persons, while recognising that the distinction of mind in persons and groups is more an epistemological and practical distinction than an absolute one.

The unconscious as applied to persons

Sigmund Freud and the dynamic unconscious

I discuss Freud in this section because understanding of persons is paramount in his work and his method is focused on the analytic pair. However, the person and the social system are not as separate, as might at first seem. Many regard Freud as one of the greatest social theorists of the twentieth century and his theorising has inspired many forays into social understanding (e.g., Adorno et al., 1950; Brown, 1959; Marcuse, 1955, 1964; Reiff, 1966, 1979; Slater, 1966). His work on identification, narcissism, and group psychology is the foundation of much of our understanding of group dynamics and the person in Freud is always linked to the family and its social and historical context. None the less, in this chapter, I am breaking this connectedness down into its component parts (as does the TEF model) for ease of understanding and for allowing a focus on different elements within the complexity of human psycho-social dynamics.

Contrary to popular views, Freud's major contribution was not to discover "the unconscious", but to discover the use of free association—a method for exploring unconscious processes. "The poets and philosophers before me discovered the unconscious. What I discovered was the scientific method by which the unconscious can be studied" (Lehman, 1940).[1] Freud's work is most often traced back through a historical link to the work of Mesmer and Charcot through the application of magnetism and hypnosis (Rabstejnek, 2011). But the influence of philosophy, given Freud's wide reading, cannot be dismissed.

What, then, is the unconscious that Freud examined? Too often, the unconscious is seen as a "location" or storehouse and Freud sometimes writes as if it were. However, his main emphasis is that it is a system of the mind within which certain processes take place. In his paper on "The unconscious" (1915e), he talks of the system unconscious as one of three systems of mind. This is not a static storehouse view.

Freud's ideas have formed a foundation for our understanding of unconscious processes and his specific theory of repression—motivated forgetting—adds a new perspective to that found in pre-psychoanalytic ideas.

> We have learned from psychoanalysis that the essence of the process of repression lies, not in putting an end to, in annihilating, the idea which represents an instinct, but in preventing it from becoming conscious. When this happens we say of the idea that it is a state of being "unconscious", and we can produce good evidence to show that even when it is unconscious it can produce effects, even including some which finally reach consciousness. (1915d, p. 166)

In many ways it seems as if Freud has taken the concept of the unconscious from the philosophers and turned it on its head. For instance, whereas we see in Schelling and the German Romantics an ambition to understand how an intelligent and self-conscious world arose from an infinity that was unconscious, in Freud, we see an unconscious built through a process of repression occurring through personal and social history. Ideas that are repressed were once conscious. However, this difference might be more apparent than substantial because, despite the contribution of his theories of repression, Freud also recognises a primordial unconscious of inherited instincts that push for expression, much as the infinite spirit of Schelling wills its own realisation. Freud's interest is in the dynamics of this push for consciousness and in the opposing forces of repression that resist this, themselves unconscious.

A greater difference between the earlier views of the unconscious and the Freudian perspective is in Freud's rejection of a teleological emphasis such as is found in Schelling's work. In Schelling, it is the subordination of the unconscious to consciousness that enables its participation in love.

> Freud's dark principle (the id) is held down by consciousness. According to Schelling, the dark ground, when it acts in accordance with love, *holds itself back*; it defers to the light not because its desires are out of proportion to the modicum of pleasure reality can afford, but only by subordinating itself to consciousness can it participate in love. (McGrath, 2012)

We might, at first, argue with McGrath here, because the repressing action of the ego is itself part of the unconscious in Freud; the holding down is not strictly by consciousness, but by those unconscious egoistic forces pressing for individual survival. Yet, then again, the repression is from an ego once conscious and a superego shaped by social forces.

Schelling's description is partly present in Freud's idea of sublimation, where erotic love in a way holds itself back and is transformed into tender love, and in Ernst Kris's notion of regression-in-the-service-of-the-ego (Kris, 1952), where regression is not regarded as pathological, but as a means by which the unconscious might express itself creatively and, thus, actualise itself. None the less, the implication in Schelling is that the willing of the unconscious is *in order for* spirit to achieve self-recognition and connection with the other through love (and—as it was actualised in the fall—hate); hence, the teleological underpinning of the idea. There is a fulfilment or greater purpose stretching back, as it were, to pull the spirit forward. Freud's scientific deterministic disposition, on the other hand, looked to the psyche as primarily determined through personal history and repressive forces.

In Freud's work, the instincts or drives become represented in thoughts (1915c, 1923b). Whereas the person can flee anxiety-provoking stimuli that arise in the external world, the anxieties arising in relation to instinctual representations require different methods of escape; hence, the use of repression. Through this mechanism, the instinctual representations are forced back into unconsciousness. However, because thoughts have many associations in consciousness, more distant associations with the repressed thoughts might escape the repression and stay in consciousness. It is through these associations that the psychoanalytic method approaches the unconscious material.

> In carrying out the technique of psychoanalysis, we continually require the patient to produce such derivatives of the repressed, as in consequence either of their remoteness of their distortion, can pass the censorship of the conscious. Indeed the associations which we require him to give without being influenced by any conscious purposive idea and without any criticism, and from which we reconstitute a conscious translation of the repressed representative – these associations are nothing else than remote and distorted derivatives of this kind. During this process we observe that the patient can go on spinning a thread of such associations, till he is brought up against some thought, the relation of which to what is repressed becomes so obvious that he is compelled to repeat his attempt at repression. (Freud, 1915d, p. 149)

Freud's early theories are based on an idea of the mind as being formed and altered through psychic energy that is either bound to particular thoughts (cathected) or unbound and experienced as anxiety. Increasingly, his later theories became more focused on the symbolic processes of meaning making. Anxiety became not simply unbound energy, but a signal that a repressed idea or wish might become conscious and, thus, a threat to the ego and the person's narcissistic investments. In this later thinking (*The Ego and the Id*, Freud, 1923b), Freud moved to a model of the mind based on id, ego, and supergeo: three systems of mind roughly representing (i) instinctual forces, (ii) the part of the mind in touch with perception, conscious reasoning and reality, and (iii) the conscience and ego ideal. This model lies over his older model of the systems unconscious (ucs), preconscious (pcs) and conscious (cs), with the id as totally and always unconscious and sections of each of the other two systems being either conscious or unconscious. Many later psychoanalysts tend to avoid the idea of psychic energies as described by the early Freud, and the theory of id, ego, and superego has become dominant in the popular mind. None the less, repression *is* an energetic term—pushing ideas out of mind—and the idea of the unconscious has always been formed with the implication of energetic forces. "The nucleus of the ucs consists of instinctual representatives which seek to discharge their cathexis; that is to say, it consists of wishful impulses" (Freud, 1915e, p. 186).

Moreover, the very ideas of psychological defence and psychic conflict imply forces that act on one another: the theory of the defences being a foundation theory for psychoanalytic psychotherapy (for example, Malan, 1999) and, later, for ideas of social defences (Jaques, 1955; Menzies, 1970).

Although a powerful psychic force, repression is never whole or complete. Freudian psychoanalysis is concerned with the return of the repressed: how repressed thoughts influence current thinking, feeling, and actions. The method of Freudian psychoanalysis attempts to retrieve repressed thoughts and free the person from their domination.

So, we have, in Freud's idea of the unconscious, a dynamic system of the mind where threatening thoughts (instinctual representatives) are kept from consciousness, but not from having an impact on other thoughts, feelings, and behaviours. As Freud says, "a repression is something very different from a condemning judgement" (Freud, 1918b, pp. 79–80). Freud's analysis of dreams, parapraxis, jokes, and symptoms gives a picture of repressed ideas seeking to express themselves, to return to consciousness, at times cleverly evading the censorship of the conscious ego by mechanisms such as displacement and condensation (the primary mechanisms of dream work), processes that Freud describes as primary process thinking, or by rationalisations, denial, reaction formations, or other such defensive mechanisms. Perhaps the most ingenious mechanism if we are to anthropomorphise these processes, as Freud does for descriptive clarity (even as late as 1938 describing a defensive process as "artful" (Freud, 1940e)), is where the defence mechanism is "won over" so that the defence itself expresses the repressed thought (the hand-washing rituals of the obsessive neurotic being a prime example). The washing both represents the thought *and* represents the dismissal of the thought. Similarly, both loving and hating attitudes can be expressed in the same symptom. Freud calls these compromise products and describes such a defensive solution in his case study of the Wolf Man, whose obsessive thoughts linked God to faeces "in which a part was played no less by an affectionate current of devotion than by a hostile current of abuse" via the patient's anal eroticism (Freud, 1918b, p. 83). Clever! Such mechanisms illustrate how the ego itself is partly unconscious; striking deals as it were between combating forces. These ideas expressed by Freud through metaphors of attack and defence, censors and evaders, bring images of an internal world of conflictual systems that require neutralisation and provide a vision taken up more fully by later object relations theorists who describe an inner world of objects and partial objects striving among each other for expression in the experience of the person (subject).

The inner world as a place of conflict and turmoil is not new. The Ancient Greeks wrote this into their plays, where the conflicts between the gods paralleled and interacted with the internal conflicts of the human protagonists, as did Shakespeare, where the forces were often as much between natural forces as within human political intrigue. Inner conflict and turmoil is also at the centre of the tussle between temptation and piety, as portrayed in the great religions. However, for Freud, the turmoil has its developmental roots specifically in childhood sexuality and its conflict with the repressive forces of social mores and authority. For psychoanalysis, the nursery is the crucible of conflicts rather than the heights of Mount Olympus.

Within this picture of an active influential unconscious, in so far as unconscious ideas seek expression and other forces seek to prevent this, there is also the view of a rather unchanging scene. The system unconscious is regarded by Freud as entertaining no doubts or uncertainties, is free from internal contradictions, not altered over time, and pays "little regard to reality" (1914e, p. 186). Repressed material, it appears, is held in the grip of an extremely conservative and illogical system of mind, out of touch with reality and subject to phantastic satisfactions. Some more recent authors have taken up this view and regard this conservative and illogical system as an internal somewhat dictatorial "establishment" (Bion, 1970; Hoggett, 1997). We shall come to this later.

Freud's whole oeuvre is large and, of course, contains contrasting and conflicting ideas developed throughout his lifetime. This is natural in so far as an idea—such as the unconscious—is worked through and developed in the light of practice and experience. The determinist stance that drove him to create psychoanalysis as scientific by the standards of his time is matched by the influences of a more hermeneutic tradition or, beyond this, as a psychoanalytic method *sui generis* (Long, 2001). Freud follows Descartes in so far as "Lacan argued that the true significance of the *Cogito* was not perceived until Freud, who identified the true subject as the subject of the unconscious, the existence and nature of which is only detectable via the mediation of symptoms" (Restivo, 2013, p. 54).

Freud's unconscious, while emphasising the dynamic forces of instincts and repressions, also owes much to the influence of the romantic philosophers.

Jung and the collective unconscious

An understanding of the unconscious from the framework of the TEF cannot proceed smoothly from the categories of person, system, and context if we try to force a consistent reading of any one theory into these categories. This is already evident with Freud, whose theory of groups is returned to in a later section of this chapter. Jung's ideas of the collective unconscious and the archetypes must be mentioned in looking at the concept of the unconscious and its effects on the lives of individuals. For Jung, there are layers within the unconscious: the personal and the deeper, more primitive collective. The personal unconscious contains repressed ideas, traumas, and images, the shadow self and the inferior function of personality (either introverted or extraverted according to its opposite, the superior or consciously expressed function). The collective unconscious refers to inherited unconscious contents that are the same for everyone.

> The collective unconscious is a part of the psyche that can be negatively distinguished from a personal unconscious by the fact that it does not, like the latter, owe its existence to personal experience and,

consequently, is not a personal acquisition. While the personal unconscious is made up essentially of contents which have at one time been conscious, but which have disappeared from consciousness through having been forgotten or repressed, the contents of the collective unconscious have never been in consciousness, and, therefore, have never been individually acquired but owe their existence exclusively to heredity. Whereas the personal unconscious consists for the most part of complexes, the content of the collective unconscious is made up essentially of archetypes. (de Coster, 2010, p. 1)

Jung differed from Freud specifically around this issue and in his belief that Freud's exclusive focus on sexuality was too limited. He believed that the unconscious was a source of creativity beyond repressions. Freud's idea of sublimation has really only scratched the surface of this. Although Jung made no direct reference to Schelling's work on mythology, it might be argued that Schelling's perspective, through the influences of the nineteenth century romantics, influenced Jung's work on art, mythology, and the cultural expression of archetypes. Jung identified twelve major archetypes through his intensive studies of different cultures. They are unconscious representations of common human experience throughout our evolution and express deep human emotion: for example, the archetypes of the "hero", the "wise man", or the "innocent". "Consciousness rests upon and is organized by its archetypal forms and foundations. Dig far enough into an intense inner experience and you eventually come to the mythological, ageless themes that indicate an activated archetype" (Chalquist, 2015).

Jung worked extensively with psychotic patients whose hallucinations and delusions gave him indications of a collective as well as a personal unconscious. He viewed the personality as containing many "complexes"—"emotionally charged clusters of associations, usually unconscious and gathered around an archetypal center" (Chalquist, 2015). Freud has, of course, made the Oedipus complex central to his theorising and he also saw the importance of myth in understanding the human psyche. For Jung, the complexes arise from the need to adapt to reality and an inability to do so, either constitutional or due to external influences. Psychosis was the result of such an inability, but normal people also have unconscious complexes.

Jung is known mostly in organisational work for his theory of psychological types (Jung & Baynes, 1921), understood as emanating from four functions: sensation, intuition, thinking, and feeling. These functions are modified by the character types of introversion and extraversion. Although seen as consciously operating character types, Jung saw both extraversion and introversion as operating at an unconscious level in opposition to the main type. That is, if extraversion was operating in consciousness, introversion was unconsciously present, and if introversion was operating in consciousness, extraversion was unconsciously present. Still used extensively today, the Myers–Briggs Inventory (MBTI) was developed from the work of Jung by Isobel Briggs Myers and Katherine Cook Briggs from their own researches in the 1940s (Myers et al., 1998). It follows the deep interest in finding personality traits and dispositions that has captured western approaches to psychological measurement for the seventy years since the Second World War.

The unconscious in Jung's work is more closely linked to the Romantic philosophers views than is Freud's conceptualisation. The archetypes point to deeply embedded, species-wide cultural forms unconsciously transmitted across the generations that are a source of life and creativity and a kind of historical record of human culture. This echoes some of Schelling's ideas propounded in his history of the ages. There is an aesthetic dimension to the balance of conscious and unconscious expressions of the personality; for example, his ideas on anima and animus and introversion–extraversion. The unconscious not only holds the past but, through the will of the individual, it holds the future (Jung, 1939). While Freud works against the kind of teleological explanations popular in the nineteenth century, Jung, in some sense, embraces them. However, we must think of these two conceptualisations in their own historical contexts. Freud wanted to locate psychoanalysis within the science of his times—despite the tendencies in his work that are antithetical to empiricism and positivism—and to eschew the idea of teleology as it was understood in the biological sciences of the nineteenth century. The idea of teleology contains many meanings.

1. That final causes exist.
2. The idea of design or purpose in nature: the purpose for which things exist.
3. The idea that phenomena are guided not only by mechanical forces but that they move towards certain goals of self-realisation.

While it is accepted nowadays in science that human activities are guided to some extent by purpose and the vision of futures, early twentieth century science had a greater emphasis on the chemical, biological, and social efficient causes of behaviour, including psychosis and neurosis. Darwin's theory of evolution, for example, strongly argued against final causes in nature (see *Encyclopedia Brittanica* and Dictionary.com).

The idea of the unconscious in both Freud and Jung does contain notions of purpose, albeit in Freud these are part of the repressed unconscious and the unconscious drives of the id, while in Jung they also stem from strivings embedded in collective human history.

Object relations theory

Object relations is not a unified theory but a group or school of theories that understand the psyche as consisting of relations between "internal psychic objects". In a simple rendition of the idea, the internal object might be "an internal loving mother", or "a critical person", or "a powerful dictator". The whole idea of an internal critic—the conscience—was already well established as an idea before psychoanalysis. But object relations theories describe multiple inner objects, felt to be either good or bad. Internal objects are multi-faceted and complex and involve constellations of thoughts, feelings, and desires. "In essence, the term 'internal object' means a mental and emotional image of an external object that has been taken inside the self" (Bott Spillius et al., 2011). Here, "external object" is the object of some instinctual satisfaction or anxiety, usually a person but sometimes a "part-object", such as a breast or penis internalised very early in life as representing (for example) nurturance or withholding, power or loss. The internal object is partly a representation based on the infant's and later the adult's perception of the external object and partly a phantasy fuelled by projections into the external object and then reintrojected into the self, such phantasies being representations of primitive instinctual drives. Felt to be real and active, the internal objects are able to give the person pleasure or pain. They tend to take on a dynamic life of their own and very often conflict with each other.

This conceptualisation is a continuation of the idea of internal conflict described by Freud but with a complex understanding of how internal objects become established as part of the internal life of persons through processes of projection and introjection; incorporation and engulfment. One might hear in these ideas an echo of medieval notions of "possession" but formulated now in terms of psychological processes.

A founding figure in this "school" is Melanie Klein. Klein is usually respectfully referred to as Mrs Klein (which somewhat underscores her interest in infancy as a non-medical psychoanalyst, perhaps through the unconscious association to the Mrs by her followers). She analysed the early experiences of infancy in her adult patients as well as analysing children through watching and analysing their play activities. While, in Freudian analysis, interpretation of recalled past experiences is common, Klein's methods spend more time in analysing the current transference to the analyst. Freud had discussed transference in the case that he published as "Dora" (Freud, 1905e). This concept holds the idea that analysands transfer their feelings and thoughts about important others in their life to the analyst during psychoanalysis.

Following a paper by Ferenczi, Klein elaborated the concept of projective identification, a major concept dealing with the dynamics of internal objects and underscoring the emotional relatedness between people. Ferenczi was Klein's first analyst and influenced her thinking extensively. Many of the ideas contained within the object relations school can be attributed originally to him, but some of his practices and ideas led to his being marginalised within the psychoanalytic circle (Benedek, 1993; Kahn, 1998). The Melanie Klein Trust defines the concept:

Projective identification is an unconscious phantasy in which aspects of the self or an internal object are split off and attributed to an external object. The projected aspects may be felt by the projector to be either good or bad. Projective phantasies may or may not be accompanied by evocative behaviour unconsciously intended to induce the recipient of the projection to feel and act in accordance with the projective phantasy. (www.melanie-klein-trust.org.uk/ accessed 18 August 2014)

In addition to the defensive aspect of these dynamics—that is, casting out unwanted parts or protecting vulnerable parts of the self by projecting them into others—there is a manipulative and controlling aspect in relation to others.

> Phantasies of projective identification are sometimes felt to have "acquisitive" as well as "attributive" properties, meaning that the

phantasy involves not only getting rid of aspects of one's own psyche but also of entering the mind of the other in order to acquire desired aspects of his psyche. In this case projective and introjective phantasies operate together. (www.melanie-klein-trust.org.uk/ accessed 18 August 2014)

Internal objects may be more or less conscious and can include internal representations of self and other (Kernberg, 1968). The processes of projective identification are usually regarded as unconscious. While analysis enables people to begin a process of awareness, it is often through recognising the dynamic after, rather than during, its occurrence at an experiential level, due to the primitive and automatic manner in which it operates. Analysis of the transference allows something of the immediacy of the unconscious processes to be recognised, as does recognition of countertransference in the analyst. In addition, reflection on the possibility of projective identification before action allows the ego greater contact with reality.

For object relations theorists, the idea of unconscious processes operating within and between people through the dynamics of internalised objects builds on and expands Freud's views. Early infancy and relations with the mother take on more prominence. Unconscious phantasies are elaborated and a major therapeutic tool lies in the transference dynamics between analyst and analysand. For example, in exploring difficulties in the analytic process, Waska (2013, p. 63) says, "projective identification is an internal phantasy that often colours interpersonal dynamics potentially drawing the analyst into intra-psychic and interpersonal acting out of the patient's unconscious object relations". The analyst's task is to help the patient understand and process his or her unconscious phantasies through examining their appearance in the transference and in the countertransference, where the analyst finds "himself or herself forced to occupy the place assigned to him or her by the unfolding of the transference, or to confront the alternative of remaining outside the link" (Puget, 2002, p. 133). These ideas are nascent or implicit in Freud's work on unconscious processes.

Jacques Lacan: the unconscious structured as a language is structured

Lacan believed that Freud had been grossly misread and misinterpreted over the years, particularly in his translation into English. In

proposing a return to Freud's original texts, his early seminars cri-
tiqued readings by the schools of ego psychology and object relations
in particular (although he was an admirer of the contributions made
to the field by Melanie Klein, Wilfred Bion, and Donald Winnicott,
who were influential in the field of object relations but not typical of
the school).

He was particularly interested in Freud's early writings and ideas
that included Freud's formulation of the subject's relation to unconscious processes in his Project for a Scientific Psychology. Lacan
adapts the work of linguist Roman Jakobsen concerning the relation
between the signifier and the signified and applies the ideas of
metaphor and metonymy (major processes in our use of language) to
Freud's ideas of condensation and displacement (primary process).
Thus, in the relation between the signifier and the signified, metaphor
involves a condensation of signifiers (e.g., what does a word "mean")
and metonymy a displacement of signifiers (e.g., what does the slip-
of-the-tongue "mean").

Like Freud, he regards the subject's relation to unconscious processes to be manifest in the processes of speaking, both processes
being structured by difference—the meaning of a signifier being an
effect of its difference from other signifiers. Hence, the aphorism: the
unconscious is structured as a language is structured, that is, on the
basis of difference. Lacan understood the subject's relation to his or
her experience as being in relation to three registers that are inextricably bound up with each other: the Imaginary, the Symbolic, and the
Real registers. Experience in relation to the Imaginary is in terms of
what we experience perceptually as a contiguous space–time bounded
reality. In simple terms, it is that register of perceptions, images, and
thoughts that we think of as describing our everyday reality. The
terms in which we experience this everyday reality, however, are
shaped by the relation to the Symbolic register with its structuring of
difference. This shaping means that the relation to difference in the
Symbolic register mediates the ways in which we experience the
Imaginary.

The effects of our relation to the Symbolic are most apparent in our
relation to language, where the meaning of words or phrases as signifiers is defined not so much by what they refer to as by their difference from what we are not saying. The signifier "father" can be
used as an example. So, for instance, the Symbolic father shapes the

experience of the Imaginary father. However we experience the father through perception or imagination (a happy or sad father; a hostile or loving father), this experience is shaped by, or given meaning to (contained by), the relation to what "father" means as a difference within a family as an institution. The subject's relation to the register of the Real is then a relation to that which disrupts the contiguous and bounded nature of the Imaginary and to that which escapes signification, falling outside the Symbolic. Experience in relation to the Symbolic register is in terms of the chaining of signifiers in the unconscious, which might or might not be articulated in the subject's speech, hence the gaps in conscious associations identified by Freud. For Lacan, the *interpretive unconscious* (sometimes referred to as the transference unconscious, or the Imaginary Unconscious) is a relation to the chains of signifiers that are not articulated in consciousness, while the *real unconscious* is a relation to gaps in the unconscious structuring of difference itself. Thus, with the interpretive unconscious, unconscious signifiers do not stand rigidly for an object or idea in perception. The relation between the two may be changed according to the context of other unconscious signifiers. Lacan describes this as the signifier "sliding" across the signified. This understanding of the unconscious leads Fazioni (2012, p. 5) initially to say, "the unconscious is not the place of irrational instincts or our psychical inner coffer. It is a logical–dialectical system that is interpretable by the psychoanalyst as a literary text": that is, an unconscious that can be interpreted. But, he goes on to argue, psychoanalysis is not simply a hermeneutic exercise. Following Lacan, it is an ability to "work with a subject without reducing the subject to his representation" (Fazioni, p. 11). Lacan's notion of the real moves us beyond hermeneutics.

Entering into this picture is then the relation to the real unconscious and the notion of "desire", Lacan's word for that which is familiar to readers of the Strachey translation of Freud as "wish", although desire holds more of the relation to the lost object that Freud theorised. The lost object is that which cannot be repeated, constituted by gaps in the unconscious structuring of difference in relation to which the subject experiences the partial drives. Lacan identified these partial drives as oral, anal, phallic (the relation to signification), scopic (the gaze), and invocatory (the voice). As with Freud, in Lacan the subject's relation to desire is a manifestation of the relation to these partial drives, with the complication that our ego misrecognises this relation as a demand, our relation to desire being defined more by what is missed in the pursuit of satisfying these demands. The relation to desire is, therefore, shaped by the relation to the Symbolic that functions like the Law—the law of the father in the oedipal context.

The ways in which a desire manifests itself in the form of a demand is, therefore, a social concept originating in those places where the Imaginary's body and the Symbolic's organisation of difference intersect in everyday reality: Lacan describes these places as cuts in the ego's boundaries where the inside–outside difference in the Imaginary breaks down and there is also a relation to a gap in the Symbolic—the erogenous zones, for example, the lips, the anus, the sexual organs, but also the gaze and the voice. Because these cuts in the ego's boundaries are shaped by the relation to the Symbolic, they are signifiers and not simply the body parts of everyday reality. They stand in the place of desire, representations of desire taking the form of demands that can never be fully satisfied because of their relation to what is lost to the unconscious—a loss that is not just repressed, but that is radically unknowable.

Towards the end of his work, Lacan referred to the subject's particular relation to this radical unknowability as the subject's sinthome, taking up a relation to this sinthome being "true to desire"—the Lacanian understanding of the psychoanalytic ethic. The sinthome here is not analysable in the sense of being a signifier, but is an expression of the subject's enjoyment of the unconscious (*jouissance*) and holds together the knot of the Symbolic, Imaginary and Real.

> The sinthome is what is left after going through the enigma of the formation of the unconscious and its repetitive and never-ending productions of meaning. . . . The symptom has something to say; there is communication taking place on the level of the symptom. . . . The symptom lives in the domain of the transference unconscious, whereas the sinthome is a consistency detached from the production of meaning . . . on a certain consistency of jouissance. (Restivo, 2013, p. 157)

Lacan has extended the idea of the unconscious through his distinctions between the registers of the Imaginary, the Symbolic, and the Real and through his exploration of sexual difference and *jouissance*. While there is an element of the unconscious that can speak and be interpreted, there is also that which cannot be spoken, that is outside signification and can only be experienced through *jouissance* and its expression in sexuality and art.

Bion and the unconscious infinite

Wilfred Bion took the idea of unconscious process and transformed it. While Freud and Klein formulated their theories predominantly around sexuality, the life and death instincts, and the oedipal family configuration, Bion developed a metapsychoanalysis around epistemology (Grotstein, 1997). His focus was on how emotional experience was transformed into thoughts and how the mind develops in order to think those thoughts. In this he builds upon a small section of Freud's paper on the unconscious, which states, "It is a very remarkable thing that the *Uncs.* of one human being can react upon that of another, without passing through the *Cs.* This deserves closer investigation . . ." (Freud, 1915e, p. 198).

Bion does engage in this further investigation, for it is this phenomenon, considered as incontestable by Freud, that indicates a system of thoughts independent of conscious thinkers. This will be an important idea for thinking about the unconscious in groups and organisations later in this chapter.

Bion took forward Klein's ideas on projective identification. He introduced the ideas of container–contained, whereby the container is able to accept projections and, through a process of reverie, is able to transform the projected material. In this view, projective identification can be regarded as a form of communication. The prototypical example of such communication is the projection of distressing experiences from infant to mother who, as container, through reverie and a capacity to think, is able to transform the distressing experience into an experience that is tolerable. This is then transmitted back to the infant. In this extension of the concept of projective identification, the dynamics are between people, not simply an intrapersonal phantasy. Clarke describes this:

> For Bion (1962), therefore, projective identification is part of the thinking process. Originally a procedure for "unburdening the psyche of accretions of stimuli" (Bion, 1962, pg 31) phantasy is projected into the container, and in a reprocessed form projected back into the projector. The point is that bad or intolerable feelings are transformed by the

recipient and are made tolerable. Bion calls this process of transformation the "alpha function". If, as Bott-Spillius[sic] (1988) notes, "all goes well", then the projector, the infant, eventually introjects this function of transformation and thus develops a means of thinking and tolerance of frustration (Bott-Spillius[sic], 1988, pg 155). (Clarke, 2014)

Bion was convinced, from his study of psychotic phenomena, that the psyche needs not simply to express and protect itself but needs to pursue truth in order to develop. While knowledge is often conscious, truth is rarely in the realm of conscious knowledge. For Bion, "O" is ultimate truth, unattainable in its totality, and resides not in sensory knowledge and learning, but in a deeper non-sensory understanding of emotional experience.

Bion (1965, 1970) would frequently cite Milton's phrase, "the deep and formless infinite" in regard to his comments about "O." . . . Bion's picture of the Unconscious, along with that of Winnicott and Matte-Blanco, conveys an ineffable, inscrutable, and utterly indefinable inchoate formlessness that is both infinite and chaotic—or complex—by nature. *It is what it is and is always changing while paradoxically remaining the same.* From this point of view, Freud's instinctual drives and Klein's paranoid–schizoid and depressive positions can be understood as secondary structures, strategies or filters, to assist the infant in mediating this chaos. (Grotstein, 1997)

While Freud, in his later theories, had conceptualised the psyche primarily as consisting of structures (the id, the ego, the superego), Bion remained with Freud's earlier ideas of systems and their functions (Symington & Symington, 2002), developing his ideas about the processes of thinking and coming to understand the truth in things. Taking the way we use language figuratively in relation to thought and emotion (e.g., chewing over an idea or not stomaching an experience), he explored the process of thinking in terms of digestive processes—incorporating or expelling thoughts as if they were good or bad food. He believed that the capacity to think grew from such bodily processes in order to think about the environment. Only more recently in our evolutionary history have we come to think about ourselves and our own thinking.

It is this idea of thought as object, and thinker as subject that opens for us a new view of unconscious process. Thinking develops as alpha function organises emotional experience into preconceptions. When such preconceptions match or "mate with" a realisation, a concept is developed. In a patterned way, "constant conjunctions" of thoughts begin to emerge and "selected facts" serve to centre these conjunctions within models or theories: a theory about what a certain experience means or about what name should be given to a class of objects, for example. This is an all too brief description of Bion's view about how thinking develops largely unconsciously in the person (for a fuller description, see Bion, 1963, 1965, 1967; Grotstein, 2007). We must move to an understanding of the unconscious in groups and organisations to link the theory of the development of thinking, with the notion (later in Bion's work) that thinking develops in order to deal with thoughts. Before that, I examine briefly the relation of unconscious process to creativity because this will become important when discussing unconscious processes at a social level.

Creativity and the unconscious

For Freud, the return of the repressed was most healthily expressed in the process of sublimation. He saw the creative artist as steering a path between trauma and artistic creation. This linked creativity closely with unconscious process. Such an idea is further expressed in the work of Kris (1952) and Ehrenzweig (1967). The artist is seen to move between regression and rationality, unconscious scanning and conscious focus, playful free association and careful evaluation. But, in Freud's conception, creativity is a solution to the problem of anxiety and repression rather than a direct expression of the unconscious. Perhaps a rather harsh critic in this regard, Whyte says,

> Freud neglected one of the most important, had nothing fresh to say about it, and seems only to have mentioned it in passing: the general character of the unconscious mental processes which underlie the appearance of novelty in all creation, imagination and invention. (Whyte, 1962, p. 68)

Schelling's idea of the unconscious as a source of creativity is revived in the work of Wilfred Bion. Bion's epistemology places unconscious processes at the heart of creativity. This is implicit in his naming the unconscious as infinite, with all possibility. The "artfulness" during symptom formation described by Freud and noted earlier in this chapter is part of that creativity, as is the creative *jouissance* of the sinthome as described by Lacan. The play of primary process underpins the possibility of new solutions. Moreover, the processes delineated by Bion in his clinical practice as he traces how emotional experience is transformed are essentially creative. The emergence of constant conjunctions and selected facts occur in primary process thinking during reverie or during dreaming when unconscious process has free rein.

> Although the extraordinary creative idea may originate in a dream there is reluctance to admit this for it is embarrassing to acknowledge the irrational. Einstein was honest enough to admit that the solution to the general theory of relativity, after years of fruitless calculations, came from a dream "like a giant die making an indelible impress, a huge map of the universe outlined itself in one clear vision" (Brian, 1996, p. 159, in Lawrence & Long, 2010, p. 220)

Christopher Bollas captures and blends Freud's idea of repression together with Bion's idea of thoughts requiring a thinker in his concept of the unconscious as "the unthought known": the unconscious that holds that which is known or has been known but is currently unable to be thought (Bollas, 1989). A major part of this is that ideas become available to the infant as actions before he or she can give them language. This leads us to question of what prevents the thinking. Psychoanalysis has proposed the answer variously, among others, as: narcissistic threat (Freud), social anxieties (Neo-Freudians), annihilation anxieties emanating from death instincts (Klein), and nameless dread (Bion). We can consider further the question of what prevents the thinking of thoughts by persons when we consider role, system, and context.

In concluding this section, we can state that the unconscious as understood in terms of the person in the twentieth and twenty-first centuries, albeit with influences from systems and contexts, has been dominated by Freud's conception of repression and by his use of free association in exploring unconscious processes. We are affected by things that we once knew but had good reason to forget and that we spend some degree of energy in keeping out of mind. This manner of regarding the unconscious leads to methods by which we attempt to recover memories, or to work through re-enactments of past experiences. It implies a somewhat wilful ignorance and a depth psychology that can be mined in the person. It demands an exploration of personal biography with personal meanings. It understands mind as split and conflicted.

Unconscious processes in groups or organisations and systems

It is not simply individuals who get caught in unconscious processes. Groups, teams, organisations, and societies also are subject to such dynamics. The transforming experience framework points to this through its focus on role, system, and context. If we follow Bion's ideas of the unconscious infinite, we can comprehend this as not contained within the boundaries of the person, but stretching across boundaries, roles, and systems. We can say that unconscious process is a property of the group, much as language and other symbolic and signifying processes are properties of the group. The group-as-a-whole has unconscious assumptions, beliefs, and arguments that influence how it acts, perceives, and feels through its representatives. This may be discerned when all group members act, think, or feel similarly, as in group-think (Janis, 1972) or basic assumption thinking (Bion, 1961; Long, 1996; Lawrence et al., 1996; Turquet, 1974).

An additional complexity is evident, however, when, during a group task, group members have differing thoughts and feelings leading to the propensity to act in different ways. While each may be acting out of individual propensities, we can also say that each represents something about the state of the group-as-a-whole. It is easy to see the differences in terms of personal differences, but this will be misleading when we want to understand the group. One person alone might be representing something about the group that is important in their collective work. Others might be representing a defence against that representation. Just as when Freud explained the trickiness of the symptom that unconsciously both expresses and defends against a taboo thought, so group members could represent different aspects of an overall group dynamic, expressing and defending against particular ideas or inclinations. Averaging individual responses to find meaning will lose this understanding. The whole is greater than the sum of its parts. It is in the differences within the group that we can come to identify its unconscious process as well as through its members' similarities. Taking a Lacanian perspective, the various group roles might each be conceptualised as signifiers in the signifying chain that is the group dynamic (Long, 1991).

Although there are many theories that apply psychoanalytic ideas, including the unconscious, to examine large-scale societal and political dynamics, I do not have space here to examine them. Rather, I note the influence of the concept of the unconscious on broad social theory. As outlined at the beginning of this chapter, my aim is not a comprehensive review of theories of the unconscious, but to examine a small number of theories that illuminate how the concept has been developed and transformed, especially by systems thinking.

Socio-analysis is a term coined to describe the study of groups, organisations, and society from a psychoanalytic and systems theory perspective (Bain, 1999; Long & Sievers, 2012). Others have termed this "systems psychodynamics" (e.g., Gould & Stein 2006; Gould et al., 2004; Hirschhorn, 1988; Obholzer & Roberts, 1994; Stapley, 2006, to name but a few). The discipline grew out of work done by Bion, Rickman, Bridger, Main, and others during and after the Second World War. As psychoanalysts and social scientists, these pioneers worked in officer selection with the British army and at Northfield hospital with soldiers psychologically damaged by the war. They regarded the problems they faced in these tasks as involving systemic dynamics rather than purely issues about individuals or about interpersonal relations (Trist & Murray, 1990). The distinction between interpersonal and group or system dynamics is critical. Interpersonal dynamics involve direct person-to-person communication—perhaps among several people. System dynamics mediate that direct relationship through a third position, that of the system, its purposes, and tasks. So, systemically, persons are related to one another by means of their positions in the system (i.e., their roles related to tasks—see Long, 1992), not by means of a direct relationship. Their differences of position and role and the relations between them are key to our understanding of group dynamics.

As with psychoanalysis, the theories in the field of socio-analysis are extensive. But before looking in more detail at socioanalytic ideas of the unconscious we should look at relational psychoanalysis to recognise a shift in the subject/object relation.

Relational psychoanalysis

Jessica Benjamin (1988) and others are described as relational psychoanalysts. These analysts have a major focus on interpersonal as well as intrapersonal dynamics, recognising the effects of the analyst as a subject in relation to the subject of the analysand. Benjamin stresses the needs for recognition and assertion in relations between people, using the master–slave dynamic outlined by Hegel. The mutual needs in the relations between subjectivities are highlighted, whatever the power relations. Like the object relations theorists, inner phantasy life is regarded as important.

Relational psychoanalysis changes the language used in analysis in order to stress the effects of the analyst as subject rather than as a distant objective element in the analysis. Analysis is seen as an inter-personal encounter. The unconscious dynamic becomes one that is engaged by both parties, analyst and analysand. This emphasis begins a greater focus on the analytic dyad as a system, hence the inclusion of relational psychoanalysis in this section. It contains ideas that behaviours, situations, and dynamics are unconsciously co-created.

Group dynamics

For Freud (1921c), the dynamics of the group rest on identification. Each member identifies with the leader (or a leading idea) in their ego ideal (part of the superego) and identifies with one another in their egos. The dynamic of identification might be quite unconscious, although its effects and the feelings of loyalty (to the leader) and simi-larity (to other group members) are conscious. The difference between the dynamics of libido—love for the self or other—and the dynamics of identification—the wish to be like the other—are significant in the understanding of group behaviours. Both operate at a social level.

Bion developed ideas on groups from his work with them in the 1940s and 1950s. In this period, he focused on group culture and the manner in which group members collectively protected themselves from the anxieties present in group life. Here, in an extension of Freud's ideas about groups, he established the idea of basic assump-tions in group life. These assumptions centre on how the group mem-bers collectively relate to the leader in their attempts to avoid anxiety. Naming dependency, flight/fight, and pairing as phantasy cultures, he describes the effects these have unconsciously on the behaviour of group members and how they can derail the consciously planned work of the group. A large literature has grown around the idea of basic assumption behaviour in groups and in investigating their relation to the work group (e.g., French & Simpson, 2015; Gould, 2015; Rioch, 1970).

Basic to the relation between individual and group is a network of what Bion terms proto-mental processes. This is an unconscious network of processes directly emanating in the group. "The sphere of proto-mental events cannot be understood by reference to the individual alone, and the intelligible field of study for proto-mental events is the individuals met together in a group" (Bion, 1962, quoted in Morgan-Jones, 2010, p. 224).

Also,

> The proto-mental system I visualise is one in which physical and psychological or mental are undifferentiated. It is a matrix from which spring the phenomena from which appear – on a psychological level and in the light of psychological investigation – to be discreet feelings only loosely associated with one another. It is from this matrix that emotions proper to the basic assumption flow to reinforce, pervade, and on occasion, to dominate the mental life of the group. (Bion, 1961, p. 89)

Bion is clear that the proto-mental matrix does not cause the basic assumptions in a linear fashion, but that they are related more in a patterned or circular manner: emotion triggering assumptions and assumptions sustaining emotions. The proto-mental matrix provides an explanation for Bion's concept of individual valency: how individuals are drawn to join in particular basic assumptions (Morgan-Jones & Torres, 2010). This theory of proto-mental processes is reminiscent of the earlier philosophical position of Herder, who argued that body and mind were not distinct, but basically one and the same. This view is now taken to the level of the group where a matrix of emotion crosses individual body boundaries.

Bion returned to social ideas later, following his more intensive study of psychosis and his development of a theory of thinking. In this later work, he identifies the ways in which individuals and groups are related to one another. This is done within a language that emphasises the social nature of humans, or what he terms "groupishness". This groupishness becomes evident as an internalised system as well as a contextual system for the person. For example, he describes the relation of a social establishment to a radical thinker in terms of his theory of thinking. The social establishment is parallel to the established mind of the thinker, with established thoughts that serve both understanding and defensiveness toward the chaos that a new idea might bring. The radical, or "messiah", brings a messianic idea that will disturb the social establishment (say, a ruling elite), much as a new idea or experience demanding a new idea will disturb an established mind. Peace of mind will be disturbed in both cases. Bion describes three forms of relatedness. First, in the relation between the establishment and the messiah, the mind and the new idea might be commensal, that is, both go along without really influencing one another in a form of denial that they ever came in contact. Alternatively, in a second form, the relation might be parasitic, where one or the other destructively gains at the expense of the other. In an extreme case, the new idea might completely destroy the establishment, leaving no container for it to grow within, such as in a psychotic breakdown of the mind, or in a social rebellion that has no containing governmental structure and consequently diffuses in competitive or envious dynamics. A third form of the relation is symbiotic. Here, the contact between the two might be creative. The establishment is able to contain and nurture the new ideas (Bion, 1970).

These ways of conceptualising the effects of new thoughts show the tenuous relation between thought and thinker that we saw when discussing the theory of thinking in the section under the person. Constant conjunctions of thought occur through the experience of the person within a system (group, organisation, society). The conjunctions are both within and between people. They attempt to organise and bring into being the unconscious infinite that flows within and between. It is only through the structure of consciousness—structured by the boundaries created by language and culture—that the flow becomes contained and held. Yet, this containment, this bringing to consciousness, is never complete:

> "Thoughts without a thinker" derive from "O." They are the "unborns," the "intimations of immortality" that we seemingly experience as located within our inner cosmos, but they are placeless, unlocatable. They cannot be found because they can never be the object; they can only enhance our sense of subjectivity. (Grotstein, 1997)

This is reminiscent of Schelling's unconscious in God that wills actualisation in order to be known: cf. the thought that needs to find a thinker.

The idea of a proto-mental matrix, the relation between thoughts and thinkers, and the relation of a new thought to the establishment are ideas that are critical to Bion's view of the unconscious as it operates in a group or social system.

The theory of social defences

Since the pioneering work of Jaques (1955) and Menzies Lyth (1988, 1989), a complex theory of organisation as a defence against painful emotions has emerged in the literature. Hinshelwood and Skogstad (2000), for example, describe an anxiety-culture-defence model that is indicative of a social defence theory. Hirschhorn (1988) describes how normal anxieties arising from everyday work—especially during workplace communications and the taking up of authority—give rise to defensive chains of behaviour. Basically, these theories state that anxieties originating in people's responses to their work tasks, when experienced repeatedly and by many within an organisation, lead to a collective defence. Such social defences could permeate the organisational culture and structures so fully that the defensive mechanisms undermine the tasks that the organisation should be undertaking in order to prosper. Furthermore, just as with personal defences, the social defence might create secondary anxieties and dysfunctional symptoms. All this occurs outside of the consciousness of the organisational players and with evidence to indicate that because the dynamic serves a socially defensive purpose, that is, many people have a stake in its continuance, it is part of the repressed unconscious.

The idea of unconsciously formed social defences has been developed and extended beyond organisational to societal dynamics (e.g., Armstrong & Rustin, 2015; Krantz, 2010; Long, 2006, 2008; Long & Sievers, 2012) and to country level dynamics (Boccara, 2013, 2014). It seems that the size of the system is no impediment. In these instances, the anxieties or other distressing emotional responses are in relation to large systemic threats such as perceived national traumas, economic crises, natural disasters, or other wide-scale challenges to a relatively comfortable *status quo*. These theories extend the idea of unconscious processes beyond the individual psyche to broad collective dynamics.

Group relations

The systems psychodynamic perspective, together with social defence theory, has informed a method of exploring group dynamics known as group relations conferences. This method began at the Tavistock Institute of Human Relations (TIHR) and the first such conference was held at Leicester University in 1957 (see Aram et al., 2009; Brunner et al., 2006; Fraher, 2004, who provides a history of the group relations movement; Miller, 1990; Rice, 1965).

Group relations work has been particularly influenced by the object relations school of psychoanalysis and by the work of Wilfred Bion. It studies the systemic and unconscious dynamics that occur within and between groups. The conference is designed as a temporary organisation with the task of learning about group dynamics. The conference staff members are managers of the temporary organisation and from their "collective management" they provide consultancy to the conference members in their learning task. This task is carried out through the "here and now" study of group dynamics as they occur in different group settings. Alongside these "here and now events" are conference events that review what has occurred and events that consider the application of learning from the conference to members' workplaces.

The importance of group relations to the intent of this chapter is that the conferences enable a direct exploration of unconscious processes in groups and social systems where the focus is on the system rather than the person. The method is akin to clinical psychoanalysis except in its systemic focus and in the primarily educational, rather than therapeutic, purpose. This is notwithstanding that clinical psychoanalysis also has an educational purpose. Through group relations methods, systemic unconscious processes are hypothesised and explored directly in the temporary organisation. This has led to such explorations also being undertaken in workplaces, not directly through the conference method, but through workplace cultural analyses, role analyses, socio-technical analyses, and other forms of socio-analytic interventions (see the journals *Socioanalysis* and *Social and Organizational Dynamics* for examples). The transforming experience framework first developed through the Grubb Institute and now the Grubb Guild grew within this context.

Perverse social dynamics

Much has been written about narcissism in leaders and narcissistic social dynamics; also about psychotic organisational dynamics

(Sievers, 1999, 2008). From my own studies, I have identified dynamics in organisations that include a narcissistic component alongside a particular configuration of defences and ideologies that echo the perverse position in individuals (Long, 2008). I explore five key aspects of perverse dynamics: (i) the narcissistic position where individual pleasure and gain is regarded as more important than the purposes and gains for the group or society; (ii) the use of denial as a major defence, where denial involves knowledge of, and belief in, both A and not A at the same time (involving "turning a blind eye"); (iii) the engagement of accomplices in the perversion; (iv) the use of instrumental power and ideology; (v) the pervasive cycle of unconscious perversion and its links to corruption. Using this definition of perverse dynamics, I analyse a variety of emotional states in organisations such as pride in Long Term Capital Management (LTCM) in the USA, greed in Parmalat in Italy, and envy in professional organisations. The perverse dynamics involved led to the downfall of managers and even of the organisations themselves, with wider implications for their stakeholders.

As an example, HIH Insurance was the second largest insurance company in Australia (see Long, 2008). The stories from HIH were not primarily about corruption, embezzlement, or illegal activities, despite the criminal convictions given to two of its directors. HIH's problem was that subtle and unconscious processes were operating—assumptions, unspoken agreements, turning a blind eye. The board gave in to pressure (*from the CEO*) and responded with fear and withdrawal from their responsibilities. The CEO retained a narcissistic and overbearing outlook. He hired "mates" on to his board—mates he hoped would not question his decisions. Important decisions were driven through when players likely to question them were absent. To understand what occurred does not require that we understand the big financial issues. We need to understand what happens between people in close group settings. In this case, the board neglected its duty and became lazy about its processes, manipulated by senior managers who believed that they knew best and would be able to pull the organisation out of any difficulties. In addition, the board was manipulated so that important decisions were made when members with an opposing view were absent.

The unconscious examined here is a social process lodged in the assumptions, structures, and culture of the organisations involved.

This is not an unconscious embedded in a single mind defined within the confines of a nervous system, or even an individual mind emergent from that nervous system. It is a process between people located in their institutions. This perspective is examined more fully in the section about the unconscious and context.

The unconscious through a socio-analytic lens

What has changed in the conceptualisation of the unconscious through a socio-analytic perspective? I can identify the following.

- Unconscious process is understood to occur collectively and systemically. The mechanisms through which it operates include projective identification, mirroring, parallel process, symptom formation, defensive processes, and collective unconscious assumptions. These concepts build on the ideas of identification and libidinal connections put forward initially by Freud and the group basic assumptions articulated by Bion (1961). They are extended also in the work of other European and South American analysts (Hinshelwood & Chiesa, 2002).
- Unconscious process is a property of the group rather than the individual. It is expressed through persons (particularly persons in their organisational roles)—their actions, thoughts, and feelings—much as the structure and dynamics of language (a group property) is expressed though a speaking individual.
- Individual persons come to contain aspects of the unconscious infinite depending on their roles, personal biographies, valencies, and experiences.
- Different groups unconsciously represent something of a whole organisation or of a whole institution, much as persons unconsciously represent something of the group-as-a-whole. This is notwithstanding that representation may also be conscious.
- Unconscious neurotic, psychotic, and perverse defensive dynamics operate at a group level.
- Creative processes and the emergence of new ideas is dependent as much upon the boundarylessness of the unconscious infinite as it is on the capacity of people to create boundaries to contain the new ideas. This is because the boundarylessness allows the development and transfer of thoughts across thinkers.

The socio-analytic or systems psychoanalytic perspective has embraced the ideas found within the psychoanalytic approach to persons, groups, and societies but has added a systems perspective. This has expanded the idea of the unconscious more fully from an intrapersonal and interpersonal process to a social process.

Conceptualising a group unconscious has been done in many ways that range from the extrapolation of individual to group dynamics (the least satisfactory solution because the individual and group systems are not identical) through to seeing the group-as-a-whole with its own system dynamics (Kaes, 2002; Puget, 2002). It is perhaps misleading to frame this as a group "mind" in the same sense that an individual has a mind, but a consciousness and an "unconsciousness" beyond the individual is a compelling proposition. The collective sensibility of a group is described by Halbwachs (1992), who explores "collective memory" as a socially constructed shared memory derived from the shared experiences of group members. Sievers (2015, personal communication) takes this idea, together with Bollas's notion of "evocative objects", into a sensitive exploration of family memories evoked by a photograph of himself as a small boy. There are parallels between individuals and groups that can give rise to hypotheses about either system. The TEF generally takes the view that the dynamics of person and of group are different and influence the experience of person *qua* person and of person in role. However, the TEF diagram is of interacting persons, systems, contexts, and source. These are integrally linked and cannot really be understood in isolation.

Unconscious process and context

I repeat here what is said in Chapter One of this book. Context is the environment within which a social system occurs. That environment includes the physical, political, economic, social, historical, international, and emotional context for the system. What is currently occurring in the context will have an effect on persons, organisations, and social systems.

Sometimes, we might not be aware of contextual issues, but they still affect us. For instance, climate change and its effects on species survival might not seem to affect us directly, but loss of some insect species could affect food production and the direct effect on us might be in prices. Similarly, we might be unaware of the way we perceive different groups of people due to political or economic contextual issues and their presentation in the media and, hence, the effects this has on our judgements and decisions about them.

Awareness of context allows us to discern the resources and connections that may be found there. The experience of connectedness to context enables the use of resources in a sustainable, rather than an exploitative, manner.

The social unconscious

The idea of a social unconscious was first framed by Eric Fromm:

> ... each society determines which thoughts and feelings shall be permitted to arrive at the level of awareness and which have to remain unconscious. Just as there is a social character, there is also a 'social unconscious. (Fromm, 1962, p. 88)

The social unconscious is an important aspect of group analytic psychotherapy, founded by S. H. Foulkes (see Foulkes, 1986[1975]). This form of therapy makes interventions to the group-as-a-whole conceptualised as having an unconscious mental field across all members. Foulkes states,

> When a group of people, by which for our purposes I mean a small number of persons, form intimate relationships, they create a new phenomenon, namely, the total field of mental happenings between them all ... The point I wish to stress is that this network is a psychic system as a whole network, and not a superimposed social interaction system in which individual minds interact with each other. This is the value of thinking in terms of a concept which does not confine mind, by definition, to an individual. (Foulkes, 1990[1971], p. 224)

While his description of the unconscious matrix of "mental happenings" that is a property of the group rather than the individual resonates with Bion's ideas of a proto-mental matrix (both had ideas of the group-as-a-whole), Foulkes differs from Bion. He disagrees with what he considered as Bion's idea of the transference of the internal dynamics of the person to the group. Instead, he refers to a social unconscious that consists of social contexts that are generally not detected. He regards the community as the primary focus and that the inner processes of the individual are internalisations of the forces operating in the group (Foulkes 1990[1971]).

Hopper, following Foulkes, discusses the psychoanalytic idea of transference in terms of context. Transference occurs in the person as an unconscious replication of past events or attitudes to a current situation or person. But the context is critical. Hopper says,

> In attempting to contextualise a transference is it possible and is it therapeutically useful to explore a full range of events on the dimensions of time and social psychological space? How far from the so-called "here and now" should we go? The later phases of life? The structure and function of social institutions, not only now but also in a person's past? Should we take account of events which occurred even before a person was born and were located in another country? (Hopper, 2003 p. 105)

These questions of context are important when we consider understanding unconscious issues in a cross-cultural setting. What is embedded in the institutions and histories of different cultures becomes embedded in unconscious processes of communication (Volkan, 2001, 2005). The concept of the social unconscious, according to Hopper, refers to the existence and constraints of social, cultural, and communicational arrangements of which people are unaware:

> unaware insofar[sic] as these arrangements are not perceived (not known) and if perceived are not acknowledged (denied) and if acknowledged are not taken as problematic (given) and if taken as problematic are not considered with an optimum degree of detachment and objectivity. (Hopper, 2003, p. 127)

Fromm, Foulkes, and Hopper take the idea of the unconscious and centre it in the idea of social unawareness. This concept of the unconscious refers not to simple ignorance, but adds an almost wilful non-acknowledgement of social and cultural issues that are harmful to work and wellbeing. As with other group and social perspectives on the unconscious, it shares in the idea of collective denial and of turning a blind eye, but it adds a political dimension. The social unconscious implies, on the one hand, a possible attitude of detachment from the common good. On the other hand, it includes reference to those impediments to social justice that lie in inequalities of information. This is a different dimension in thinking about unconscious dynamics. These dynamics are no longer simply transposed from the psychodynamics of the "person" to the larger systems of social and organisational dynamics, however valid and helpful that might be. The social system, with its politics and ethics, is now an integral part of an idea of the unconscious.

Of relevance here are the theories of Rene Girard, a French-American anthropologist and theologian. Girard (1977) argues that the central dynamic of human relations is "mimesis": the human tendency to imitate others and to reciprocate actions. His focus is on the reciprocal effects of violence through revengeful cycles that escalate and threaten to destroy communities, whether these might be family feuds, tribal animosities, or wars. Such a dynamic was a major problem for humanity in its evolution from animal groups to human communities. The cycle of mimetic violence was enacted through what Girard terms the scapegoat mechanism. A victim is chosen, agreed on by all parties, and sacrificed so as to prevent further reprisals. This model, Girard claims, is held for all primitive religions where sacrifice is central and later religions where sacrifice, if not of life but of desire, is a hallmark. The scapegoat mechanism held, at least to hold communities together internally, despite the fact that religions themselves have come to be the cause of violence. Girard regards the operation of this mechanism and of all scapegoating as unconscious in the sense that were communities or groups aware of the scapegoat as a mechanism, it would not work to prevent mimetic escalation. He considers the development of law through religion as a largely successful attempt to stop this dynamic.

Girard does not subscribe to the idea of the Freudian repressed, or dynamic unconscious. He uses the term more in the sense of a social unawareness of a social and cultural process. In this, he is close to the ideas of Fromm, Foulkes, and Hopper. In his view, Christianity is different from other religions because Christ exposed the scapegoat dynamic by consciously addressing it through his own willing sacrifice (Girard, 1986). Christianity in its true message, he says, recognises that violence should not be answered by further violence, whether mimetically or through the use of an innocent victim. The Christian response to escalating violence is not through reprisal and consequent sacrifice, but through non-violence and forgiveness. Girard has more recently written on modern terrorism, saying that globally we are returning to mimetic violence, alarmingly, at a planetary level, and seem caught still in the old cycles of escalation and scapegoating (Girard, 2009, 2010). The terrorist position of suicide bomber, he argues, is not self-sacrifice in the sense of exposing the scapegoat mechanism, but is a perpetuation of it. Violent responses also escalate further violence.

Whether or not one subscribes to Girard's theological views, his ideas have been influential in understanding the unconscious social dynamics of the scapegoat mechanism and the operation of mimesis at an intergroup or even international level.

Political context

An examination of this area leads into the vast disciplines of politics and social theory: areas that this chapter can only hope to approach minimally. However, it is important to consider issues of power relations, many of which occur at unconscious levels. Freud was not without an understanding of the importance of the political context: "One thus gets an impression that civilization is something which was imposed on a resisting majority by a minority which understood how to obtain possession of the means to power and coercion" (Freud, 1927c, p. 6).

Understanding context provides a reading of dynamics from the outside in and is more in line with sociological and political thinking than traditional psychoanalysis. Such a reading resonates with some readings of Lacan's ideas on the unconscious; for instance:

> Indeed, we have to note that the Lacanian unconscious is a radical critique of the modern individualism (from naturalism to liberal democracy and human rights theory) because it implies that what determined the subject (the linguistic unconscious) is not an inner–intimate property of the subject. . . . Our psychoanalysis teaches us that the subject is a non-individual category, linguistically but also socially and politically produced. (Fazioni, 2012, p. 8)

However, psychoanalysis as a discipline and a practice has not always pursued the political context in any institutionalised way.

The group relations work described earlier has, throughout its history, an interest in power relations. The "politics of relatedness"—

a term coined by the Leicester group relations conferences of the 1980s—refers to a description of the power relations found among groups and organisations and that are part of the context for social systems. Power and authority are differentiated. While power is regarded as influence, whether by force, guile, or open persuasion, authority is understood as legitimate power. The legitimacy comes from the group and its agreed purpose as represented through duly appointed persons. Thus, from this perspective, organisational authority can be seen to rest in roles rather than persons. Khaleelee and White (2014) argue, for example, that group relations has always had a focus on aiding the development of personal authority.

Increasingly, none the less, the issue of retained personal authority has become important in organisations subscribing to democratic ideals. Personal authority is the power legitimately held by the person *qua* person. It is the authority to make one's own decisions as a person with rights constrained only by the law. Chattopadhyay and Malhotra (1991) and Chattopadhyay (2014) argue that people give over vast amounts of personal authority to an organisation when making an employment agreement. This authority to make decisions is given over to the organisational group, often a hierarchy, and then delegated down from the most senior to subordinate roles. But personal authority is also retained, perhaps at a pre-conscious or subliminal level, ready to be exercised should this be necessary. In many organisations, people might be promoted and given status within the organisation because they use initiative and personal authority in their roles. Moreover, despite, at times, the operation of strong peer and superordinate pressures, people might retain their own ethical standards and authority to act on these when organisational ethics become dubious. This is especially so in those contexts where the law is supportive of individual rights. In the light of these contextual issues, there remains a tension in taking up the authority placed in a role because, although the authority is tied to role, how that is interpreted and acted upon relies on the person.

The nature of authority, its expression, and responses to it, both conscious and unconscious, are critical concepts for those interested in the unconscious, right back to Schelling. It seems always to be present, whether in the form of spirit, gods, truth, nature, or reality and always operating through processes of which we are largely unconscious. Psychoanalysis has privileged the paternal function as the source of authority—Lacan stating the "name-of-the-father" as a central signifier in both culture and psyche. It is this function in the family and in society that articulates and binds the law; the glue of society. Without symbolic paternal authority and its associated maternal position, some argue, lawlessness and social breakdown occurs (see, for example, Schwartz, 2003). Yet, others argue that the apparent lessening of paternal authority in current democracies requires us to move away from the paternal–maternal dyadic understanding of authority in order that we find new ways to understand the foundations of authority in networked societies and organisations, less based on hierarchical authority than those of the past century and earlier.

We can, none the less, find multiple ideas about authority in a broader literature. Mitchell (2003), for example, addresses and challenges the primacy given by psychoanalysis to the impact of parental authority by elaborating the role that sibling relationships play in the psychological development of children. Gould (2015) and Chattopadhyay (2014) each describe personal authority as that taken up by the person acting on personal conscience or personal desire, although such descriptions of personal authority really only describe outcomes rather than sources of such authority. The links between personal authority and narcissism might be worth exploring as a dynamic explanation. In fact, if we remember Schelling's theories, we see a nascent formulation of such a link in the necessary struggle of the inward turning ego that then allows for the creation of "other": the whole idea of authority requiring the ego–other duality.

Reiff (1982) elaborates on paternal authority as only one form among others. He names the paternal function as "interdictory authority", the authority of the establishment and the God of the Old Testament that says "Thou shalt not!" But he also describes "remissive authority" as an authority that forgives transgressions—such as demonstrated through Christ of the New Testament—and "transgressive authority" as that authority taken up in defiance of the law. In his later writings, posthumously published, Reiff (2008) argues that repression, rather than the force described by Freud as resisting unconscious instincts, is best described as repression of the human yearning upward towards the sacred: the possibility of sacred interdicts guiding us.

> What is holy terror? Is it the fear of a mere father; in a phantasmagoric enlargement, Freud's idea is silly. Holy terror is rather fear of oneself,

fear of the evil in the world. It is also fear of punishment. Without this necessary fear, charisma is not possible. To live without this high fear is to be a terror oneself. A monster. And yet to be monstrous has become our ambition, for it is our ambition to live without fear. All holy terror is gone. The interdicts have no power ... A great charismatic does not save us from terror, but rather conveys it. (Reiff, 2008, p. 6)

He has some views comparable to those of Girard (Humbert, 2015), in so far as his formulation states that culture requires the operation of interdictory as well as remissive and transgressive authority: the latter exemplified by the "triumph of the therapeutic" following Freud that he regards as a dominant motif of societies based in the therapeutic. It is perhaps interesting to see the current split between the fundamentalists (of any persuasion) and liberals in the light of interdictory *vs.* transgressive authority patterns.

An important but not much cited paper (at least, not cited as much as it deserves) was written by Redl (1942). This paper describes many different forms of leadership and the authority taken up by leaders and does follow from Freud's contributions on group psychology (1921c). Although his examples are taken from the schoolroom and the teaching function, they are more broadly relevant. The emphasis is on what he terms the "central person" who becomes the focus of a group dynamic and holds authority because of this dynamic. The central person might be the object of identification on the basis of love or fear, for example. The central person could also be the object of the drives—libidinal or aggressive. These forms take in traditional psychoanalytic ideas of identification with the father and the paternal function, the development of the conscience and ego-ideal, as well as the literature on identification with the aggressor. But the central person might also be someone who provides support for the egos of other group members by providing drive satisfactions through initiatory acts (the ringleader, the "bad influence", or the "good example", depending on circumstances), assuaging guilt, serving and supporting defences, or acting as an example of an unconflicted personality in conflicted situations for others. This description of how central persons draw group dynamics around them as a magnet draws metal is reflected in Bennis and Shepard's theory of group development (1956) and later theories of social defences against anxiety (Armstrong & Rustin, 2015; Jaques, 1955; Menzies, 1970).

While, in some ways, each of these ideas might seem still to take us back to a unitary source of authority in the One as described by Schelling and other philosophers (remission, transgression, and personal authority are taken up alongside or against such authority, for instance), sources of authority in the very process of group dynamics and sibling relationships appear more descriptive of networked and virtual social relations. How multiple authorities are related to a central or dispersed model is a problem for current scholars.

Perhaps of most interest to a history of the concept of the unconscious are those authors that combine Marxist and Freudian ideas to study the ways in which political domination is enacted: the Frankfurt School of critical theory, for example. Adorno and colleagues' (1950) study of the authoritarian personality, Marcuse's ideas of surplus repression (1955, 1964), and Fromm's ideas of "social character" and "social unconscious" (1962) each examine the part unconscious processes play in political repression. While the Freudian repressed unconscious is an important concept for these authors, it is taken into the political arena and its meaning is extended and altered. No longer is repression simply a force to remove anxiety in the individual by an ego that cannot bear some aspects of reality; the impetus for repression now comes from one section of society in order to dominate another. This domination is done under cover in ways that are not immediately obvious, but that result in great inequalities.

Whereas those who are socially repressed might explicitly discern conscious domination, unconscious social repression is not always immediately evident. Marxist theory coins the term "false consciousness" to describe a condition whereby populations are unable to see repressive situations for what they are. It is a "systematic misrepresentation of dominant social relations in the consciousness of subordinate classes" (Little, 2014). But, rather than being a process located within the psyche, Marxists such as Althusser argue that inequalities are lodged in the institutions, dominant ideologies, and political power structures of society. In this analysis, the capitalist system itself creates false consciousness in both the *bourgeoisie* (the bosses) and the proletariat workers. "Althusser argues ideology is profoundly unconscious – it is a structure imposed involuntarily on the majority of men" (Brewster, 1969). The work of Jurgen Habermas (1971) in the tradition of critical theory seeks to uncover the effects of political ideologies.

The idea of unconsciousness is here a notion of unawareness, but an unawareness that is the result of repressive mechanisms embedded in societal structures and processes. This is not a simple state of "out of mind" or "not yet in mind". It is a state of mind that has been brought about by unconscious political force, a force not necessarily physical but psychological. Due to power differentials and associated domination, unconscious social effects occur.

The idea of false consciousness has been criticised by postmodern thinking in so far as it implies that if there is a truth that is being disguised, how would that be discovered or even possible? While Žižek (1989) agrees with this critique, he does argue for the influence of ideology but, in contrast to some of the critical theorists, sees there is no way around this influence. People both know that they are subject to ideologies and yet go along with their dictates. Drawing on the Lacanian idea of "the one-supposed-to-know", Žižek argues that even if people do not themselves have knowledge, they believe that authorities do and, hence, they act with a sense of free will in their choices due to a misguided sense of trust. This occurs despite the widespread distrust of traditional authority in postmodern societies (Sharpe, 2015). It is a political representation of the perverse position (Long, 2008).

Political hegemony is a strong contextual issue. Some examples of work that consider this are Jameson (1982), who studies how literature is unconsciously permeated by politics, and McAfee (2008) who

> argues that . . . when some are effectively denied . . . participation, whether through trauma or terror, instead of democratic politics, there arises a political unconscious, an effect of desires unarticulated, failures to sublimate, voices kept silent, and repression re-enacted. (Back cover notes on his book)

McAfee takes up the idea of a "political unconscious" in the shaping of subjectivity where "development is a matter of moving from speechlessness to participation" (McAfee, 2008, p. 22).

Hoggett (2006) takes a directly psychoanalytic approach in his examination of the institutionalisation of many political and interpersonal dynamics: for example, indifference and cruelty. His interest (2006, 2009) is focused on the role of emotion in shaping our social experiences in many different social arenas. He says (2009, p. ix) that "politics, as researched and taught in universities does not have much to say about the role of identity in politics and still less to say about the role of emotion". His own work attempts to rectify this as he explores emotions and unconscious dynamics present in political contexts such as the dynamics of welfare (Hoggett, 1997, 2000, 2006), the mobilisation of democratic movements (Hoggett, 2009; Hoggett & Thompson, 2012); and perverse societal structures (Hoggett, 2010). His stress on the importance of emotion is critical, but understanding its importance as just one avenue to the truth, not necessarily the only access. Analysis of current society shows that the personal character-istics of public figures now enter our assessment of them to a greater extent than ever. We expect our politicians and public figures to show emotion.

Following the work of Hochschild (1983), Hoggett takes up the idea of "deep acting": a notion that commercial employees do not simply put on a face for the customer but deeply believe in the prod-uct or service they are selling, despite such beliefs being socially manufactured. The bases of such beliefs are unconscious and operate in "illusional space". This space allows for co-operation, but also for unconscious collusion. Deep acting within illusional space is sup-ported through mass corporate marketing, the push of large organi-sations for all employees to subscribe to a corporate vision, values, and mission—even the word calls forth a religious zeal—and through unconscious identificatory dynamics; all this is linked within a culture of celebrity where private lives are commercially on display. This illu-sory space is also the space within which we misguidedly assess public figures. Hogget warns,

> We must learn to judge public men and women on the basis of the consequences of their public actions rather than on the basis of their private lives or on some feeling for the authenticity of their personal-ity. (Hoggett, 2006, p. 16)

When we come to examine the political context and its influence on roles in large systems and institutions, we move into examining the machinery of government. Bruno Boccara (2013, 2014) describes "country romances"—collective illusions about a country—that become defensively enacted in government policy. Following Volkan's notion of the chosen trauma of a large group or country, a trauma that shapes the culture, phantasies, future directions, and actions of the group, Boccara (2014) describes how countries come to have romances developed from their histories that unconsciously form an identity and guide their citizens. The country identity he describes as "the-country-in-the-mind", echoing Armstrong's (1997) "institution-in-the-mind" to give emphasis to the psychic dimension at play. Boccara examines several countries to identify their current identities as based in historical traumas and successes. These traumas and successes become the basis for "romances" that have a strong impact on policies developed by governments. This dynamic is easy to recognise and may be quite conscious—such as the country romance in my own country, Australia, that involves an identity of egalitarianism, mate-ship, and some sense of rebelliousness derived from early convict and settler days and later reinforced by the story of Gallipoli. But things are not as simple as this. Policies often seem to run counter to the romances and myths due to changing circumstances—Australia is no longer a colony but a multi-cultural society with mineral wealth. So, defences are formed as Freudian compromise products, including the romance alongside its reaction. Following the failures and infighting within what had seemed a promising Labour government in Australia, there is a reactive defence along the lines of Orwell's *Animal Farm* where all are equal but some are more equal than others, socio-economic divisions in the country being on the ascent and cuts to health and education affecting the poor.

In the case of Bolivia, Boccara's research using socio-anaytic dialogue groups names the important historical influences as (i) the Spanish conquest and colonisation; (ii) Potosi (where silver was minted) and the exploitation of silver; (iii) the war of the Pacific with Chile. Each of these events, felt as traumas that degraded and exploited Bolivians, laid down indelible traces in the identity of Bolivia, not just indigenous Bolivians. For example, an important myth of utopian life in pre-Columbian society is of a society without private property. This is retained in the current identity as "*reciprocidad* or reciprocity . . . an intense network of personal relations available as instruments of economic insurance and implied a greater willingness to accept directives from the group" (Boccara, 2014, pp. 136–137). This sits alongside suspicions about strangers with conscious and unconscious beliefs that the other is always an exploiter. As with individuals and groups, so with countries: social defences are raised to deal with the anguish and anxieties associated with the traumas. In the case of

Bolivia, Boccara names defences associated with magical undoing, whose psycho-social significance is to "undo Potosi" (Boccara, 2014, p. 152). Such defensive ideologies then impregnate government policy.

In contrast to the political organisation of nation states, corporate multi-nationals, and hierarchical institutions, the electronic age, with its networked structures utilising social media, has developed new forms of distributing authority. Some of these might support the *status quo* through advertising and the spread of popularism such as is found in the cult of celebrity, but, equally, some have fuelled social activisim and protests against oppressive authority. Although it appears that such social movements are leaderless, Western (2014) argues that a form of "autonomist leadership" operates. He defines leadership as "a psycho-social influencing dynamic" (Western, 2014) and argues that current networked social movements build on the personalisation of society through social media:

> . . . personalisation of society becomes a personalisation of these move-ments, which have less rigid identifiable causes, political programmes or collective identities than previous social movements. This facilitates wider participation so that individual activists can personalise their political commitment. The Occupy movement epitomised this. Its "We are the 99%" slogan embraced everybody (except the evil 1 per cent). This enables individuals to personalise the movement to their own ends. Individuals form intimate networks and sub-groupings, they create personalised blogs, tweets and Facebook identities and attract like-minded individuals. (Gerbaudo, 2012, in Western, 2014)

Leadership and authority are taken up in informal ways through cliques and cells within the network. Western approaches a central problem for these social movements: their disavowal of the idea of leadership because of its links with formal authorities (a disavowal fuelled by emotional ideology) and the actual operation of leadership within the network.

> Drawing on the psychoanalytic work of Jacques Lacan, the disavowal of leadership represents a desire for a world that is freed from author-itarianism and power-relations. The affective investment in being "leaderless" is to unconsciously seek pure jouissance (Lacan, 2007), which means to unconsciously identify with the fantasy of obtaining excessive enjoyment, a utopian fantasy that is unobtainable. The idea

of being leaderless acts as the objet petit a, the object that temporarily offers relief by filling the gap, and at the same time symptomatically points to the lack of, and the repressed desire for, leadership. (Western, 2014)

He says that this dilemma must be accepted and resolved for the future success of these movements.

Authors such as McAfee (2008), Hoggett (1997, 2006, 2010), Boccara (2014), and Western (2014) are examples of those who take a psycho-social and political view of the unconscious. While McAfee names more overt forms of political oppression and their unconscious operation society-wide, Hoggett looks at how emotional states cannot be suppressed or dismissed in organisational and social life. They often reflect conscious and unconscious social repression. Boccara examines policy-making in terms of unconscious defence mechanisms and provides an understanding of mechanisms that link the repressed unconscious at a social or collective level with unconscious processes in institutions. Western approaches social networking and examines some of the unconscious dynamics present in the social movements sustained through social media. In each of these approaches, unconscious processes influence behaviour within large groups and networks.

The unconscious as source

Everything has an origin. That is its source. Everything has an origin except the very beginning: the original origin. This very beginning is *The Source* whether one regards this as God, the Big Bang of physics, Bion's "O", or infinity. Or perhaps there is not one such source but many in many different universes. In the TEF, source is that which gives meaning, is a bedrock, gives energy and purpose, and is beyond ego.

Returning to Schelling, the eighteenth-century philosopher who first extensively explored the idea of the unconscious, we come squarely before the idea of unconscious as source. Referred to first as "unground" and then as "ground", the unconscious precedes all consciousness. It is infinite. It is an attribute, if not *the* attribute of God. It contains within it freedom of will for good or for evil, and Schelling spends much effort on exploring the origins and necessity of evil within the free will that is the very basis for the unconscious infinite becoming actualised, eventually, into consciousness and self-consciousness.

Schelling's later work took him into the area of myth and stories. He saw these as telling a fundamental truth about human history. Myths come from primordial thoughts arising beyond human conscious control. Schelling's thinking here precedes that of Jung and Levi-Strauss, in so far as his God can be understood through the lens of myth (Woodard, 2012).

Peircian philosophy and the associative unconscious

Engaging the idea of the unconscious for all my working life has led me to think about unconscious processes in many different ways. When working on my doctoral thesis, later published as Long (1992), I described the reciprocal relations between "person as system" and "person as an element within a system", such as a group or society. These are not the same, although I may refer to both as "me". I am a member *within* my family and yet my family is *within* me, internalised and influencing my thoughts, feelings, and decisions. Which is the container and which the contained, and in what circumstance? Much of western thinking and psychology has taken the individual as a fundamental element with group at best an emergent system of interacting persons and at worst an accumulation of quite separate individuals. But what if we take group as fundamental? And what if we describe persons as developmentally growing those containers that will contain the internalisation of multiple groups throughout their biographies? What if the connections *between* persons within those groups, across their internalised representations in different persons, are stronger than the connections *within* the person? What if the social glue is stronger than the internalised compromises that the person attempts in order to maintain sanity among their internalised, sometimes warring, groups?

Following Harre (1979, 1984) and Watzlawick and colleagues (1974), this was the perspective I endeavoured to pursue, finding support from Freud (1921c), from my particular reading of several other psychoanalytic theorists, and from my forays into social theory. I came to see that the repressed unconscious, as described in psychoanalysis, belongs to individual biography more than to social history, despite the understanding of unconscious social repression and illusion provided by the neo-Freudians and the Marxist Freudians. The associative unconscious, as I call it, seems to me to have more to do with unconscious connections between people. The associative unconscious is somewhat akin to Jung's collective unconscious, except that he stresses more the hereditary component, seeing the archetypes as similar in each person. I have come to think that Jung's collective unconscious is just one part or aspect of the associative unconscious. My view is that the group and society are systems of many interconnected different parts, each of which is unique, but each of which fits together to make a whole. This is the emergent system aspect, except that if we take the idea that the social precedes the individual, that the singularity is fundamental to the diversity, then it is the person or the subject who is emergent.

This view became more fully developed following my work with group relations methods and then especially with social dreaming (Lawrence, 1998, 2003, 2007). It has links to Neri's description of "syncretic sociality" taken from Bleger (Neri, 2004) that he describes metaphorically (following Freud's idea about the dream) as like the invisible underground network of fibres linking individual mushrooms. This is the mycelium, the oldest living organism that can be enormously extensive. The associative unconscious grew as an idea of a vast unconscious network of thoughts in social systems and, hence, between people, accessed through dreams, art, literature, social knowledge, and through free association. This is the conceptual underpinning of the social dreaming matrix and other methods that access the associative unconscious (Long & Harney, 2013).

Maurita Harney and I describe the associative unconscious as

> a mental network of thoughts, signs, and symbols or signifiers, able to give rise to many feelings, impulses and images . . . The associative unconscious as a system holds a set of processes of symbolisation constrained only by current expressions. (Long & Harney, 2013, p. 8)

This should be qualified by the notion that signs may be sensate as well as symbolic and are lodged in nature as much as in culture. Peirce notes three major classes of signs: iconic, indexical, and symbolic. The icon bears close resemblance to its object, a map or picture, for instance. An indexical sign stands in relation to its object by means of causation: smoke is a sign of fire. A symbol is related to its object by way of convention, a linguistic convention: for example, "cat" is a symbol for a furry feline. Signs are a tripartite combination of a sign vehicle—say, smoke, an object—the fire, and an interpretant, which is the means by which meaning occurs. This is in contrast to the sign in Saussurian linguistics, where signifiers and signified form just two parts of the sign. In Peirce, the interpretant is the third aspect: the sign means something to someone or something else. A smell can be a sign for a dog; a colour can be a sign for a bee. This is a semiotics of meaning. The network of signs and potential signs in the associative unconscious ranges across all those noted in Peirce's semiotics so that we can understand it as the crucible of meaning and, hence, of the creativity of new meanings.

The associative unconscious, or unconscious associations, are infinite. The associations are all that is implicate (Bohm, 1980) in the signs, symbols, and signifiers available to any set of interacting thinkers. Associations are only limited by biological impediments, personal and social repressions, cultural constraints, and technological limitations (i.e., current constraints). Access to the associative unconscious is through methods that stimulate and allow free association among people (see Long & Harney, 2013 for a description of such methods).

We attempt to think in linear logic in our day-to-day lives, even though at times we think and act in seemingly illogical ways. Freud's method of free association showed that there is an underlying stream of logic to everyday thinking—the logic of the primary process. Dreams, parapraxes, and symptoms are all clues to the primary process logic and the contents beneath the surface of consciousness. When free association is practised by a group of people, underlying patterns can be discerned. The associations made—to dreams, photographs, artwork, literature, cultural institutions, and memories—form patterns that inform us about the primary process within the culture of the group. Rather than consciously searching for the implications and meanings within our cultural products (which include dreams, artwork, industry, etc.), collective free association can provide an alternative path leading to new meanings. These emerge from the patterns. Accessing unconscious thoughts or potential thoughts through associations makes available hitherto consciously unthought possibilities: new hypotheses to explain otherwise inexplicable, surprising observations.

The Peircian philosophy of abductive logic provides background to the associative unconscious. Whereas inductive and deductive forms of logic confirm propositions already formulated, abductive logic brings forward new ideas in the form of hunches or best guesses.

> Peirce introduced the term "abduction" to describe the initial, creative phase in scientific inquiry, the phase of discovery sometimes described as "a flash of insight" whereby a hypothesis is formed to explain some surprising fact. Peirce saw abduction as a form of logic, alongside but different from, and irreducible to, induction and deduction. Elsewhere he calls it a method of inquiry. It has the following form:
>
> A surprising fact, C, is observed.
>
> But if H were true, then C would be a matter of course
>
> So, . . . (hypothetically) . . . H is true. (Peirce, 1903: CP 5.189) (Long & Harney, 2013, p. 11)

Ginzberg and Davin (1980) note that abductive logic and abductive enquiry is used in crime detection, art authentication, and psycho-analytic enquiry. Observations or clues are used to formulate hypotheses about causes. These are later either substantiated or rejected through further enquiry, as in normal science. But the careful obser-vation of signs and clues is the first step. This method is described in Voltaire, Conan Doyle, and Poe and can be seen in the work of psycho-analytic case studies (see, for example, Freud). Just as the detective perceives surprising facts or the psychoanalyst uses free-floating attention without any particular memory, desire, or irritable reaching after facts (Keats in Bion, 1970), so associative thinking provides a matrix or mental field where unconsciously the environment of possi-ble links and signs is scanned so that working hypotheses—patterns of causes—might be developed. This is the method that is so uncon-sciously used by artists (Ehrenzweig, 1967) and in social dreaming. Accessing the associative unconscious to formulate hypotheses can be the first step in creative enquiry.

Beyond the network that is the associative unconscious, however, is the "irreducible vagueness": that which can never be known due to the complexity of occurrences in the universe. "Not only can we not know all it is that we do not know, we cannot know with absolute certainty all that there is to know about anything" (Chiasson, 2001). It

is the gap between signifiers that is the real of experience: the differences that cannot be symbolised. The associative unconscious can
point us to these gaps but cannot fill them.

It is within this perspective that I put the hypotheses of the unconscious as source. The associative unconscious is a network and a
process of unconscious thinking that belongs to the system and its
context, rather than to the individual person. We cannot apprehend it
as a whole, we can only, as it were, dip into it through our collective
associations. It is accessed through free association, reverie, meditation, the arts, music, and other collective endeavours that suspend
ego. It can be a source of reaching towards truth, beauty, and transcendence into a place of greater good. It can also bring forward associations of human frailty, vulnerability, cruelty, and horror. These are
part of our human reality and experience. How we choose to work
with the meanings we collectively create at any one time from this
source is our choice. The unconscious provides and consciously we
must choose. Different groups at different times do this. Such a formulation links back to Schelling's ideas on the unconscious as unground
and the basis of all that is conscious.

Conclusions and the future of the unconscious as an idea

This chapter has traced some of the history of the idea of the unconscious using the transforming experience framework of person, role,
system, context, and source. A theoretical framework is simply a scaf-
fold within which ideas can be developed and examined. I have used
the framework to study the unconscious from pre-psychoanalytic
ideas, through the psychoanalytic perspective on persons, systems,
and contexts, and I have added the hypothesis of the unconscious as
source. Following Schelling, who explored the idea of unconscious in
the early nineteenth century, this hypothesis is not surprising. Freud's
revolutionary examination of the repressed unconscious and Jung's
ideas on the collective and creative unconscious were all present
embryonically in the works of the romantic philosophers, initially
stemming from nature philosophy and spirit as realised in the
creation of nature.

In this examination, I think we can conclude that unconscious
processes are defined in a multiplicity of ways and that the concept of

the unconscious is multi-faceted. There is much about ourselves, our cultures, and nature of which we are not conscious. This is to be expected because consciousness itself is a specific organ, limited and bound. The unconscious has been conceptualised as ground to consciousness, that which is prior to consciousness and necessary for its emergence. With psychoanalysis, the focus is primarily on the repressed or dynamic unconscious, where, none the less, the id as ground based in human inheritance remains a foundational concept. Socio-analysis brings forward the importance of social systems and their contexts. The unconscious becomes something between people, found in the structure and culture of social relations and bound into the fibre of institutions. The associative unconscious is conceived of as a mental network of possibilities.

Where might we take the concept of the unconscious in the future?

First, there is the extension of socio-analysis and psycho-social thinking. As Scanlon says,

> a more informed "psycho-social analysis" . . . might take place in "the in-between places" where people can weep and rage and mourn together. These discussions might be informed by psychoanalytic ideas – but psychoanalysis also needs to be better informed by a "socio-analysis" of the deep social structures of the group, the social and the community. (ISPSO listserv communication, December 2014)

Further exploration of the associative unconscious is one pathway.

Other possibilities come from other fields. Perhaps an area of great future interest is that of biosemiotics. Climate scientists are showing us that human activity has a dramatic effect on nature and whereas in the past cultures have attempted to subdue or even conquer natural forces, there is now a greater need to understand how human culture is part of nature rather than separate from it. Biosemiotics takes the stance that communication at any level of organism is intentional. Signs within nature hold knowledge, much of which is unconscious. They range from the complex languages of human cultures through the simple tropisms of plants. The meaning of a sign depends on the relationship between the sign vehicle, the object, and the interpretant (the processes elicited by the sign vehicle). For instance, the information within the sign for fire might be as follows: sign vehicle = smoke, the object = fire, the interpretant = the thought of fire (whether in a human or animal, or even the unconscious reaction of other flora, such as in the biological make-up of plants in bush fire or wildfire prone areas whose seeds can germinate only under conditions of fire). Nature holds many messages through her signs. In terms of evolution, "an organism is a message to future generations that specifies how to survive and reproduce" (Sharov, 2015).

Understanding more of the biosemiotics within the earth-as-an-organism may give us a deeper understanding of what is unconsciously available to us as earth inhabitants and integrally part of that system. While the intentionality in biosemiotics appears as teleological (a stance rejected by psychoanalysis in its acquiescence to the science of the day), that view is from a mechanistic perspective. Intentionality is not a property simply of conscious will, but a systemic property of living, evolving organisms (Harney, 2014).

Another area might be in the neurosciences. Eisold (2009) describes the "new unconscious" informed by developments in cognitive psychology, neuroscience, systems thinking, and research into emotions. He describes the "cognitive unconscious":

> Consciousness may not grasp all the data we receive and the responses we construct, but the cognitive unconscious works constantly to keep us informed, abreast of what adaptation requires that we know about our environment. (p. 32)

And he argues for the "emotional unconscious":

> . . . there does seem to be increasing agreement that, having developed in the process of evolution, our emotions are not only indispensable but, like cognition are largely organized outside of consciousness . . . our behavioural reaction precedes our conscious emotional awareness. (pp. 38–39)

No doubt these and other developments in neuropsychology will tell us more of what Kahneman (2011) calls "thinking fast"; the sort of thinking that occurs automatically below the level of consciousness and greatly influences conscious reflections (named as "thinking slow") that take more time. Much of the experimental work that he cites gives the impression that our conscious reflections are but justifications or rationalisations for what we initially decide unconsciously in a reflexive manner, based on learning and experience as well as instinct (an idea familiar to psychoanalysis). This dualistic version of the brain during decision-making is discussed by Greene (2014) as a basis of moral decision-making. Greene argues that we are biologically and evolutionarily shaped to make decisions about values and moral behaviours that serve to support our nearest and dearest—families and communities—through close group ties of identification. In contrast, our values might be quite different to other cultures whose members are linked to their communities or tribes. Even if we have moral values such as "all people are equal and have equal rights", we tend automatically and emotionally to act to preserve close interpersonal relations rather than serve a "common good" that is more distant (an observation supported through corporate as well as individual behaviour (Bakan, 2003; Long, 2008). Greene argues for a rational utilitarian meta-morality in order to overcome a species-limited moral heritage, while recognising that our instinctual responses are also necessary. But the dilemmas about moral decisions based on distinctions between unconscious, instinctual, and emotionally linked behaviour and conscious rational calculation are not so much solved by Greene through his appeals to utilitarianism as further defined through neuropsychological and philosophical investigations as an indication of the dominance of unconscious processes.

More specific investigations are also being made into the neuropsychological basis of the unconscious processes described by psychoanalysis. Berlin (2011) reviews several articles that explore what she refers to as "a revival and re-conceptualisation of some of the key concepts of psychoanalytic theory . . . the processes that keep unwanted thoughts from entering consciousness" (Berlin, 2011, p. 5). She concludes her review by stating that

> unconscious processes appear capable of doing many things previously thought to require deliberation, intention, and conscious awareness such as processing complex information and emotions, goal pursuit, self-regulation and cognitive control. (p. 20)

Yet, she also concludes that we still know little about the processes that foster or allow interchanges between conscious and unconscious thinking. Fertuck (2011) agrees that "unconscious processes are more adaptive, smarter and survival oriented than previously assumed by psychoanalysis" (p. 46) and believes that we will only learn more through individual case analysis rather than pursuing ideas of repression or dissociation more generally. This holds for case studies at an organisational and social level.

There have been, and continue to be, many ways of understanding what is meant by unconscious processes and the unconscious. Psychoanalysis presents us with an unconscious that is dynamic, largely repressed, and that influences our conscious everyday lives. Also within psychoanalysis there are differences and the unconscious unfolds itself to our view from many perspectives. Socio-analytic and systems thinking have expanded the frame within which we see unconscious processes operate. Have the new and evolving ways of seeing the unconscious strayed so far from Freud's view that we are seeing a quite different concept? They challenge the ideas that we have about mind, its nature, and location. Are they a return to earlier perspectives, but with new methodologies for exploring such perspectives? They echo the idea of unconscious as nature and the ground of being. Or are they additions that enrich the concept from its very beginnings so that now we must think of many types of unconsciousness and many different unconscious processes at the level of person, system, role, context, and source?

Note

1.   Credit for tracking this one down goes to Jeffrey Berman. He believes the remark was made in 1928 to Professor Becker in Berlin. www.freud.org. uk.about/faq/. Accessed 8 October 2014.

References

Adorno, T. W., Frenkel Brunswick, E., Levinson, D., & Sanford, N. (1950). *The Authoritarian Personality.* Berkeley, CA: University of California Press.

Age of the Sage.com (2014). Schopenhauer philosophy. sage.org/ philosophy/schopenhauer_philosophy.html.

Aram, E., Baxter, R., & Nutkevitch, A. (Eds.) (2009). *Adaptation and Innovation: Theory, Design and Role Taking in Group Relations Conferences and Their Applications. Volume 2.* London: Karnac.

Armstrong, D. (1997). The institution-in-the-mind: reflections on the relation of psychoanalysis to work with institutions. *Free Associations,* 7(41): 1–14.

Armstrong, D., & Rustin, M. (2015). *Social Defences Against Anxiety: Explorations in a Paradigm.* London: Karnac.

Aurelio, M. S. G. (2012). Schelling's aesthetic turn in the system of transcendental idealism. www.kritike.org/journal/issue_11/aurelio_june2012.pdf.

Bain, A. (1999). On socio-analysis. *Socio-Analysis, 1*(1): 1–15.

Bakan, J. (2003). *The Corporation.* London: Random House.

Benedek, L. (1993). What can we learn from Ferenczi today? In: L. Arron & A. Harris (Eds.), *The Legacy of Sandor Ferenczi* (pp. 267–277). Hillsdale, NJ: Analytic Press.

Benjamin, J. (1988). *The Bonds of Love: Psychoanalysis, Feminism and the Problem of Domination.* London: Pantheon Books.

Bennis, W. G., & Shepard, H. A. (1956). A theory of group development. *Human Relations, 9*: 415–437.

Berlin, H. (2011). The neural basis of the dynamic unconscious. *Neuropsychoanalysis, 13*(1): 5–31.

Bion, W. R. (1961). *Experiences in Groups.* London: Tavistock.

Bion, W. R. (1963). *Elements of Psychoanalysis.* London: Heinemann [reprinted London: Karnac, 1984].

Bion, W. R. (1965). *Transformations.* London: Heinemann [reprinted London: Karnac, 1984].

Bion, W. R. (1967). *Second Thoughts: Selected Papers on Psychoanalysis.* London: Heinemann [reprinted London: Karnac, 1984].

Bion, W. R. (1970). *Attention and Interpretation.* London: Tavistock.

Boccara, B. (2013). Socioanalytic dialogue. In: S. D. Long (Ed.), *Socioanalytic Methods* (pp. 279–300). London: Karnac.

Boccara, B. (2014). *Socio-Analytic Dialogue: Incorporating Psychosocial Dynamics into Public Policies.* Lanham, MD: Lexington Books.

Bohm, D. (1980). *Wholeness and the Implicate Order.* London: Routledge.

Bollas, C. (1989). *The Shadow of the Object: Psychoanalysis of the Unthought Known.* New York: Columbia University Press.

Bott Spillius, E., Milton, J., Garvey, P., Couve, C., & Steiner, C. (2011). *The New Dictionary of Kleinian Thought.* London: Routledge.

Brewster, B. (1969). Althusser glossary. www.marxists.org/glossary/terms/althusser/. Accessed 18 November 2014.

Brown, N. O. (1959). *Life Against Death: The Psychoanalytic Meaning of History.* Middletown, CT: Wesleyan University Press.

Brunner, L., Nutkevitch, A., & Sher, M. (Eds.) (2006). *Group Relations Conferences: Reviewing and Exploring Theory, Design, Role Taking and Application.* London: Karnac.

Chalquist, C. (2015). A glossary of Jungian terms. www.terrapsych.com/ jungdefs.html. Accessed 6 March 2015.

Chattopadhyay, G. (2014). Exploring the phenomenon of the denial of personal authority. *Socioanalysis, 15*, online @ www.grouprelations. org.au.

Chattopadhyay, G., & Malhotra, A. (1991). Heirarchy and modern organisation: a paradox leading to human wastage. *Indian Journal of Social Work*, L11(4): 1–28.

Chiasson, P. (2001). Peirce's logic of vagueness. www.commens.org/ encyclopedia/article/chiasson-phyllis-peirce%E2%80%99s-logic-vagueness. Accessed 27 June 2014.

Clarke, S. (2014). Projective identification: from attack to empathy. *Kleinian studies ejournal. www.psychoanalysis-and-therapy.com*. Accessed 28 August 2014.

Culler, J. D. (2002). *The Pursuit of Signs: Semiotics, Literature, Deconstruction*. New York: Cornell University Press.

Das, S. B. (2014). Friedrich Wilhelm Joseph von Schelling (1775–1854). *Internet Encyclopedia of Philosophy*. www.iep.utm.edu/schellin. Accessed 11 September 2014.

De Coster, P. L. (2010). The collective unconscious and its archetypes. (http://archive.org/stream/TheCollectiveUnconsciousAndIts Archetypes_100/ArchetypesAlongJung_djvu.txt. Accessed 1 November 2014.

Dictionary.com. www.dictionary.com

Ehrenzweig, A. (1967). *The Hidden Order of Art*. London: Trinity Press.

Eisold, K. (2009). *What You Don't Know You Know: Our Hidden Motives in Life, Business and Everything Else*. New York: Other Press.

Elam, K. (1986). *Shakespeare's Universe of Discourse: Language Games in the Comedies*. Cambridge: Cambridge University Press.

Encyclopedia Brittanica www.brittanica.com.

European Graduate School (EGS) (2014). *Johann Gottfried Herder – Biography* (www.egs.edu/library/johann-gottfried-herder/biography).

Fazioni, N. (2012). Unconscious and subjectivity: intersections between psychoanalysis, philosophy and science. *Avello Publishing Journal, 1*(2): *The Unconscious*, 1–17.

Fertuck, E. A. (2011). The scientific study of unconscious processes: the time is ripe for (re) convergence of neuroscientific and psychoanalytic conceptions: commentary. *Neuropsychoanalysis, 13*(1): 45–48.

Ffytche, M. (2011). *The Foundation of the Unconscious: Schelling, Freud and the Birth of the Modern Psych*. Cambridge: Cambridge University Press.

Foucault, M. (1970). *The Order of Things: An Archaeology of the Human Sciences*. London: Tavistock.

Foulkes, S. H. (1986)[1975]. *Group Analytic Psychotherapy: Method and Principles*. London: Karnac.

Foulkes, S. H. (1990)[1971]. The group as matrix of the individual's mental life. In: E. Foulkes (Ed.), *Selected Papers*. London: Karnac.

Fraher, A. L. (2004). *A History of Group Study and Psychodynamic Organizations*. London: Free Association Books.

French, R., & Simpson, P. (2015). *Attention Cooperation Purpose: An Approach to Working in Groups Using Insights from Wilfred Bion*. London: Karnac.

Freud, S. (1905e). *Fragment of an Analysis of a Case of Hysteria. S. E., 7*: 7–122. London: Hogarth.

Freud, S. (1914c). On narcissism: an introduction. *S. E., 14*: 73–102. London: Hogarth.

Freud, S. (1915c). *Instincts and their Vicissitudes. S. E., 14*: 117–140. London: Hogarth.

Freud, S. (1915d). Repression. *S. E., 14*: 146–158. London: Hogarth.

Freud, S. (1915e). The unconscious. *S. E., 14*: 166–204. London: Hogarth.

Freud, S. (1918b). *From the History of an Infantile Neurosis. S. E., 17*: 7–122. London: Hogarth.

Freud, S. (1921c). *Group Psychology and the Analysis of the Ego. S. E., 69*. 69–143. London: Hogarth.

Freud, S. (1923b). *The Ego and the Id. S. E., 19*: 12–66. London: Hogarth.

Freud, S. (1925h). Negation. *S. E., 19*: 235–239. London: Hogarth.

Freud, S. (1927c). *The Future of an Illusion. S. E., 21*: 3–56. London: Hogarth.

Freud, S. (1940e). Splitting of the ego in the service of defence. *S. E., 23*: 271–278. London: Hogarth.

Fromm, E. (1962). *Beyond the Chains of Illusion. My Encounter with Marx and Freud*. New York: Simon & Schuster.

Gardner, M. (1975). Not Freud's discovery. *The New York Review of Books*, June 12. http://www.nybooks.com/articles/archives/1975/jun/12/not-freuds-discovery/

Ginzberg, C., & Davin, A. (1980). Morelli, Freud and Sherlock Holmes: clues and scientific method. *History Workshop, 9*: 5–36.

Girard, R. (1977). *Violence and the Sacred*. Baltimore, MD: Johns Hopkins University Press (1979).

Girard, R. (1986). *The Scapegoat*. Baltimore, MD: Johns Hopkins University Press.

Girard, R. (2009). On war and the apocalypse. First Things. www.firstthings.com/article/2009/08/apocalypse-now. Accessed 14 October 2014.

Girard, R. (2010). *Battling to the End: Conversations with Benoir Chantre*, M. Baker (Trans.). Michigan, MI: Michigan State University Press.

Glover, N. (2009). *Psychoanalytic Aesthetics: An Introduction to the British School.* London: Karnac.

Gould, L. (2015). Correspondencies between Bion's basic assumption theory and Klein's developmental positions. Human-Nature.com, http://human-nature.com/free-associations/bion.html. Accessed 6 March 2015.

Gould, L., & Stein, M. (2006). *The Systems Psychodynamics of Organisations: Integrating the Group Relations Approach, Psychoanalytic and Open Systems Perspectives.* London: Karnac.

Gould, L., Stapley, L., & Stein, M. (Eds.) (2004). *Experiential Learning in Organizations: Applications of the Tavistock Group Relations Approach: Contributions in Honor of Eric J. Miller.* London: Karnac.

Greene, J. D. (2014). The cognitive neuroscience of moral judgment and decision-making. In: M. S. Gazzaniga (Ed.), *The Cognitive Neurosciences V.* Cambridge, MA: MIT Press.

Grotstein, J. (1997). Bion's transformation in "O" and the concept of the "transcendent Position" www.sicap.it/merciai/bion/papers/grots.htm Accessed 13 November 2014.

Grotstein, J. (2007). *A Beam of Intense Darkness: Wilfred Bion's Legacy to Psychoanalysis.* London: Karnac.

Habermas, J. (1971). *Knowledge and Human Interests.* Boston, MA: Beacon Press, 1971.

Harney, M. (2014). Peirce and phenomenological naturalism: a semiotic contribution to Merleau-Ponty's ontology of nature. Paper presented to Reconceiving Naturalism Conference: Swinburne University, April.

Harre, R. (1979). *Social Being: A Theory for Social Psychology.* Oxford: Blackwell.

Harre, R. (1984). Social elements as mind. *British Journal of Medical Psychology, 57*: 127–135.

Herder, J. G. (1774). *On the Knowledge and Sensation of the Human Soul.* Cambridge: Cambridge University Press.

Hinshelwood, R., & Chiesa, M. (Eds.) (2002). *Organisations, Anxiety and Defences.* London: Whurr.

Hinshelwood, R., & Skogstad, W. (2000). *Observing Organisations: Anxiety, Defence and Culture in Healthcare.* London: Routledge.

Hirschhorn, L. (1988). *The Workplace Within.* Boston, MA: MIT Press.

Hochschild, A. (1983). *The Managed Heart: Commercialisation of Human Feeling.* Berkeley, CA: University of California Press.

Hoggett, P. (1997). The internal establishment. http://human-nature. com/hraj/hoggett.html. Accessed 10 December 2014.

Hoggett, P. (2000). *Emotional Life and the Politics of Welfare*. Melbourne, Australia: Macmillan.

Hoggett, P. (2006). Putting emotion to work in the feeling state. *Socio-Analysis, 4*: 15–32.

Hoggett, P. (2009). *Politics, Identity and Emotion*. St Paul, MN: Paradigm.

Hoggett, P. (2010). Government and the perverse social defence. *British Journal of Psychotherapy, 26*(2): 202–212.

Hoggett, P. (2012). Fairness and the politics of resentment. www.social-policy.org.uk/lincoln2012/Hoggett%20P5.pdf. Accessed 6 December 2014.

Hoggett, P., & Thompson, S. (Eds.) (2012). *Politics and the Emotions*. London: Continuum.

Hopper, E. (2003). *The Social Unconscious: Selected Papers*. London: Jessica Kingsley.

Humbert, D. (2015). Desire and the politics of anti-culture: Rene Girard and Phillip Reiff on the mystique of transgression. Thorneloe College, Laurentian University. http://transformingviolence.nd.edu/assets/26602/humbert_paper.pdf. Accessed 6 March 2015.

Jameson, F. (1982). *The Political Unconscious: Narrative as a Socially Symbolic Act*. New York: Cornell University Press.

Janis, I. L. (1972). *Victims of Groupthink: A Psychological Study of Foreign Policy Decisions and Fiascos*. Boston, MA: Houghton Mifflin.

Jaques, E. (1955). Social systems as a defence against persecutory and depressive anxiety. In: M. Klein, P. Heinmann, & R. Money-Kryle (Eds.), *New Directions in Psychoanalysis* (pp. 478–498). London: Tavistock.

Jung, C. G. (1939). The symbolic life. A talk presented to the Guild for Pastoral Psychology. www.jung.org/readingcorner.html. Accessed 6 March 2015.

Jung, C. G., & Baynes, H. G. (1921). *Psychological Types* or *The Psychology of Individuation*. London: Kegan Paul, Trench, Trubner.

Kaes, R. (2002). Psychoanalysis and institutions in France. In: C. R. Hinshelwood & M. Chiesa (Eds.), *Organisations, Anxiety and Defences* (pp. 97–124). London: Whurr.

Kahn, S. R. (1998). Ferenczi's mutual analysis: a case where the messenger was killed and his treasure buried. http://pandc.ca/?cat=sigmund_freud&page=ferenczi_mutual_analysis.

Kahneman, D. (2011). *Thinking Fast and Slow*. Harmondsworth: Penguin.

Kernberg, O. (1968). The treatment of patients with borderline personality organization. *International Journal of Psychoanalysis, 49*(4): 600–619.

Khaleelee, O., & White, K. (2014). Speaking out: global development and innovation in group relations. *Organisational and Social Dynamics, 14*(2): 399–425.

Krantz, J. (2010). Social defences and twenty first century organizations. *British Journal of Psychotherapy, 26*(2): 192–201.

Kris, E. (1952). *Psychoanalytic Explorations in Art.* New York: International Universities Press.

Lacan, J. (1977). *Ecrits.* London: Tavistock.

Lawrence, W. G. (1998). *Social Dreaming @ Work.* London: Karnac.

Lawrence, W. G. (2003). *Experiences in Social Dreaming.* London: Karnac.

Lawrence, W. G. (2007). *Infinite Possibilities of Social Dreaming.* London: Karnac.

Lawrence, W. G. (Ed.) (2010). *The Creativity of Social Dreaming.* London: Karnac.

Lawrence, W. G., & Long, S. D. (2010). The creative frame of mind. In: W. G. Lawrence (Ed.), *The Creativity of Social Dreaming* (pp. 212–233). London: Karnac.

Lawrence, W. G., Bain, A., & Gould, L. (1996). The fifth basic assumption. *Free Associations, 6*(1): 1–20. www.acsa.net.au/articles/thefifthbasic assumption.pdf.

Lehman, P. R. (1940). Freud's contributions to science. *Harofe Haivri, 1* and cited by Trilling, L. (1940), "Freud and literature" in *The Liberal Imagination.* www.freud.org.uk/about/faq/. Accessed 8 October 2014.

Little, D. (2014). University of Michigan. www-personal.umd.umich. edu/~delittle/iess%20false%20consciousness%20V2.htm. Accessed 18 November 2014.

Long, S. (2001). Working with organizations: the contribution of the psychoanalytic discourse. *Organisational and Social Dynamics, 2*: 174–198.

Long, S. D. (1991). The signifier and the group. *Human Relations, 11*(1): 389–401.

Long, S. D. (1992). *A Structural Analysis of Small Groups.* London: Routledge.

Long, S. D. (1996). Psychoanalysis, discourse and strange lists: these are a few of my favorite things. Paper presented to the 1996 ISPSO Symposium in New York.

Long, S. D. (2006). Organisational defences against anxiety: what has happened since the 1955 Jaques paper? *International Journal of Applied Psychoanalytic Studies, 3*(4): 279–295.

Long, S. D. (2008). *The Perverse Organisation and its Deadly Sins*. London: Karnac.

Long, S. D., & Harney, M. (2013). The associative unconscious. In: S. D. Long (Ed.), *Socioanalytic Methods* (pp. 3–22). London: Karnac.

Long, S. D., & Sievers, B. (Eds.) (2012). *Towards as Socioanalysis of Money, Finance and Capitalism: Beneath the Surface of the Financial Industry*. London: Routledge.

Love, J., & Schmidt, J. (2006). Introduction. In: Schelling, F. W. J., *Philosophical Investigations into the Essence of Human Freedom*, J. Love & J. Schmidt (Trans.). Albany, NY: State University of New York Press.

Malan, D. (1999). *Individual Psychotherapy and the Science of Psychodynamics* (2nd edn). Oxford: Butterworth Heinemann.

Marcuse, H. (1955). *Eros and Civilization: A Philosophical Enquiry into Freud*. New York: Beacon Press.

Marcuse, H. (1964). *One Dimensional Man: Studies in the Ideology of Advanced Industrial Society*. New York: Beacon Press.

Matthews, B. (2012). *Schelling: Heretic of Modernity. An Intellectual Biography of Friedrich Wilhelm Joseph von Schelling (1770–1854)* (http://philosophyproject.org/schelling/. Accessed 11 September 2014).

McAfee, N. (2008). *Democracy and the Political Unconscious*. New York: Columbia University Press.

McGrath, S. J. (2012). *The Dark Ground of Spirit: Schelling and the Unconscious*. London: Routledge, E version.

Menzies, I. E. P. (1970). *A Case Study in the Functioning of Social Systems as a Defence Against Anxiety: A Report on the Study of a Nursing Service of a General Hospital*. London: Tavistock.

Menzies Lyth, I. E. P. (1988). *Containing Anxiety in Institutions: Selected Essays Volume 1*. London: Free Association Books.

Menzies Lyth, I. E. P. (1989). *The Dynamics of the Social: Selected Essays Volume 2*. London: Free Association Books.

Miller, E. J. (1990). Experiential learning in groups 1: the development of the Leicester model. In: E. Trist & H. Murray (Eds.), *The Social Engagement of Social Science. A Tavistock Anthology. Volume 1: The Socio-Psychological Perspective* (pp. 165–185). Philadelphia, PA: University of Philadelphia Press.

Mitchell, J. (2003). *Siblings: Sex and Violence*. London: Wiley.

Morgan-Jones, R. (2010). *The Body of the Organisation and its Health*. London: Karnac.

Morgan-Jones, R., & Torres, N. (2010). Individual and collective suffering of organisational failures in containment: searching for a model to explain proto-mental dynamics. *Socioanalysis, 12*: 57–76.

Myers, I. B., McCaulley, M. H., Quenk, N., & Hammer, A. (1998). *MBTI Handbook: A Guide to the Development and Use of the Myers–Briggs Type Indicator* (3rd edn). Sunnyvale, CA: Consulting Psychologists Press.

Neri, C. (2004). Genius loci: the spirit of a place, the spirit of a group. http://lnx.claudioneri.it/wp-content/uploads/2013/05/genius-loci-the-spirit-of-a-place-the-spirit-of-a-group.pdf. Accessed 12 November 2014.

New World Encyclopedia (2014). Friedrich Wilhelm Joseph von Schelling. www.newworldencyclopedia.org/entry/Friedrich_Wilhelm_Joseph_von_Schelling#Mythology_and_the_unconscious. Accessed 10 November 2014.

Obholzer, A., & Roberts, V. (1994). *The Unconscious at Work: Individual and Organisational Stress in the Human Services*. London: Routledge.

Pistiner de Cortinas, L. (2009). *The Aesthetic Dimension of the Mind: Variations on a Theme by Bion*. London: Karnac.

Puget, J. (2002). Contributions from South America: the group-as-jigsaw-puzzle to the incomplete whole. In: C. R. Hinshelwood & M. Chiesa (Eds.), *Organisations, Anxiety and Defences* (pp. 125–142). London: Whurr.

Rabstejnek, C. V. (2011). History and evolution of the unconscious before and after Sigmund Freud. http://www.houd.info/unconscious.pdf.

Redl, F. (1942). Group emotion and leadership. *Psychiatry, 5*: 573–596.

Reiff, P. (1966). *The Triumph of the Therapeutic: Uses of Faith after Freud*. Chicago, IL: University of Chicago Press.

Reiff, P. (1979). *Freud: The Mind of the Moralist* (3rd edn). Chicago, IL: University of Chicago Press.

Reiff, P. (1982). Sacred order: what pictures reveal and conceal. Lecture given to the Seminar on the Sociology of Culture, in conjunction with the National Gallery of Victoria, Melbourne, 4 August.

Reiff, P. (2008). *Charisma: The Gift of Grace and How It Has Been Taken Away from Us*. New York: Vintage Books.

Restivo, G. (2013). Jouissance and the sexual reality of the (two) unconscious. PhD Thesis: Auckland University of Technology. http://aut.researchgateway.ac.nz/bitstream/handle/10292/6053/RestivoG.pdf?sequence=3.

Rice, A. K. (1965). *Learning for Leadership: Interpersonal and Intergroup Relations*. London: Tavistock.

Rioch, M. (1970). The work of Wilfred Bion on groups. *Psychiatry: Journal for the Study of Interpersonal Processes, 33*(1): 56–66.

Ryle, G. (1949). *The Concept of Mind*. London: Hutchinson, 1984.

Schelling, F. W. J. (1942). *The Ages of the World*, F. de Wolfe Bowman Jnr (Trans.). New York: Columbia University Press.

Schelling, F. W. J. (2006). *Philosophical Investigations into the Essence of Human Freedom*, J. Love & J. Schmidt (Trans.). Albany, NY: State University of New York Press.

Schopenhauer, A. (1893). Psychological observations. In: *Studies in Pessimism*. http://ebooks.adelaide.edu.au/s/schopenhauer/arthur/essays/chapter 9. Accessed 11 November 2014.

Schwartz, H. (2003). *The Revolt of the Primitive: An Enquiry into the Roots of Political Correctness*. New Brunswick, NJ: Transaction.

Sharov, A. (2015). Biosemiotics. https://home.comcast.net/~sharov/biosem/welcome.html. Accessed 12 March 2015.

Sharpe, M. (2015). Slavoj Zizek. *International Encyclopedia of Philosophy*. www.iep.utm.edu/zizek/. Accessed 12 March 2015.

Sievers, B. (1999). Psychotic organization as a metaphoric frame for the socio-analysis of organizational and inter-organizational dynamics. *Administration and Society, 31*: 588–615.

Sievers, B. (2008). The psychotic university. *Ephemera, 8*: 238–257.

Slater, P. E. (1966). *Microcosm: Structural, Psychological and Religious Evolution in Groups*. New York: Wiley.

Stapley, L. (2006). *Individuals, Groups and Organizations Beneath the Surface*. London: Karnac.

Symington, J., & Symington, N. (2002). *The Clinical Thinking of Wilfred Bion*. London: Routledge.

Trist, E., & Murray, H. (Eds.) (1990). *The Social Engagement of Social Science. A Tavistock Anthology. Volume 1: The Socio-Psychological Perspective*. Philadelphia, PA: University of Philadelphia Press.

Turquet, P. (1974). Leadership: the individual and the group. In: G. S. Gibbard, J. J. Hartmann, & R. D. Mann (Eds.), *Analysis of Groups: Contributions to Theory, Research and Practice* (pp. 349–371). San Francisco, CA: Jossey-Bass.

Volkan, V. D. (2001). Transgenerational transmissions and chosen traumas: an aspect of large-group identity. *Group Analysis, 34*(1): 79–97.

Volkan, V. D. (2005). Large group identity and chosen trauma. Online Journal, *Australian Psychoanalytic Society, 6*.

Waska, R. (2013). *Real People, Real Problems, Real Solutions: A Kleinian Psychoanalytic Approach with Difficult Patients*. Routledge, E Book.

Watzlawick, P., Weakland, J., & Fisch, R. (1974). *Change: Principles of Problem Solving and Problem Resolution*. New York: Norton.

Western, S. (2014). www.ephemerajournal.org/contribution/autonomist-leadership-leaderless-movements-anarchists-leading-way

White, A. (1983). *Schelling*. New York: Yale University Press.

Whyte, L. (1962). *The Unconscious Before Freud.* New York: Basic Books.
Wicks, R. (2011). Arthur Schopenhauer. In: E. N. Zalta (Ed.), *The Stanford Encyclopedia of Philosophy.* http://plato.stanford.edu/archives/win2011/entries/schopenhauer.
Woodard, B. (2012). Exploding gods, Schelling, myth and the absolute. www.academia.edu/1756880/Exploding_Gods_Schelling_Myth_and_the_Synthetic_Absolute. Accessed 2 October 2014.
Žižek, S. (1989). *The Sublime Object of Ideology.* London: Verso.

CHAPTER FOUR

Reframing reality in human experience: the relevance of the Grubb Institute's contributions as a Christian foundation to group relations in the post-9/11 world*

John Bazalgette and Bruce Reed

In this chapter, we propose to draw on two icons to frame what we have to say, exploring how iconic images have shaped the modern world and both helped and hindered our understanding of it. We explore briefly the differences between the anxieties mobilised by these images and the boundary markers of interpretation, which encoded those images with meanings designed consciously and unconsciously to contain anxiety. Against the backdrop of these images and their interpretations, we investigate the relevance of the methods and shorthand explanations for our own and others' behaviour. Yet, icons can also be dangerous. Unless we remain alert to their limited purpose, the structure they offer can become reified and we risk treating them as more real than the world they help us to understand. Human beings seek ways to stabilise thinking about their complex, often confusing, environment. One way to manage our temptation to respond irrationally to the anxieties of life is to rely on

---

* This chapter is a transcription of a presentation by Bruce Reed to the Great Britain and Ireland Group Relations Forum at the Tavistock Institute, 21 February 2003. It was first published in 2005 in *Journal of Organisational & Social Dynamics*, 5(2). Unattributed quotations are from the 2003 transcription.

frames of reference that can structure, shape, and give meaning to experience, enabling us to feel as if the world is rational and orderly. Icons are symbolic markers that help to organise complex, sometimes contradictory, events in ways that orientate us to reality. As Rowan Williams (2000, p. 2) put it, an icon is "a window into an alien frame of reference that is at the same time the structure that will make definitive sense of the world we inhabit". Although they do not constitute rationality directly, they provide applications of group relations to the study of those negative and positive projections lying behind the mobilisation of anxiety by threatening global events. In particular, we suggest how the approach to group relations in theory and practice which seeks to bring the human sciences and Christian experience into relation with each other, as developed at the Grubb Institute, can provide one way to develop a "window into an alien frame of reference", a window which might enable us to better manage our anxieties and take responsibility for our own behaviour by becoming more accountable for how we are implicated in what happens around us.

Icons for two succeeding generations

Icon No. 1: The mushroom clouds that hung over Hiroshima and Nagasaki on 6 and 9 August 1945.

For forty-five years after August 1945, the world lived in the shadow of having seen terrifying examples of the human capacity to deliver mass destruction from a great distance with little risk to the deliverer. Both the spread of nuclear weapons and the constant threat of their use during the Cold War between the world's capitalist and communist "tribes" meant that two generations lived with the possibility of nuclear war and understood that possibility to be inextricably linked with the capitalist–communist split across the world. This possibility and its interpretation consciously and unconsciously affected local, national, and international structures, strategy, and everyday life. In this sense, the icon of nuclear destruction provided a way to make "definitive sense of the world" in which we lived by providing a mutual "Other" on to whom destructiveness could be projected.

Icon No 2: The vivid image of smoke and flame as passenger aircrafts smashed into the Twin Towers on 11 September 2001.

The destruction of the World Trade Centre opens up questions of great complexity. Both the ubiquity of the weapons of destruction used on September 11th and the relative anonymity of the perpetrators point to the greater amorphousness or boundlessness of this threat. "International terrorism" is the name given to the "enemy", an opponent whose profile and character are shadowy and intangible. Both the USA and the UK have initiated a "war on terror" in response, first invading Afghanistan and then Iraq. However, these interventions seem not to have successfully contained the problem of terrorism even in those two countries.

The difference between these two icons is stark. Where we used to split the world into "East/communist" and "West/capitalist", with all the underlying formal and informal controls needed to maintain a basic world equilibrium, we now lack a comparable boundedness or way to frame our anxieties; to define a definable Other on to whom we can project our own murderous natures, and, through that definition, devise ways of controlling their implications. The destruction of the iconic Twin Towers has not yet provided us with a way to make "definitive sense of the world" in which we live. Neither geographical boundaries nor ideological characterisations of readily available persons, groups, and countries as "evil" can provide satisfactory foci for the projection of our murderous capabilities. We are being tempted to frame the "battle lines" in religious terms, principally Judeo-Christian–Islamic ones. Yet, such a frame not only is inaccurate, it also relies on religious stereotypes that foster fundamentalist emotional positions, thus fuelling further aggression.

Another, possibly more complex, way to read this event is to see it as the sign of the impending collapse of such seemingly "Goliath-like" yet brittle architectural structures erected to represent western-based trade interests under the impact of "David-like" blows of two unarmed civilian aircraft, hijacked by highly motivated men from poorer nations, armed only with the simplest of weapons. On this reading, one sees the destruction of these symbols of economic and political might as an indication of the real though masked fragility of the power of the wealthiest nations to attack at the hands of those poorest whom they have victimised, marking the event as a contemporary icon of the widening gap between the planet's rich and poor. Yet, this, too, rests on a stereotypical conceptualisations and justifications of violence.

If these frames remain inadequate, how can we find boundaries that might contain the new turbulence that is characteristic of today? Can we find ways to define differences, which can enable us to distinguish between "enemies" and "friends" without merely mobilising stereotypes? As Clinton said in 2001,

> The purpose of terrorism is not military victory; it is to terrorise, to change your behaviour if you're a victim by making you afraid of today, afraid of tomorrow and, in diverse societies such as ours, afraid of each other. Therefore, by definition, a terror campaign cannot succeed unless we become its accomplices and, out of fear, give in. (Clinton, 2001)

The relevance of group relations

"Group relations" is an approach to the study of human behaviour within and between groups, growing out of the work of the Tavistock Institute in the mid-1950s. The underlying discipline has applied psychoanalytic concepts of unconscious behaviour, drawing especially on the thinking of Melanie Klein. It might be that the very inchoateness of these times represents an opportunity for group relations as a field: challenging us to consider what "group relations" is at heart today. Is it a *training method* for increasing professionalism among leaders and managers? Is it a *marketing method*, publicising a specialism by which a body of consultants can attract and build up clients and earn a living? Is it a *career path*, whereby a person moves from being a conference member to joining a training group, to getting invited on to staffs, to setting up one's own conference programme? Or is "group relations" a *philosophy* for critiquing life in today's world through a *process of identification with the other* which questions widely held assumptions about how we human beings live together on this planet, enabling us to develop another way to make sense of our experience of living together by challenging us to transform our behaviour, our roles, and our social, political, and economic structures?

Global political and economic structures in the second half of the twentieth century were bounded by the differentiation of the world into a capitalist–communist split, always against a threat of mass destruction. Not surprisingly, the earliest group relations conferences, which emerged out of the work of Tavistock Institute staff in the Second World War, developed within the context of this cultural and political bifurcation. Events such as the Campaign for Nuclear Disarmament in the UK, the Cuban missile crisis in October 1962, women's peace demonstrations against the USA's airforce base at Greenham Common, and the escape of communist spies such as George Blake and Kim Philby from British prisons, provoked group relations thinkers such as Ken Rice and Pierre Turquet to wonder whether their theories might provide a different kind of "window into an alien frame of reference" that was both practically relevant to the world and to how to run a conference (see Preface in Miller, 1976). Drawing on the work of Melanie Klein, Wilfred Bion, and others, these pioneers began to consider how thinking in terms of splitting and projection might provide a fruitful frame within which to explore global reality. (In this regard, it is also important to remember that Wilfred Bion's own formative experiences included being in the Tank Corps in the First World War and rehabilitating soldiers at Northfield Hospital in the Second World War.)

As a result, conference preparatory staff meetings in the 1960s and 1970s began by reflecting on the political and social relevance of the forthcoming conference and upon the meanings that could be discerned by exploring the processes of splitting and projection at group, institutional, and societal levels. Only after tentative working hypotheses had been formulated about the wider political, economic, and social context did work on the programme of events begin. Indeed, Gordon Lawrence recounts that Pierre Turquet would "lead the staff outside the immediate 'skin' of the conference to . . . a questioning of the state of contemporary societies in the world" (Lawrence, 1979, pp. xiii–xiv).

In what ways can group relations continue to develop to respond to the challenges of living in an increasingly tumultuous twenty-first century? In order to answer this question, we turn next to the history of the thinking of Bruce Reed and the development of the Grubb Institute, charting experiences from the late 1940s until 2003.

The Grubb Institute and its methodological innovations

In 1969, Bruce Reed founded the Grubb Institute, "whose purpose is to energise people to transform their behaviour individually and corporately as they gain insight into their experience of human systems, institutions, communities and personal relations when seen in the context of the Christian faith" (Reed, 2003). Reed trained in Australia as an architect, but was also educated in theology at Moore College, Sydney, Australia and at Cambridge University, becoming an ordained priest in the Church of England and Chaplain of Fitzwilliam House (now Fitzwilliam College) in the early 1950s. His increased involvement in pastoral counselling had a subsequent influence on his approach to the field of group relations:

> Beginning from a position of counselling people about their Christian faith in the context of the realities of society, I left Cambridge and offered to direct the Follow Up for the Billy Graham Crusades in the mid-1950s. At the end of every meeting I went through the hundreds of cards that had been filled in about those who had come forward at the end of Dr Graham's presentation. The brief I gave myself was to select cards from professional people, some of whom were in key positions in society in business, government, education and social service. I phoned them, met with them, first singly, then in small groups. It was quickly evident that, while they may have seen going to church as a new and important activity, more significant questions were on their minds about what difference this made to their everyday responsibilities in the wider, secular world in which local and global movements affected the decisions that people made. (Reed, 2003)

Wanting to help people make connections between the "wider, secular world" and their religious values, Reed and others founded the Christian Teamwork Trust in 1957. As he put it, "Christian Teamwork was set up to address directly the questions brought to us, called 'concerns', which led to people reflecting about what the Christian faith meant in the practical terms that faced them in their work". They formed diverse teams "to work together to tackle those concerns in the most professional way we could", but engaging directly with the question of what relevance their experience as Christians and the teaching they were now taking note of had to their work lives.

Examples of the composition of these early teams illustrate the possible range of application of principles to practice: an international marketing executive exploring the ethics of marketing; an engineering company executive concerned about how to work justly on labour-management relations; an individual who wanted to establish dignified independent living arrangements in the community for the elderly; explorations of questions of authority and leadership among young people; support programmes for discharged prisoners; ways to support the mentally ill outside of hospitals.

Drawing on his theological training, Reed worked with key concepts, such as "corporate personality"—the group as a greater self, and "representation"—the individual as expression of the tribe or group, both of which he saw as embedded in scripture. A key theologian writing about corporate personality was Aubrey Johnson (1942). But Reed's encounter with group dynamics, with which he first connected in the mid-1950s through a friend in Finland introducing him to the National Training Laboratory's T-groups, led Reed to become involved with "studying what people were doing in the 'here-and-now'". This led to his formulating a central question that remained the key motivation for his work for fifty years, fundamentally shaping the approach and techniques he developed: "If I believe that God exists, I must assume that He is present in this group. If He is present, what is He doing and what real signs might I look for to test my assumption?" (Reed, 2003).

Reed found ways to answer this question, which he used to develop specific methods of consultation to groups and for running conferences, initially through his subsequent contacts with Dick Herrick, Harold Bridger, and then, later, Ken Rice, Pierre Turquet, and Margaret Rioch, all three of whom he met at the Leicester Conference in 1963.

> The whole notion of experiencing feelings and being able to name them—dependence, hope, fear, love, hate—opened up exactly the lines of thought that I needed. In particular I now had a way of having an experience myself and being able to think about it. This has enabled me to see the relevance of named experience to my own understanding of life which I had until then been exploring through theological study. (Reed, 2003)

Following the Leicester conference, Christian Teamwork ran its own conference, "at first directed by Ken with Pierre, but then on our own behalf" (see Rice, 1965, pp. 3, 173, 179, 189). The Grubb was, in this way, the first organisation to adopt what has become known as the "Tavistock group relations method", followed nine months later by the Washington School of Psychiatry in the USA.

Early on, it became clear that the innovations Reed inaugurated, combined with his sensitivity to working across differences, could have a wider relevance, a point we shall come back to later. He worked well with Rice and Turquet, despite the latter's atheism, even taking Rice's advice to "transform Christian Teamwork from . . . a counselling service into an applied social research institute, taking the name of The Grubb Institute". He became interested in how group relations stimulated him to think about his experiences "as a human being". These experiences led him to investigate his own assumptions and those made by others "and to seek to test them even to destruction", which, in turn, shaped the Grubb Institute's process of innovation and experimentation.

Structural developments

Although the Grubb Institute had already experimented with shorter four- and six-day conferences rather than the traditional fortnight of the Tavistock–Leicester Conference (Rice, 1965, pp. 173, 179), in 1968 they launched a very important innovation known as the Behaviour in the Working Environment conference (BWE), a

> six month non-residential course designed to give participants time to digest the experience of the course, becoming familiar with previously unfamiliar ideas and their application while . . . still in contact with staff and their fellow members. [It] opened with a full week group relations conference, including familiar here-and-now events, followed by six weekly Consultation Group sessions, another full week's course and a further six weeks of Consultation Group sessions.

These ran from 1968 to 1973, when the contraction of the economy following the oil crisis made the model more expensive than most professions at the time could afford.

During this course they

> . . . made a vitally important discovery. We had been preoccupied with how participants could go about building their learning into their places of work. To address this, in the second phase of Consultation Groups, participants were invited to bring in a colleague to work with them on a practical issue they needed to tackle together. It became clear from this that, in the context of the Consultation Group, those who had not attended a conference could get in touch with and work

with their own experience of their workplace in a way that was comparable to what conference participants could do. This offered them the same kinds of insight into unconscious processes in the workplace as those who had attended the two week long conferences. This realisation—that one could generate conference type learning without attending a conference—led to the development of what we called Organisational Role Analysis, which is now the Institute's way of working experientially in a one-to-one setting with those who head up working systems. (Reed, 2003. See also Reed, 1976; Mant, 1976, and, for later developments, see Newton et al., 2006)

This structural innovation of partnering conference participants with those from the outside in a participant's own work community is one of the many experimental structural innovations in conference design inaugurated at the Grubb Institute whose wider applications have yet to be fully plumbed. This innovation, which offers an opportunity for learning to colleagues who may be unable to attend an entire conference series or events, helping foster wider understanding of the operation of unconscious obstacles to group co-operation within and beyond an organisation, deserves further exploration and analysis.

Another innovation, launched in 1974 after an experimental run with Barry Palmer, was the introduction into conferences of what we called the Median Group.

> We described this in the brochure as "a group of between 18 and 24 members—the size of many councils and committees—which is too large to be taken in at a glance but not so large that members can remain anonymous" (Brochure, 1974). Our experience as staff led me to conceive of the dynamics of this size of group as expressing the necessarily unstable relationship between a fantasied "included group" and the fantasied "excluded ones". Throughout the life of the group, participants move between experiencing themselves as either being included consciously and/or unconsciously in a sub-group of others, or feeling excluded from such a group and isolated from everyone else. No one feels that they are part of the "included group" for any length of time. Some may never feel a part of it. (Reed, 2003)

The relevance of this innovation to the discussion at hand concerns the ways that the fluid and flexible nature of those who felt "in" or "out" might be particularly appropriate as a learning environment in which to explore the fluidity of boundaries between "us" and "them" in our post-9/11 world, and, because it awakens such protean anxieties, might stimulate thinking about the arbitrariness of stereotypes and other "othering" practices. Given that the British Cabinet usually comprises between twenty and twenty-four members, this insight is of particular relevance in understanding the dynamics of intra-government relations and the underlying folly of Tony Blair's decision during his period of government to have members of Cabinet address each other in Cabinet meetings by their personal names rather than by role designation, as was the custom before.

Two further structural transformations of group relations experiential learning design are worth mentioning. The first is the way that Reed and other members of his staff undertook a review of the ways that staff and director roles can become stuck, thus inhibiting learning. In the mid 1970s, Reed became increasingly aware that,

> having functioned many times in the role of staff member and Conference Director, there were many things that I was taking for granted as I designed and led conferences. In particular I realised that I could no longer be sure that I understood the reality of the experience of a member.

He returned to a Leicester–Tavistock fortnight conference as a member, which brought to the foreground for him about "how little time the members have for reflection, being incessantly involved in all sessions . . . [T]he members truly live in the *here-and-now*".

Finding the event one of those "transforming moments for me as a Christian" he began to realise "just how members create a hierarchical picture of the conference system as a whole in their own minds, which can play into unconsciously manipulative behaviour by staff members". John Bazalgette had a similar experience when he returned to the member role after fifteen years. Subsequent Grubb Institute conference designs attempted to address this in three ways. First, they attempted to break the hierarchical position of staff by "holding the Large Group as the first two or even three *here-and-now* sessions, creating circumstances where members knew enough about each other to choose the Small Group membership for themselves" (Reed, 2003).

Second, they tried to break through the

natural human proclivity to see consultant staff in exaggerated ways—demonising or idealising them . . . [by] creating a space for reflection by all the conference participants—members and staff—that had not been present in conferences at that point.

In 1978, working with Gordon Lawrence and David Gutmann, they introduced the "Praxis Event" early in a conference sponsored by the Tavistock Institute and the Fondation Internationale de l'Innovation Social (FIIS Paris).

In this Event, the task was negotiated with the members by the Conference Director and, once a statement had been agreed, the consultant staff as a whole relinquished their management role, which was taken on for the duration of the event by the Conference Administrators. This meant that all the conference participants, consultants and members could now "take authority to be out of their framed, ordered places in the conference life so that they could look at the regular framed events with fresh wonderment". Staff and members engaged with each other on the basis of the same role, with no use of "interpretations". (Reed, 2003; see also Lawrence, 2000, p. 141)

In the Praxis Event, "each participant had to develop his or her own way of exploring reality rather than rely on a 'staff role' to do it for them". With the exception of the overall conference boundary and general resource issues that the administrators handled as conference management, "all internal boundaries—time, space, membership of group or solitary working—were handled by each person taking part in the Event". One of the key results of the event, and the reason why it has been continued and is relevant to the present discussion of managing boundaries in our more chaotic age, is that it provided an especially salient way to bring to the foreground the underlying dynamic human issues and created a context in which to "explore how they are expressing their here-and-now experience of reality in practical action with others" (Brochure of the Grubb International Conference "Being, Meaning, Engaging", 2003).

The multiplication of such opportunities for applied learning would be one way to address the issues of power and authority in various work and social contexts that beset us today. In fact, Grubb has continued its efforts to provide members with as much authority as possible by handling "work on application in a way which gives members choice to work individually on issues declared in advance, with the opportunity to ask to work with specific consultants, though their choice is not guaranteed", calling this method Praxis Event II, since it continues to focus on the members' experience of the inter-action of theory and action but does so now in the context of their working institutions. As we shall discuss further, several principles that Grubb has evolved out of its work with institutions in context might be adapted further for work in other settings in ways that can address the particular anxieties which are represented in the destruc-tion of the Twin Towers.

The third and final structural innovation Grubb launched was to challenge the conventional combination of the role of conference director with being a consultant in the Large Group, which Reed began to think distorted the perceived power of the director. Instead, he developed an approach "to keep the director out of all *here-and-now* events until the Institutional Event", an innovation which has been replicated by some other directors elsewhere.

Conceptual developments

In addition to these structural innovations, Reed and others began to modify some of the concepts they had inherited from Ken Rice, espe-cially related to the concept of *primary task*, defined by Ken Rice as "the task that must be performed for an institution to survive" (Rice, 1963, pp. 13–14) and placed renewed emphasis on the proper under-standing of this term as a process of discovery that emerged in the light of reflection on experience and the analysis of reality, rather than a purpose defined in advance of action. Stressing instead that the term was meant to provoke a spirit of enquiry, a desire to find out what is happening in institutions, Grubb Institute work began to use the terms *aim* (intended outcome) and *operating process* (method of enquiry) in order to remain open-ended as to outcomes.

What became significant at Grubb has implications for our post-9/11 world. As we search for new ways to stimulate dialogue in differ-ent community settings, which can encourage conversation to generate its own purpose, remaining open to what happens, we are likely to stimulate, in a covert way, some of the same anxieties about the unexpected that have been mobilised by the wider political context. This becomes an opportunity that, if properly structured, can lead to group exploration of those anxieties in rich and rewarding ways. Of course, this stress on openness, or the

> lack of closely specified outcomes still presents problems for those from business, civil service and similar settings, who tend to think in terms of precisely defined and controlled results, and who are suspicious that such open-endedness implies lack of discipline and focus.

None the less, it is exactly this suspiciousness that we must continue to investigate creatively, since it seems emblematic of the very anxieties mobilised in the contemporary global context. Consequently, the Grubb Institute has continued to use these key concepts both in conferences and in our research and consultancy.

Several other conceptual developments were important, but one of the key ones has been the development of the Reed theory of oscillation (Reed, 1978), which became a core text for theological students during the 1980s and 1990s. Bringing together

> thinking about the function of religion in society viewed from the two perspectives of the human sciences disciplines of psychodynamic and systemic thinking . . . with Christian theology, this theory postulates that life is lived moving between two modes. One mode is where we are taking practical action in the world, seeking to realise our beliefs and meanings (whatever these may be) while functioning autonomously, mobilising our capacity to take risks. (Reed, 2003)

Reed named this "intra-dependence", where the object upon which one is dependent is internalised, providing an internal reference point to the person. The swing toward the second mode of dependence occurs because "we encounter obstacles and resistances . . . become despairing and seek security, and regress to a place in which to experience to dependence . . ." This second mode he named "extra-dependence", where the object which is depended upon is external to the person.

Reed understood that this oscillation process was natural, for both individuals and groups. It is a normal process whereby individuals retreat, as it were for security, from the world, to be replenished, reconstituted, so as to be transformed back to being able to act effectively once again. In fact, he argued, a stable and healthy society relies upon the underlying structures that facilitate shared regression and transformation in ways of which we are largely unaware. If the cultural and political context is designed to facilitate it, in this second mode we can acknowledge our dependence—upon others for comfort and reassurance, upon writings or music, upon an institution (say the family or even the nation), [and] at the deepest level . . . upon God (this may be Allah or other manifestation of the divine).

However, he also argued that

a major issue in present day British society is that we are in a stage of deep transition where the familiar symbols and institutions (the monarchy, the church, parliament, etc.) that used to facilitate shared national regression to extra-dependence, no longer serve that purpose effectively.

The crisis of underpinning structures and shared values to which Reed alluded seems to have been amplified at the national and international level by the symbolic impact of 11 September on confidence in any institutions and symbols, except weapons and institutions of destruction, to provide us with security and renewal. In addition, since one representation of the meaning of 11 September, to which we referred earlier, connects to religious conflict itself, the ability to explore "where God is" in this context becomes even more complicated. None the less, we continue to believe that it is now all the more important to consider how understanding the experience of reality can be provided by religious belief and spirituality at a corporate level.

The context of conferences and the relevance of context to transformative group relations work

In this last section, we return to one of the themes established at the outset and offer some comments on how to develop a new iconic "window into an alien frame of reference", which might enable us to better manage our anxieties and take responsibility for our own behaviour in the post-9/11 world. First and foremost is the need to be aware that any social or individual transformation requires taking account of those contextual pressures that influence meaning and behaviour, even though individuals and groups remain wholly or mainly unconscious of them. As Reed emphasised, conference directors need to remain

> attentive to the wider political and economic context. The threats and opportunities for transformation more and more [provide] the back-cloth to conferences. Although continuing to pay attention to the personal level of resistances and resources, we [should seek] to grasp realistically the impact of the global context.

The Grubb Institute is, of course, not alone in this. Alastair Bain and Gordon Lawrence had been seeking the same in such conferences as their Explorations in Global Group Relations in Australia in 1994 and 2002, and we at Grubb did it in conjunction with FIIS in Maryland USA in 1998.

The significance of context is not limited to the fact that it provides only a setting for conferences and other group relations work, but that, in Reed's assessment, it very much is the shaping force and drive of the work itself. Describing his own experiences, Reed noted how

> As I saw things happen across the world—the explosive growth and impact of the HIV/AIDS virus, the ethnic "cleansing" in the Balkans and Central Africa, the growth of the "greed is good" culture across the Western world, with the attendant corporate scandals of Enron and other companies—I was faced with the question "What part of me is represented there? And what reality-based action can I take when I have uncovered that part of me?" (Reed, 2003)

Such an attitude raised for Reed the question about how leaders needed to become more aware of how to "identify aspects of . . . unconscious processes within institutional life in its real context, in ways that enabled those in positions of accountability . . . to influence what was happening at deeper levels". Yet, this question of account-ability extends beyond the issue of what official leaders do in response to a situation. Systems thinking allows us to see how we are all impli-cated in an event, even if we are not directly connected to it.

Systems thinking postulates that every part is reflected in the whole and that the whole is more than the summation and the expression of all parts. Ken Rice's thinking was based on systems theory, especially drawing on Kurt Lewin and Ludwig von Bertalanffy. He focused particularly on boundary management between system and context. As experience and thinking has gone further, the scope of systems thinking has been extended. The work of Gregory Bateson, Boscolo, Cecchin, and Palazzoli, Maturana and Varela, and others have focused on the energised interactions between parts and wholes. For example, when a holographic plate is broken the hologram can be reproduced from every fragment. Of course, what might be the "whole" in a micro-system is itself also a "part" in a macro system. Thus, whatever happens in the world is thought of as being related in some way (even if we cannot perceive the link) with the whole of the rest of the world. Systemic thinking enables the other to remain the other, that is, different from me, while still becoming one, that is, a person. In the Judeo-Christian tradition, this concept is expressed in the Second Commandment, which describes an intergenerational connection through the indication that God visits sins of the fathers to the third and fourth generations, although also showing mercy to thousands. This Commandment introduces a corporate dimension to sin—if one person sins, all are implicated, or held responsible, in some way, which leads to a different understanding of the nature of "original sin". Thus, as the aircraft smashed into the World Trade Centre, thinking systemically means seeing how each of us was vicariously a part of the hijacking and also a part of those who perished in the disaster. Similarly, we are all implicated in both the invasion and the reconstruction of Iraq.

The destruction of the Twin Towers—the twenty-first-century icon—represents, then, another context for exploration of what blocks accountability and responsible action in contemporary life, but it differs from other contexts, as we explored at the outset, because we do not seem to have any adequate maps available, however limited, with which to make sense of the alien frame of reference represented by this icon. If, during the second half of the twentieth century, Hiroshima and the "Cold War" created a climate of fear across the globe, it seemed containable because the "iron curtain" marked a boundary across which splitting and projection could be rendered manageable and because of the creation of the United Nations with its Security Council. Yet, the aftermath of the Twin Towers atrocity has not yet been accompanied by the development of any comparable structure (despite the weakening of the UN by the invasion of Iraq), except a potential one between Islam and what might be called a Judeo-Christian "alliance". Yet, this division might be more fabricated than real, but, if it becomes embedded, will, without doubt, be an extremely dangerous one for the world.

Group relations and the twenty-first century

In this current, fluid state of the world, what questions must we in the group relations community of knowledge and practice now address? The following seem most pressing:

How can group relations thinking help us discover a way into the alien frame of reference symbolised by the destruction of the Twin Towers that confronts the realities of the world today?

In what ways does the group relations' structure enable us to make definitive sense of the world we inhabit?

What are the inherent weaknesses in group relations thinking against which we must guard?

We live in the post-Renaissance, postmodern, individualist culture. Two concepts are central to group relations and yet alien to most western cultures: understanding oneself, not as an "individual" but in terms of "corporate identity", and the recognition that we are embroiled in unconscious processes which spring, not simply from us as individuals, but which are part of the wider systems within which we take roles.

The concept of corporate identity is still present in some contemporary cultures. Nelson Mandela describes, in his autobiography, how he was brought up to see his own identity in ever widening circles: as a member of his family, his clan, his tribe, his nation, and his people (Mandela, 1994). He learnt that each person is the embodiment of both their own uniqueness and of the corporate entity of which they are a part. It is probable that much of Mandela's universal appeal is that this corporateness is clearly evident in the way he relates to whomever he meets. George Alagiah, the BBC broadcaster who grew up in Ghana, has described the concept of corporate personality as "the uniquely African spirit of *ubuntu* . . . The notion that one person's humanity is inextricably linked to the perception of humanity in others" (Alagiah, 2001, p. 233). The late Bishop of Winchester, John V. Taylor, who was an African specialist, said, "The European assumption is: I think, therefore I am (real). The Africans assumption is: I belong, therefore I am (real)". This means that, in order to feel real, we need a way to relate the person (a part) dynamically to the whole—be it a family, a tribe, a company, a country, or whatever. The concept of "role" can provide that.

A role connects the person effectively and efficiently to the system, potentially to both the greater benefit of the system and to the greater sense of fulfilment for the person. Indeed, to learn to work in role is a major opportunity for personal development.

We have come to recognise that in systemic thinking. "Role" involves two aspects: an *inward discipline* whereby the person "grows" the role in his own mind, first from identifying his own desire, and then from how he understands the system within which he will take a role: this means understanding the system's purpose and what the person's desire can contribute to the system. From this mental work, the person can begin to consider and to determine her own behaviour and to manage herself in the system's context. We have come to call this aspect the "psychological role". At the same time, there is the observable evidence of the "outward behaviour" to which others respond, drawing on their expectations of what they want from the person and how they interpret what they see the person doing. These expectations create an influential part of the context for the person, which she must take into account as she forms the psychological role in her own mind and which affects how she develops the self-discipline which she exercises in relation to how she behaves. We call this external factor the "sociological role".

Applying this concept in group relations work in the context of our post-9/11 world suggests the importance of investigating the ways that our projected desires can conflict in the wider system with how others are seeing us, who also respond through their own complex role definition process. A group relations conference provides a microcosm of the wider world within which we can learn to become sensitive to how others perceive us in corporate terms. This is a major implication of this application of role to the contemporary context. The study of group relations opens up a way to further this process, based on the assumption that if we can become sensitive to the *here-and-now* of a situation, we are in a position to identify our own resistances and defensive fantasies. From this, we can experience a sense of reality and, thus, of being in touch with reality itself. The test of what is experienced is whether a hitherto chaotic, seemingly unintelligible state now becomes significant and meaningful, where the person has an "aha" experience which leads to transformed behaviour. That kind of experience can become a basis for new action. In terms of the global macro-scale, we can learn to understand how those from outside the west perceive the west. For many religions, the discernment of reality is symbiotically a discernment of God at work in a situation.

For ourselves at the Grubb Institute, we have continued to be drawn to explore Bruce Reed's initial question about the reality in human experience from the 1950s: "If God exists and He is present in this group, where is He and what is He doing?" We have set out to tackle this face to face, drawing on psychodynamic and systemic thinking and our own Christian experience. We have called this approach "convergent thinking", referring to the convergence between the human sciences and Christian thinking in terms of understanding the reality of our experience. It is now the hallmark of our work.

After thirty-six years of group relations conferences (most of which had been run without specific reference to Christian thinking), in 1999 John Bazalgette directed our first full scale conference working to the title "Leadership and Authority in Systems, in the light of Christian Spirituality". Applying our learning from that prototype, in 2000 we designed a conference entitled "Being, Meaning, Engaging: Resistance and Transformation in Systems", directed jointly by Bruce Reed and John Bazalgette, and in 2002 by John Bazalgette alone. In November 2003, shortly after Bruce Reed's death, we ran our third conference under that title, this time directed by Bruce Irvine, the Institute's new Lead Consultant. It is not that we have run new "events", but we have used existing events in new ways, seeing the events as different lenses through which to explore experience of the *here-and-now*, seeking illumination of reality through the different converging spotlights of human science and faith.

The aim of these conferences is to enable people to manage their anxieties, memories, prejudices, and beliefs through the way events are constructed, so that the *here-and-now* is experienced as "reality"— from which one can start evaluating one's everyday activities differently. As a result, not only does one glimpse the *reality of that moment*, but one is also in a position to turn and look outwards and "see" the world in all its variations from two perspectives: that of psychodynamic and systemic thinking, and that of one's spiritual experience.

The intention is to gain a better purchase on one's experience of reality, not to persuade anyone of any dogma, be it a "religious" or a "scientific" dogma.

Those occasions when one has an experience of being in touch with reality we would call "transforming moments" and the process can experienced as parallel to a religious experience. On such occasions, Bruce Reed referred to God as "Ultimate Reality" following Bion's (1970) idea "I shall use the sign O to denote that which is the ultimate reality, absolute truth, the godhead, the infinite, the thing-in-itself" and in those conference moments when one experienced being in touch with reality, however fleetingly, one sharply sensed values in practice: for example, truth, peace, forgiveness, love, integrity, justice; as well as selfishness, envy, rivalry, betrayal, unfaithfulness, personal ambition, and greed. Every conference has a context of values and beliefs that presages the values attributed to experience regarding resistance and transformation, regression and development. The test of that understanding is expressed through behaviour in the real world of life and work.

In his 2001 BBC *Dimbleby Lecture*, Bill Clinton made several points that are significant to the question of how to connect group relations thinking to the changing global environment. Clinton argued that the world's future flourishing, which could enable completion of the process already begun through information technology, global energy sources, and international travel, required that the world become a "world without walls". He recognised that this necessitated human beings facing up to their differences—of race, politics, economics, religion, culture. Although it is true, he argued, that none of us wants our grandchildren to grow up behind barbed wire, or exposed to the risks of "differences", which 11 September 2001 exemplified, he cautioned us to remember that

> One of the big burdens of the modern world is . . . The marriage of modern weapons to ancient hatreds. . . . Don't you think that it's interesting that in the most modern of ages, the biggest problem is the oldest problem of human society—the fear of the other; and how quickly fear leads to distrust, to hatred, to dehumanisation, to death.

The fact that religious belief historically has been at the heart of the bitterest hatreds, and a war of beliefs seems to fly in the face of

Clinton's urging us to live inclusively, we at the Grubb Institute continue to address the relatedness of faith to learning to manage ourselves in this turbulent—nay, dangerous—context. In searching for truth using group relations insights, we have learnt two major things, not so much as major new insights, but through deepening our understanding of the significance of things we perceived before, but now with new sharpness. These two insights are (1) the relatedness of each of us to every other, and (2) the accountability that this imposes on each of us to think about how to act in the world, which we share with others who seem different from us, but whose "otherness" is part of ourselves.

> No man is an island, entire of itself; every man is a piece of the continent, a part of the main . . .
>
> Any man's death diminishes me, because I am involved in Mankind;
>
> And therefore, never send to know for whom the bell tolls;
>
> It tolls for thee. (Donne, 1997)

Group relations is a method of enquiry about ourselves not as isolates, but as parts of wholes, to put it in our language, as "persons-in-roles". We are always in relatedness, but how do we differentiate between when we are observers, delegates, or plenipotentiaries? Are we ready and able to be accountable for how we have been implicated in what happens around us? Relatedness is not wholly conscious: it is largely unconscious, so we human beings are always part of the dynamic of a bigger story than the one of which we are aware. Ken Rice started by using Bion's Small Group and progressed onwards to Large Group and Inter-Group Studies. Since his day, the Institutional Event has been developed. Now we seek to study the widest possible contexts. Perhaps Gordon Lawrence's social dreaming matrix is one way to do this, exploring both inwards and outwards.

The danger of taking Bill Clinton's comments on board uncritically is that his dream of the "world without walls" would open us up to the unmanageable effects of unconscious processes, and these are not all benevolent. It is worth remembering a frequent comment by David Gutmann: "L'inconscient est beau" (The unconscious is noble). Michael Dudley, a participant in the Institute's conference of 2001, remembers Bruce Reed saying in the conference Plenary Review "God is to be found in the unconscious and a meeting with God is not some-thing to be taken lightly" (email of condolence on hearing of Bruce Reed's death, 23 December 2003). Human beings naturally draw boundaries in order to differentiate, to defend, to prevent ourselves going mad, and to understand (and usually in that order). Clinton's unspoken challenge is to conceive of a boundary that can enable each to acknowledge the other—with all their defences and the stress that involves—while still being totally inclusive.

At the Grubb Institute, we have set out to find, make, and take our roles as members of the largest system we can conceive, that is, to become a citizen of the world. But to do that we need some frame or system boundary which both makes it intelligible and also enables us to split and project the unmanageable parts of ourselves without using other human beings as the object of those projections. To do this calls for each of us to develop the capacity to accept our incompleteness and our dependence on others, not as a sign of weakness, but of humanness. This becomes more possible when we can understand our experience of reality in terms of ourselves as persons-in-relation—as part of a whole which is greater than we can comprehend alone—which we can approach by disciplining our thought to attend to our "self", in the context of "system", and being in role. This calls us to pay attention to, and seek to relate to, those bits of ourselves that are carried by others. This is what we mean by "inclusiveness". From the perspective of the New Testament, this means learning to become a participant in the "new humanity" (St Paul's letters to the Christians in Galatia—Galatians 3.28, in Ephesus (4.22–24), and in Colosse (3.11–12).

But, because we draw boundaries, we think of the world as ruled not just by tolerant, liberal, kind human beings, but also populated by people whose intentions can be harmful, which means we also need some object to demonise. We need an "Ultimate Being", or source of value, which can be both the object of our deepest hatred and also the source of the most comprehensive love. Such a being's nature and the principles embodied in its nature would enable justice and peace to be established and maintained. Religious systems create such a being in the concept of the divine. For the three monotheistic religions, the ultimate boundary between the One and the Other is between human beings and God, not between one human being and another. In all three religions, it is forbidden to destroy other human beings in the name of one's God. It is worth noting that all three monotheistic religions trace creation and human history through the same documents. Indeed in the seventh century, many Jews, Christians, and Moslems used the term "Allah" to refer to God, and some still do so today.

The test is whether the concept of "God's Kingdom" as a system, in whatever language we describe it, can provide the secure container that will enable us flawed beings to behave inclusively under the most extreme pressure, wherever that comes from. Yet, today fundamentalism—not simply religious, but philosophical, political economic, and cultural fundamentalism—has gained a fierce hold. The boundaries that fundamentalism enacts are drawn between human being and human being. And one of the fundamentalisms in western culture which needs to be addressed, according to Archbishop George Carey in a speech to the House of Lords 1999, is what has been called "the learned repugnance, to contend intellectually, with all that is religion". Note the "all that is religion", not just Christianity, though in the UK today "Christianity" is the most frequent meaning attached to the word "religion".

Can a conference provide an adequate framework within which those vital—fundamental—boundary issues can be explored in the experience of the *here-and-now* of the conference design? Our own recent conferences give us some confidence that they can, but they need further testing. So far, we have worked with a staff that has been largely Christian or sympathetic to Christian understanding: what will happen when we incorporate practising Jews or Moslems with Christians on the staff, or atheists and agnostics? Individual thinkers have continued to press forward the case for taking spirituality seriously. Chattopadhyay (1999) has explored the importance of a spiritual perspective in conferences, and related issues, from the perspective of yoga. David Guttman and Shelley Ostroff have approached the same issue in their three-day conferences, "Body, Soul and Role", run in France, Belgium, Israel, and the UK, and Shelley Ostroff's "Group Relations and Gaia: a Conference on Health and Vitality in Institutions", run in Israel. Writings are beginning to appear about spiritual leadership and spiritual intelligence; for example, Zohar and Marshall (2001), and Briskin (1998).

To return to the icons: to Christians, the Crucifixion is an eternal icon which is offered for use in relation to all aspects of human life. If we superimpose the image of the Crucifixion of Jesus upon the image of the two aircraft crashing into the Twin Towers, not concealing them, a new icon is created and a different "alien frame of reference" now confronts us. Christ's message from the cross is that we are simultaneously both perpetrators and victims in that act: those of us involved in group relations are able to investigate at conscious and unconscious levels our part in the rich, "northern", developed world, recognising that we are also part of the poor, hungry, sick, and imprisoned of the "southern" hemisphere. Christ's followers look at the Twin Towers with the superimposed cross and can see there the consequence of their own failures and, in particular, their rebellion against God: they are challenged to accept responsibility for this atrocity (similarly with the bombing outrage in Madrid in March 2004).

To be real in facing up to that awful burden, a follower of Christ remembers that from the cross, Jesus cried out "Father, forgive them for they know not what they do". But forgiveness and release from guilt can only be activated through acceptance of accountability. We do not need to react to the pain, suffering, and sense of outrage simply by seeking revenge and retaliation. The exponents of group relations know, from our experience of here-and-now events, that by accepting responsibility, taking up our own cross, new relations and new courses of action become possible out of events that seemed irredeemable. In the language of scripture, this is the releasing potential of repentance combined with the experience of being forgiven and the receipt of God's grace (Reed, 2001).

Some remaining dilemmas

Our next step as the Grubb Institute will be to test the hypothesis that staff members from different faith positions can work together creatively in the interest of the members, and that this is possible when each staff member is secure enough in their own faith to enable them to address their experience from the perspective of learning.

Our group relations journey begins not from a position of conviction or "belief", but in a spirit of enquiry. This is a spirit of faith as opposed to belief—this is the Abrahamic spirit of not knowing where we are going. Doubt and ignorance are twin reasons for making the journey and twin resources to our intuitions (French & Simpson, 1999). Others may base their enquiry on other propositions. However, for us, the experience of certainty (belief) is a quicksand that, if we are unwary, will, in due course, entrap us. Concepts provide us with the tools that are our resources to our exploration of doubt and ignorance (faith). Differences are the "seam" which we mine in order to understand, not to stereotype. Fear and hatred are necessary features of our lived experience but these are not the kinds of fear or hatred that drive us into defensive destructive acts against others.

Truth is the object of our quest: fear and hatred can provide the energy necessary for exploration. And the truth we explore is the twin reality of the dynamic and continuing interaction between what lies within us and how that relates to what is without. The most significant hypotheses in this frame of reference are not simply about the transference and countertransference between members and staff (important though these are), but those which illuminate what the conference reflects, in the here-and-now, of the external context of the world we live in together, which is having an impact on behaviour within the conference. We are following sound scientific principles here. See, for example, Whitehead (1925, p. 3), who wrote, "It is this union of passionate interest in the detailed facts with equal devotion to abstract generalisations which forms the novelty in our present".

What do we need to do to apply these principles and concepts to address the human and global challenges referred to by people like Bill Clinton? Can group relations reveal to us and, we hope, to others; what is required of us in the realities in the global here-and-now to address those complex dynamics that led to the destruction of thousands of people, most of them individually innocent but corporately implicated simply by being members of the human race? Sher (2003), in his reflections as Director, asks how members have been affected by the "crazy images in society", suggesting that he is thinking in similar terms to ourselves.

The answer to these questions lies in developing the practice of group relations flexibly and self-critically enough to apply its own methods to itself. Yet, the temptation, which has not been resisted too well so far, has been to regard group relations as a "movement" in itself, splitting itself off into a supposed "unique" position and then fragmenting into "sects", as its different exponents believe they have the final truth (cf. the frictions within and between the monotheistic religions so far—if it has happened to them, what is there to save "group relations"?). Facing up to this fragmentation could lead us to a search for "professionalised conformity" which becomes taken for granted among group relations exponents (a new tribe, perhaps), rather than seeing every event as an opportunity to use the concepts as tools to explore the wider world in which conferences are set. If we fall for that, then the inevitable internal splits can become the causes that discredit group relations as a discipline. The late Barry Palmer commented on his experience, in notes written after taking a staff role in a conference in 1996 directed by Bruce Reed, that the "professionalisation" of staff behaviour had covered up the more fundamental questions about why run the conference at all, overlooking what members would have felt they signed up for. This note was one of the factors that pushed the Grubb Institute thinking towards seeking to develop the direction it has taken.

Our experience in the recent Grubb Institute conferences has been that by regarding the *here-and-now* as the crucible in which God works, creating, redeeming, and judging human endeavour, we have been encouraged to find that we can begin to break through those "ancient hatreds". We have found that we can achieve, through experience of the reality of the *here-and-now*, the kind understanding of the roots of our own individual and corporate behaviour, which mobilises the blessings of modern technology.

If we are to avoid being what Clinton called "emotional prisoners" on any of several "sides", and to realise globally in the twenty-first century the wealth *and* the peace that our technological sophistication can offer us, we exponents of group relations have little option but to press ahead on the lines we have described. We can seek to improve our conceptual tools, not by restricting them to conferences, but by testing and refining them in the real political, economic, and cultural settings of the world. And the signs are that across the world such things are happening, represented by such developments as our own "Being, Meaning, Engaging" and FIIS's "Body, Soul and Role". Such efforts suggest the ways that group relations might enable us to find another window on to the alien world opened by the image of those two smoking, ruined towers that opened the twenty-first century, just as Wilfred Bion, Ken Rice, Pierre Turquet, and others sought to do in the second half of the twentieth.

References

Alagiah, G. (2001). *A Passage to Africa*. London: Little Brown.

Bion, W. R. (1970). *Attention and Interpretation*. New York. Jason Aronson.

Briskin, A. (1998). *The Stirring of the Soul in the Workplace*. San Francisco, CA: Berret-Koeler Publishers.

Brochure (1974). Leadership and Authority: A Working Conference on Group Behaviour in Institutions, Trinity Hall, University of Dublin, 24–31 August.

Chattopadhyay, G. (1999). A fresh look at authority and organisation: towards a spiritual approach for managing illusion. In: R. French & R. Vince (Eds.), *Group Relations, Management, and Organization*. Oxford: Oxford University Press.

Clinton, B. (2001). *Dimbleby Lecture*. BBC TV, December.

Donne, J. (1997). Devotions. In: *Everyman's Poetry*. London: Orion.

French, R., & Simpson, P. (1999). Our best work happens when we don't know what we are doing. Presented to the ISPSO Symposium.

Grubb International Conference brochure (2003). "Being, Meaning, Engaging".

Johnson, A. (1942). *The One and the Many in the Israelite Conception of God*. Cardiff: University of Wales Press.

Lawrence, W. G. (1979). *Exploring Individual and Organizational Boundaries: A Tavistock Open Systems Approach*. London: Tavistock.

Lawrence, W. G. (2000). Beyond the frames. In: *Tongued with Fire: Groups in Experience*. London: Karnac.

Mandela, N. (1994). *Long Walk to Freedom*. London: Little, Brown.

Mant, A. (1976). How to analyse management. *Management Today*, October.

Miller, E. J. (1976). *Task and Organisation*. London: Tavistock.

Newton, J., Long, S. D., & Sievers, B. (Eds.) (2006). *Coaching in Depth: The Organizational Role Analysis Approach*. London: Karnac.

Reed, B. (1976). Organisational role analysis. In: C. L. Cooper (Ed.), *Developing Social Skills in Managers* (pp. 89–102). London: Macmillan.

Reed, B. (1978). *The Dynamics of Religion*. London: Darton Longman and Todd.

Reed, B. (2001). Our response to evil. Grubb Institute Notes.

Reed, B. (2003). Paper presented at a meeting of the Great Britain and Ireland Group Relations Forum held at the Tavistock Institute of Human Relations on 21 February 2003.

Rice, A. K. (1963). *The Enterprise and its Environment: A System Theory of Management Organisation*. London: Tavistock.

Rice, A. K. (1965). *Learning for Leadership: Interpersonal and Intergroup Relations*. London: Tavistock.

Sher, M. (2003). From groups to group relations: Bion's contributions to the Tavistock 'Leicester conferences'. In: R. M .Lipgar & M. Pines (Eds.), *Building on Bion: Branches* (pp. 109–144). London: Jessica Kingsley.

Whitehead, A. N. (1925). *Science and the Modern World*. New York: Mentor, 1960

Williams, R. (2000). *Lost Icons: Reflections on Cultural Bereavement*. Edinburgh: T&T Clarke.

Zohar, D., & Marshall, I. (2001). *SQ: Spiritual Intelligence: The Ultimate Intelligence*. London: Bloomsbury.

Daring to desire: ambition, competition, and role transformation in "idealistic" organisations

Vega Zagier Roberts and John Bazalgette

Introduction

There is considerable evidence among our clients leading "idealistic" organisations (charities, health, education, social care, faith-based organisations) that ambition, competition, and power are seen as dirty words describing undesirable and destructive characteristics often denied in themselves and attributed to others whom they would not wish to emulate. Our thesis is that this splitting off and projection of competitive and ambitious strivings (paranoid–schizoid position functioning) inhibits one's capacity for effective and creative leadership. Working with clients' desire can help them to reframe and reown these projections, and can lead to role transformation (functioning in the depressive position). Recent developments in organisational role analysis at the Grubb Institute provide a conceptual framework where desire is actively worked with as a key component of leadership development.

Case study: an executive transforming her role

The case study will be told in the first person, as only one of the authors was directly involved with Lina, a departmental director in an international charity. Promotions had always come without her need-ing actively to compete for them, and she could not identify in herself any feeling of ambition, now or ever. The story of her life was of being recognised by others, given special opportunities thanks to her com-bining hard work, passion, strong values, and a gift for relating with others, spreading oil on troubled waters, and making links between people. She had been personally "head-hunted" by the chief execu-tive, and, from the moment she took up her present post, he had been "whispering in her ear" his plan that she should succeed him when he retired in five years' time. She found these private whisperings distracting, denying having any active ambition for the post, although she was prepared to consider it should it ever be formally proposed to her.

The organisation, an international aid agency, which I shall call Capacitas, was the umbrella organisation for hundreds of indepen-dent Capacitas organisations worldwide, dedicated to promoting human rights and freedom through setting up sustainable, capacity-building projects in developing countries. A key issue that emerged very early on in our work together was that the organisation appeared to have two parallel primary tasks. One was to lead and link all the member organisations. The other was to use funding received from governments and donors to develop and support local community projects through training and supporting thousands of volunteers across three continents. These two tasks were located in the two largest departments, both run by men perceived by Lina as powerful, ambitious, and highly rivalrous. There seemed to be scope neither for debating whether either of these two core functions had primacy nor for defining an overarching core organisational purpose to which all departments might be understood to contribute.

This had a number of serious consequences. Departments were run as virtually independent fiefdoms with key decisions made through agreements between each director and the chief executive, rather than corporately in the executive board. The absence of a shared strategic vision and clarity of purpose was eroding its unique identity. This was not only affecting internal morale, but was also affecting the way the organisation was being perceived in the public arena. Donors were beginning to give less to Capacitas and more to other international aid agencies, particularly those providing highly visible crisis relief rather than quiet, less visible (but more sustainable) community projects. Finally, member organisations were falling away, either to become fully autonomous or to join forces with other aid agencies. This had financial implications in terms of loss of the income from membership fees, and also political implications as shrinkage threatened Capacitas's position as a significant player on the international aid and human rights scene.

Over the early months of our work together, Lina became increasingly aware of the consequences of avoiding this issue, without seeing any way forward, as she could not find a way to link the two competing core functions of the organisation even for herself. The organisation-in-the-mind for her was of two large but separate entities, bridged or loosely linked by the smaller departments (including her own), rather than of there being an outer containing and defining boundary. While she could see the need for a serious debate at board level around core purpose, as the newly appointed director of one of the smallest departments, she felt she could do little about this herself. She did try to discuss the question with the chief executive in their one-to-one meetings, but to no effect, as he was preoccupied with the management of this large and rather unwieldy system. She believed that the intense rivalry between the ambitious males in charge of the two main departments was the major stumbling block to the organisation's becoming more influential in promoting human rights. Her counter-strategy was to build collaborative relationships with each of the other directors, and she put considerable energy into fostering internal co-operation by initiating cross-departmental projects—useful and worthwhile work, but which had little impact on the main problems and challenges the organisation was facing. One might speculate that she managed to keep her envy of the more powerful men (the chief executive and the two directors of the big departments) out of conscious awareness by focusing on the need for more collaboration.

We would like now to focus on a sequence of three sessions over a six-month period in the second year of this consultancy.

In the first, which came soon after the announcement of an important new project, Lina was able to acknowledge how much she wanted this project to be located in her own department, and to plan her arguments for bringing this about in the face of competition from other departments to take the project on themselves. Previously, her power to influence the board had come almost entirely from her relationship and private conversations with the chief executive, and from her visibly working for the "corporate good". Now, for the first time, she would stand alone, making a public bid for something that others also wanted.

Lina did not get the project. However, the whole event led to her re-evaluating her understanding of the organisation, its purpose, and her role within it. When we next met, she brought the vision of the over-arching organisational purpose that had been eluding her for two years. It was as if clouds had rolled away to reveal a previously hidden landscape, or—to use a more psychoanalytic formulation—as if recovering her split-off ambition, envy, and competitive feelings had freed her capacity to think. She had been playing with an image that first came in a dream, of the banyan tree, the branches of which themselves become new roots, sometimes growing so large and strong that it becomes difficult to identify the original trunk. This trunk, which had been lost to sight, was the promotion of human rights, equality, and justice. The branch roots represented the myriad national organisations and community projects which supported and contributed to this core purpose ("banyan-ness"), the means to an end, rather than stand-alone ends in themselves. The work of the session focused on how she could use this insight to take up a stronger leadership role on the executive board.

By the time of the third session in this sequence, Lina's thinking had taken a further leap forward. She had retrieved a clear sense of what mattered most to her, which was her personal aspiration—her desire—to make a difference in the wider arena of social justice and human rights. This had been her desire in all her studies and previous jobs, and was the basis on which she had joined this organisation. However, this focus had become lost amid the organisational confusion, political wrangling, and her putting so much energy into bringing about internal harmony. Now she could think far more strategically than before, both about how Capacitas could have greater impact, and also about her own future. She was taking steps to develop her portfolio of skills and experience so that in three to five years she would be in as strong a position as possible to compete for

a more influential and powerful job, whether as the next chief executive of her current organisation or as a leader in another agency. She
had profound doubts whether Capacitas would prove capable of
making enough of a difference—whether it had the courage, drive,
and power to do this. Ambition, competition, and power were no
longer for her destructive forces interfering with purpose, but potential sources of strength which could be harnessed in the interests of a
larger purpose.

From a psychoanalytic perspective

Many years ago, one of us wrote a paper entitled "Is authority a dirty
word?" (Roberts, 1994). Perhaps the more crucial question now is "Is
power a dirty word?", which it seems to have become, particularly in
what we are calling "idealistic" organisations, that is, organisations
with a primary focus on serving people in need.

Lord Acton, a British philosopher, in a letter to a friend in 1887,
wrote, "Power tends to corrupt and absolute power corrupts absolutely". It is interesting that this is almost always mis-quoted as
"power corrupts" (http://oll.libertyfund.org/quotes/214), as if this is
an inevitability, presumably because of the assumed inherent self-
serving nature of mankind (or, at least, of those exemplars—never
including ourselves—who actually manage to have significant
amounts of power).

We would argue that while power can be misused in ways that
derail work on organisational (or other collective) purpose, the inability to "own" and use power equally interferes with mobilising one's
full potential in role to enable organisations to achieve their purposes.
Power is energy. Altruism as a defence against one's own (potentially
damaging) ambition and competitive strivings can severely impair
one's capacity to use power. Without power, we cannot fully exercise
authority and leadership: we cannot make things happen. Of course,
power can oppress, can be—and often is—abused. But, to turn the
notion that "power corrupts" on its head, we quote Lerner (1986, p. 2)
writing about "surplus powerlessness". He proposes that it is "powerlessness [that] corrupts ... it changes, transforms and distorts
us". Splitting and projection distort reality and diminish us, as we
know.

As a post-Second World War European from a formerly fascist country, Lina grew up with violently negative images of, and shame over, the destructiveness of power. From her student years onwards, she devoted herself to a range of reparative activities. In one of our first sessions, as part of exploring her aspirations, I invited her to project herself some decades forward and to draft an obituary that would encapsulate her life achievements. The whole piece was about the kind of person she had been. No word about any specific achievement. It was at that time that I first used the word "ambition"; a word with which she was entirely unable to connect. Ambition was self-serving and destructive, like power; like rivalry. She had been an only child, a good child who worked hard. Luckily, she had never needed to compete.

Over our first year or two, the word "ambition" had cropped up from time to time, but the emotional colour of it did not change until the series of sessions described above. It was as if the word had gradually detoxified, allowing some integration of previously split-off parts of herself. When Lina's conscious aspirations to join others in fighting injustice and protecting human rights could be connected to her previously repressed ambition, something new became possible. Instead of staying on the margins in a small department, she could invest in herself on behalf of a larger vision, authorising herself to use all the power she could muster in the furtherance of that vision. This included managing her avoidance of rivalry, and competing openly with others.

In the kind of organisations that we are grouping under the heading of "idealistic"—that is, where a key conscious motivator is to serve others—leaders appear often to be battling with an unconscious anxiety that their desires and ambitions will damage others. Competition can feel murderous, while ambition is too readily equated with being self-serving, therefore jarring with one's ego ideal. Indeed, one element that attracts some people to work in "idealistic" organisations might be a compelling reparative drive linked to unconscious guilt and anxiety that one has damaged others. The employing organisation might indeed be chosen in part to serve as a brake on unconscious destructive impulses (Roberts, 1994).

At one level, Capacitas had served Lina well. It was the perfect arena for maintaining her intrapsychic *status quo*, where she could be a "special child", a sort of golden girl, while the directors of the major departments did their "macho self-serving thing". By rendering their posturing almost absurd, she managed her rivalrous feelings, but at the cost of being unable to help the organisation develop a stronger (more power-full) voice beyond its boundaries. Furthermore, Lina's compliant "goodness" had led to her losing touch with her own desire. It made her rigid and fragile, robbing her of her real personal power. (This was not apparent—at least to me—until the transformation I have described.) Her imagination, her capacity to think, to play with dreams, images, and possibilities had been severely diminished by her need to repress her own rivalrousness. Capacitas's potential for making a difference as a whole, well-functioning organisation in its context was weakened not only by the overtly ambitious male leaders, but also by Lina's own under-performance.

As Gutmann and colleagues (1999) point out,

> envy and guilt form and fuel a vicious circle. On the one hand, envy arouses guilt in the person who looks to spoil or destroy the (human) object of envy. On the other hand, however, envy can stem directly from an even deeper guilt. It is the guilt that is experienced by those who know themselves neither to be perfect, nor to conform to the ego ideal that their own narcissism continually exalts. (p. 157)

They go on to explore how envy and desire—two responses to lack—become entangled at both the individual and the organisational level, so that repressing the one leads to repression of the other, and propose that "a fundamental task of managers consists of moving from envy to desire through the process of transformation" (p. 166). Lina's desire provoked unconscious envy. Repressing her envy had led to her losing touch with her deepest desire, to trading it in, so to speak, for the less competitive and, therefore, less anxiety- (and envy-) provoking desire to bring about peace and collaboration.

So far, we have commented on Lina's fight for the project only in relation to her allowing herself to compete. However, another significant factor that made the fight a turning-point event in her development is that she lost. This might have released her from some of the bondage of the "special child" dynamic, with its attendant conscious indebtedness and loyalty, and its unconscious anxieties and guilt, so that she could act in a more fully adult, autonomous, and accountable way.

From an organisational role analysis perspective

A traditional way of conceptualising role is as the area where person and system/organisation overlap, as in Figure 5.1 (see for example Long, 2006, p. 128).

Where the desires and strivings of the role-holder are congruent with the aims of their organisational system, personal ambition and competition for recognition or promotion become a source of collective ambition and competition: to be organisationally the best in the field, to be at the cutting edge, to have the largest market-share, and so on. Indeed, personal ambition and internal competition are often encouraged, because they can serve the interests of an organisation that needs to aim high and beat competitors.

Recent work by the Grubb Institute has expanded a two-circle model into a framework we call "transforming experience into authentic action", or, for brevity, the "transforming experience framework" (see Figure 5.2 and Chapter One of this book).

Here role is located in the overlap of three domains of experience: person, system, and context (the wider environment with its needs, meanings, and resources). This provides a way of reconceptualising roles, particularly leadership roles. Not only is there an overlap between person and organisational system as there was in Figure 5.1, but also between person and context, and between system and context.

Let us start by unpacking the three circles in Figure 5.2.

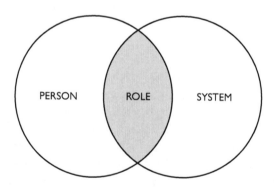

Figure 5.1.   Role.

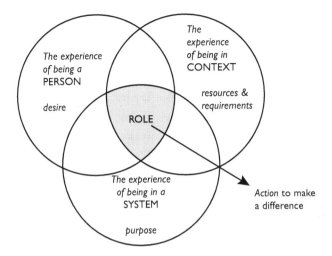

Figure 5.2.   The transforming experience framework.

Person

The word "person" is chosen deliberately (rather than "individual") to underline the view of human beings as essentially and profoundly related to others: "a nexus or network of relationships that centre in the person ... [within whom] are carried one's personal images of parents, siblings, colleagues, aspirations and fears" (Bazalgette et al., 2006, p. 106). Fundamental to the experience of being a person is the experience of desire, the underlying impetus that drives us to work at transforming ourselves and the world we live in (on however small or large a scale). Where this departs from a psychoanalytic view of the drive to reparation is that desire is not thought of as a defence against anxieties about our aggression and potential for destructiveness. Neither is it simply about "self-realisation". Rather, it is understood as one of the primary sources of energy to act in the world, connecting with other human beings to make a difference—a recognition of, and an effort to bring into play that haunting, deep human sense of yearning for "I know not what". It is this deeply human longing that makes writing such as Kahlil Gibran's *The Prophet* such a best-seller, widely used at weddings, naming ceremonies, and funerals for over three-quarters of a century (Gibran, 1926).

System

"System" refers to a set of activities with a boundary, a boundary that differentiates systems from their environment and from other systems. This enables managed connection, collaboration, and engagement through transactions across the boundary (Miller & Rice, 1967). A human system might be a formal organisation or part of an organisation such as a team or department, or it might be a family, neighbourhood, agency, etc. Each system has a purpose to which every activity within it contributes (or not!). This is different from the primary task (as defined by Ken Rice in 1958), which is about the conversion of inputs into outputs. Purpose is about why; why the system exists, why the context demands that the system exist, and, therefore, it relates fundamentally to context.

One could say that management is about achieving the primary task (the what and how of systems), whereas leadership is about discerning and articulating the purpose of the system in its context (the why), so that members of the system understand why they are doing what they are doing. Like person, system essentially exists in relationship: with other systems and sub-systems and with context. Just as the human being acting, thinking, and feeling as individual, rather than person, is cut off from mobilising his or her full potential as a human being (a kind of psychic death), so a system whose boundaries serve only to protect and differentiate it from other systems and context, rather than enable it to relate to these through managed exchanges, becomes a closed system, cut off from reality and from meaning. At best, it might survive for a time in a technical sense by continuing to produce outputs, but without a why. At worst, and over time inevitably, it cannot survive at all.

Context

"Context" refers to sources of elements of the role-holder's experience at different levels. The immediately experienced context might be the wider organisation—the department, the company. At other moments, context might be the National Health Service (NHS) or the prison service, or our society, or even the globe. For any one of us, it could be one or more of these at different moments. Working recently with the manager of a therapeutic community within a prison healthcare department, we found ourselves talking at one point about context as the healthcare unit, at another as the prison (from which, under its previous manager, the therapeutic community had kept itself as separate as possible), and, at yet another, as the wider society with its ambivalent attitudes to, and changing expectations of, the prison service.

In public sector agencies, at least in the UK, the context tends to be regarded primarily as a place of threats—to jobs, to client services and quality, to meaning. In business, the context is more likely to be read in terms of opportunities as well as threats. In reality, it is both. Old resources diminish. New ones arise. Changes in the context might indeed remove old sources of meaning, but also—even at the same time—open up new possibilities, new directions, and new meanings. Many of our public sector clients come to us with a sense of something vital having been taken from them and spoiled, so that work is no longer meaning-full for them or their staff. They might come hoping to find meaning again. But leadership requires more than the recovery of old meanings. It is about discovering new ones: addressing the question, what is the meaning of this work and this enterprise now, in the current context, and how can we influence the context to achieve purpose to the benefit not only of us inside the organisation, but to the context?—"a shift from *intention* to *attention* . . . from formation to engagement" (Armstrong, 1999, p. 150).

Purpose cannot be static, and neither can it be articulated in advance. It needs to be discovered, and, as context changes, discovered again. Shapiro (2000) identifies a crucial leadership as "making present": discovering and articulating new meanings, in particular, "discovering the link to society" (p. 136)—how people's personal values and the aims of the organisation contribute to a larger, collective, societal purpose. From a different tradition, Senge and colleagues (2005) and Scharmer (2009) have been writing about U-theory: moving first "down" the U as new sensing or reading of the context requires, letting go of old ways of interpreting and acting, to "presencing", and then moving "up" the U to "let come".

Role

In the TEF, role is about behaviour. It is her behaviour, her action-taking, that is shaped by the person's inner picture of herself as a person (including her desire), of the context (including the resources that derive from it), and of the system (including its purpose), using her feelings and experience in each domain as evidence on which to base her choice of action. Role is defined as disciplined behaviour which furthers the purpose of the system in its context. Thus, being effective in role requires one to integrate one's experience from each of the three domains of person, system, and context—integrating desire, resources, and purpose to determine one's behaviour.

Obviously, it is not only leaders who take roles. Everyone in a system takes a role and everyone who takes a role is, in effect, offering leadership to the system as a whole. However, due to their exposed position, and to their power, the clarity with which a CEO or other leader articulates the purpose of the organisation in its context can greatly influence the extent to which others can link their different roles into a collective endeavour to meet the purpose (in its deepest sense) of the organisation. This kind of leadership is defined as "revealed meaning embodied in action".

Let us now return to the TEF to focus on the areas of overlap rather than on the three circles.

Person–context

Our hypothesis is that the shift in Lina took place at several different levels. First, reintegrating previously split off parts of herself, becoming less frightened by her competitiveness and envy, freed Lina to get back in touch with her desire (person–desire). Second, she was better able to move to the outer boundary of the system she was leading and to discover or recover an understanding of the system's purpose, which had previously eluded not only her but the entire leadership group (system–purpose). From here, she could move into the third domain, focusing on context. One might say that the crucial work took place in the three areas of overlap shown in Figure 5.3.

It was only when she had worked on these three areas that Lina could fully take her leadership role, clarifying her vision of how she and her organisation could have more impact and make a more significant difference in relation to the requirements of the context. The broadening of her attention to include context freed her to think

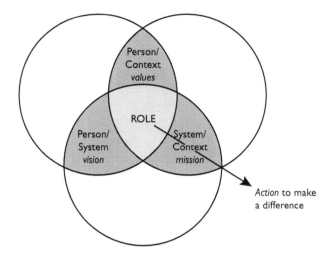

- Person–context: standing back from the maelstrom of organisational life, Lina got back in touch with her experience of, and in, the wider context, which was the original source of her values.
- Person–system: this enabled her to re-evaluate the match (and mismatch) between her desires, values, beliefs, and aspirations, and the purposes (overt and covert) of the organisation. Her vision for the organisation became clearer.
- System–context: she could then reassess the extent to which the organisation was being true to, and successful in, its mission to promote human rights.

Figure 5.3. The three areas of overlap in the person–context system.

"out of the box" and more strategically. Greater awareness of resources in the context (such as other agencies and groupings) also helped her see more clearly how she could best develop and deploy her own talents and desire to the benefit of the larger arena, thus realising more fully her own aspirations for social justice and human rights.

By putting her organisation-in-the-mind (Armstrong, 1999) into its context, she could think without so much unconscious guilt about how to become more powerful, and how to make her organisation more powerful, that is, more effective on behalf of society. She found freedom and potency, and also the capacity to "make present", first to herself and then to others.

As we were writing this paper, we started to think of these areas of overlap in a new way, linked to thinking about Lina's greater capacity to "play". Winnicott (1971) proposes that playing needs a place and a time—a place which is neither inside oneself nor outside, a potential space—and a time which is neither quite now nor quite then—a potential or transitional time, so to speak—which includes past, future, and present without being quite any one of these. Among the reasons why children play is "integration of personality": "Play can easily be seen to link the individual's relation to inner personal reality with his relation to external or shared reality" (Winnicott, 1942, p. 151). Organisational role analysis enlarged the realm of imagination, that intermediate area—neither quite fantasy nor quite reality—that sustains us, as children and as adults, between the isolation of total subjectivity and the impoverishment of total objectivity. One might think of the overlap areas of the diagram as potential spaces, neither inside us nor outside, yet also both inside and outside us—spaces which open up our potential.

Winnicott (1971, p. 59) links "the significant moment" of play with the experience of surprising oneself. In this moment, there is discovery and imagining. This joins up in an interesting way with Hutton's concept of "re-imagining the organisation" (1997, p. 66), where she describes the process of discovering new definitions of purpose across a wide range of public service institutions. The managers she describes in these case studies took up leadership roles when they were able to link system purpose with context, that is, work in the S–C overlap area.

So far, we have looked at how a leader can use and integrate experience from the three domains of person, system, and context. There is, however, a fourth domain that we are currently learning how to take into account.

Drawing on a fourth domain of experience

In introducing the concept of person, we took note of that essentially human experience of longing, indeed yearning, for "I know not what". This is the experience that can be overwhelming: when we witness the birth of a baby, when a bride and groom commit themselves to one another in the presence of others, passages of music, a fine painting, a sunset, bird-song at dawn. These kinds of experiences have been described in several ways: moments of the awareness of transcendence, or a sense of something sacred, or a feeling of spirituality. Chattopadhyay (1999), Ostroff (2000), Lawrence (2000), and Bazalgette and colleagues (2006) all choose to name these experiences in terms of spirituality, taking account of the soul, awareness of the cosmos, or belief in the divine (either in general or specific terms.). Raimón Pannikar, the Catalan theologian and philosopher, when writing about the urgency of the need for different religious perspectives and faiths to dialogue with each other, argues that:

> The human person is homo religiosus from the beginning, when human beings posed the defining questions about human nature. These are questions that initiate the most profound communication between persons (questions which always create a longing for dialogue) and are the fruit of a calling that preceded the questions themselves. (Pannikar, 2001, p. 23, translated for this edition by J. Bazalgette)

This is not only the domain of mystics and theologians. Consider Bion's concept of "O":

> . . . the ultimate reality, absolute truth, the godhead, the infinite, the thing-in-itself . . . It can be "become" but it cannot be "known" . . . But it enters the domain of K (knowledge) when it has evolved to a point where it can be known, through knowledge gained by experience . . . Its existence is conjectured phenomenologically . . . O becomes manifest through the emergence of actual events. (Bion, 1970, pp. 26, 28)

And, to quote Lawrence, we are exploring

> The capacity to be amazed and surprised by a faculty that mankind in the West is in danger of losing . . . the faculty of imaginative awareness and consciousness that takes him beyond his immediate, narcissistic preoccupations with survival in contemporary mass industrial society to link him with what may underlie existence. (Lawrence, 2000, p. 182)

The Grubb Institute began to incorporate this dimension into the TEF as "experience of oneness with the other" (Figure 5.4).

Transforming Experience into Authentic Action through Role (TEF)

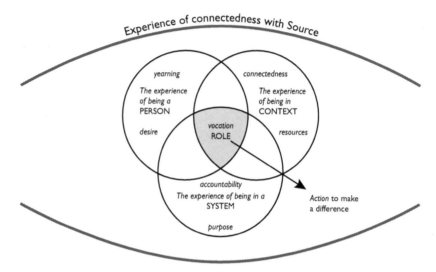

Figure 5.4.   The fourth domain of the TEF.

The Grubb Institute incorporated this dimension into the TEF initially as "experience of oneness with the other" and later as "connectedness with source" (see Chapter One).

Lina was a person with a religious faith which had always informed her life choices. She had spoken of it but—like so many leaders—she had seen it as private rather than as intrinsic to her leadership capacity. Thus, one way of understanding her point of transformation (when the image of the banyan tree came to her) is that it happened when she integrated inside herself all four dimensions represented in the framework. As a result, she understood within herself exactly how to behave in her role. She experienced a sense of direction and a new realisation of the powers that were to hand for her to use. She lost her disabling sense of guilt about "ambition" because she no longer saw her vision in personal terms, but in terms of serving others. A positive sense of duty gave her freedom to take effective action. Her faith was no longer a privatised factor in her life, but had become a true resource in her work.

For some readers, this fourth domain might feel like a no-go area, a purely private domain reserved for those with a formal religious faith, and certainly not the business of role analysis. However, we would argue that the essence of the TEF is to open up the no-go areas, a framework which serves to remind one of which domains of experience the client is and is not drawing on, and which ones we, too, might be neglecting. There is a link between "the spirit of enquiry" which we all profess, and spirituality: openness not only to uncertainty, but to that which is intrinsically unknowable.

Competition revisited

As we approach the end of this chapter, we would like to come back to the theme of "the dark side of competition". Through the case study, we have tried to illustrate two ways of looking at competition: one which we might call "competition in a vacuum", the other "competition related to purpose and context". When we started out, we saw the four domains of the TEF as being about different levels of connectedness or relatedness. But perhaps another way of understanding the four domains is as about different levels to accountability: accountability to oneself (values, beliefs, needs, desires), to one's system (to contribute to purpose), to the wider context (community, society), and to something else—humankind, life, cosmos, God?

The words "compete" and "competent" have the same Latin roots: *com*, meaning "with" or "together", and *petere*, meaning "to aim at", "seek", "strive". Along the way, the original Latin meaning was lost: "striving with" became "striving against". But think of the images on Greek vases of wrestlers or javelin-throwers. In Ancient Greece, sports competitions were fierce, not infrequently to the death. But these competitions were in the context of religious festivals, as a way to honour the gods. This framed how they fought, so what they were doing was fighting, but at the same time they were collaborating in a religious event.

However, one cannot wrestle alone. One needs an opponent, in order to wrestle together. One will win; one will lose, true. Yet, there is also something crucially important that is being done together, within a context which is larger than either or both. The dark side of competition takes over when context is forgotten. Taking system, context, and oneness-with-the-other (or the transcendent) into account enables a journey to be travelled that can move us through the destructive experience of envy and its associated rivalry (the killing off of collective purpose) to a situation where we can see how we can engage together in the repair, healing, and transformation of our world. Here, desire (ambition) can be experienced as being in touch with the life-force, or energiser, which enables us to aim for, to seek, to strive.

Desire can be perilously close to envy: it can feel like too small a gap between wanting something and wanting to destroy it (or the person who apparently possesses that which we want) and all the anxieties this evokes. Com-petition can slip into (murderous) rivalry, the killing off of collective purpose. So, we may stifle our desire and quell our competitive strivings in order to manage our envy and rivalry. But without daring to desire, there is no seeking, no competition, no reaching for the stars. If we can face the dark side of being human—our envy and competition—then we stand a chance of co-creating a world of which we can be proud. If we cannot, we will co-create a world of which we will be ashamed.

References

Armstrong, D. (1999). The recovery of meaning. In: R. French & R. Vince (Eds.), *Group Relations, Management, and Organization* (pp. 145–154). Oxford: Oxford University Press.

Bazalgette, J., Irvine, B., & Quine, C. (2006). The absolute in the present: role, the hopeful road to transformation. In: A. Mathur (Ed.), *Dare to Think the Unthought Known?* Tempere, Finland: Aivoairut.

Bion, W. R. (1970). *Attention and Interpretation.* New York: Jason Aronson.

Chattopadhyay, G. P. (1999). A fresh look at authority and organization: towards a spiritual approach for managing illusion. In: R. French & R. Vince (Eds.), *Group Relations, Management and Organization* (pp. 112–126). Oxford: Oxford University Press.

Gutmann, D., Ternier-David, J., & Verrier, C. (1999). From envy to desire: witnessing the transformation. In: R. French & R. Vince (Eds.), *Group Relations, Management and Organization* (pp. 155–172). Oxford: Oxford University Press.

Hutton, J. (1997). Re-imagining the organisation of an institution: management in human service institutions. In: E. Smith (Ed.), *Integrity and Change: Mental Health in the Marketplace* (pp. 66–82). London: Routledge.

Lawrence, W. G. (2000). *Tongued With Fire: Groups in Experience*. London: Karnac.

Lerner, M. (1986). *Surplus Powerlessness: The Psychodynamics of Everyday Life and the Psychology of Individual and Social Transformation*. New Jersey: Humanities Press International.

Long, S. (2006). Drawing from role biography in organisational role analysis. In: J. Newton, S. Long, & B. Sievers (Eds.), *Coaching in Depth: The Organizational Analysis Approach* (pp. 127–144). London: Karnac.

Miller, E. J., & Rice, A. K. (1967). *Systems of Organisaton: Control of Task and Sentient Boundaries*. London: Tavistock.

Ostroff, S. (2006). Whispers of the whole: tending to the system, by the system, for the system. In: A. Mathur (Ed.), *Dare To Think The Unthought Known?* (pp. 51–88). Tampere, Finland, Aivoairut Oy.

Pannikar, R. (2001). *El Diálogo Indispensable: Paz entre las relgiones*. Barcelona: Península/Atalaya.

Rice, A. K. (1958). *Productivity and Social Organization: The Ahmedabad Experiment*. London: Tavistock.

Roberts, V. Z. (1994). Is authority a dirty word? Some dilemmas in idealistic organisations. *Journal of Social Work Practice*, 8(2): 185–192.

Senge, P., Scharmer, C., Jaworski, J., & Flowers, B. (2005). *Presence*. London: Nicholas Brealey.

Scharmer, O. (2009). *Theory U: Leading from the Future as It Emerges*. San Francisco, CA: Berrett-Koehler.

Shapiro, E. (2000). The changing role of the CEO. *Organisational and Social Dynamics*, 1: 130–142.

Winnicott, D. W. (1942). Why children play. In: J. Hardenberg (Ed.), *The Child and the Outside World: Studies in Developing Relationships* (pp. 149–152. London: Tavistock, 1957.

Winnicott, D. W. (1971). *Playing and Reality*. Harmondsworth: Penguin, 1974.

CHAPTER SIX

Working to improve institutional strength: the challenge of taking multiple roles in multiple systems

Rebekah O'Rourke and John Bazalgette

The loss of confidence in institutions

President Barack Obama, on his visit to Ghana in July 2009, said, "Africa doesn't need strong men. It needs strong institutions" (Clinton, 2014, p. 270). He had recently been elected on a rising tide of hope (e.g., see Obama, 2006). So his remarks about "strong institutions" can be assumed to be have been made in an effort to inject hope into Africa through its institutions becoming effective in doing what they were created for, instead of hope being invested in individual persons, strong though they might be. Indeed, he was warning against the way "strong men" win control of institutions and easily become tyrants, surrounded by sycophantic followers.

Yet, at first sight, his comment appears to be a counter-cultural declaration when set against western society's general climate of the disillusionment with the capacity of institutions to tackle the challenges they were set up to address.

There are good grounds for disillusionment. There are many occasions where bureaucracy, incompetence, corruption, and malfeasance have had appalling consequences, too often at the expense of the innocent and the disadvantaged. Examples are myriad: the banking crisis which erupted in 2008; the Deep Horizon disaster in the Bay of Mexico; Enron and GSK and other companies mired in corruption. And we cannot overlook what has happened in public services, including the abuse of children by churches and local government agencies that were expected to exist to serve the vulnerable, which has effectively gone unpunished.

The general distrust of institutions is not limited to large institutions. The large ones hit the headlines and usually with causes of criminal and corrupt practices, but small and medium-sized enterprises also have problems that give weight to similar distrust.

President Obama's comment, laid alongside the scepticism, distrust, and cynicism which surround small and large institutions today, leads us to ask how what he said can be taken positively and then put into practice. Obama would believe that institutions which offer hope are ones in which those in positions of leadership understand the subtlety and complexity of taking multiple roles in them. In short, he was advocating the need for institutions that are run competently in the interest of the communities they were created to serve. Of such are strong institutions made, which provide reservoirs of hope to those communities.

A working hypothesis

Our working hypothesis, which applies to organisations of all sizes, based on our work with clients over the past couple of years, is simple but profound. It does not claim to solve everything, especially at the macro level, but it does focus on the issue of multiple roles and multiple systems. For institutions to be reservoirs of hope, this is an issue that needs to be understood and addressed.

The widespread flight from institutions is evidence of a general loss of confidence in why institutions exist. This leads to a presumption that to cope with that loss, hope needs to be vested in the individualisation of persons. Part of the reason for this is a dread of being placed under the power of others, whose motivation is unclear and cannot be trusted, or might even be assumed to be malevolent.

Much of this current thinking is based around the hope wished for from institutions, which is to meet the staff's and employees' desire for forms of escalated self-realisation. In these terms, people working in an institution work on the assumption: "This organisation principally exists because it provides those of us who work in it (or own it) with hope for ourselves". That hope might be for income, mates, status, power, a career, or security. Where providing jobs and income becomes the main reason for existence, this springs from within and inevitably leads to regression when under stress: stress which arises from being inefficiently organised and having poorly led ways of working together. Similarly, where the shareholders' return on investment is privileged over all other activities, organisations also become vulnerable because the regression that takes place in both cases is dysfunctional.

The principal destination for that regression under stress in these circumstances is the family. Families are seen as providing an archetypical *raison d'être* for a "perfect" state of human being-ness and, therefore, the primordial source of hope. In spiral dynamic terms (Beck & Cowan, 1996), this expresses a regression to purple and red memes. This centripetal mind set is conducive of tribalism.

What is not fully evident in this culture is a sense that, seen in the widest scheme of things, the assumed "why" of the family is about the survival of the family's character itself, embodied in its being the "reservoir of hope" for the individuals within it. The result is that what we have now is a narrow and vulnerable basis for hope because the "walls" of the reservoir run the risk of not being intended to take the strain. Therefore, fragmentation becomes probable. However, what is not perceived from this systemic perspective is that human survival (and, hence, the purpose of families) is about the community and, ultimately, the species. "The person is not the primordial fact: the primordial fact is the community" (quoted in Gallagher, 2010, p. 69).

However, a perverse contrary movement is also evident in today's circumstances.

Here, rather than retreating inwards in search of the unique individual, the regression is towards an ideology, religious or political, which is pursued with fanaticism, demanding compliance and conformity which defies differentiation. Here, the autonomous self is denied and hope is vested in uniformity (*vide* North Korea). This is still a purple or red meme. Again, this condition renders fruitful human life vulnerable in that it necessarily shrinks the sum of available human resources.

The question to be faced is how do we think about what an institution is for? This takes us to the concept of purpose (Bazalgette et al., 2009).

Purpose is evident when the following question can be posed: "Why does the context need this institution in this form now?" The reply to that question enables every decision and every action to be understood as connected to that answer. When that happens, everything that occurs in the system can be seen as purposeful. In this case, the reason for existence springs from outside, in terms of the difference that the institution makes in the world and which has implications inside. In spiral dynamic terms, this expresses a movement towards green, or even teal (Laloux, 2014). When this perspective is adopted, the hope that is aspired to is fuelled by the desire to further the survival and wellbeing of a community, a society, a nation, humankind, or even the planet. The moral philosopher John Macmurray (1935, p. 14) put the matter in terms of furthering the "unfolding process of human history".

So, why are these two forms of regression so prevalent and so effective in undermining the potential of institutions to be reservoirs of hope now?

The underlying force that drives is the inadequate capacity to understand how to think organisationally and systemically about the ways in which the internal structures relate to the purpose of the institution in terms of meeting the call for it to exist, springing from the context. This involves drawing boundaries that differentiate between systems, managing transactions across boundaries, and handling the consequent impact on relatedness between systems and sub-systems. This calls for a readiness to handle the reality that, in modern society systems, overlap one another and normal life involves prioritising the demands of differing systems.

It is a fact of modern life that human beings are always in at least one system and, therefore, always in a role. What springs from this state of overlapping systems is that persons are constantly taking multiple roles. This is often called "role conflict": a term that is unhelpful because it makes it appear as if the problem is resolvable by the person, who can make their own personal choice about priorities. This assumes that the person alone can always be the "reservoir of hope".

The reality is that the conflict is not between the roles, but between different systems whose priorities of purpose have not been consciously related to one another. Thus, the person in a boundary spanning role becomes an inter-system pressure point. If the person is to find freedom in working through that "conflict", his experience needs to be understood through exploring the tensions and satisfactions that spring from the relatedness between the "whys" of the different systems—their purposes. Choices about hope-filled action in role can then follow. The reality is that the essential connectedness of life on this planet cannot be ignored: the Internet, for instance, and all the manifestations that place that reality in front of us. We create systems to enable us to think about and manage our connectedness so that the best results can be achieved through that connectedness. The time of silo mentality is over, and it never was the most effective way to live and work.

An analytic framework for thinking

This chapter offers an analysis based on the interacting concepts of person, system, context, connectedness with source, and role, which outline an action pathway through complexity. This is the framework for transforming experience into authentic action through role (TEF). These linked concepts are based on a holistic understanding of what it is to take leadership and followership roles that serve purpose, enabling persons to feel authentic in grappling with the varied forces and factors which they encounter in their daily work. This equips them better as they engage with others in the way they take up their roles (Figure 6.1).

Person in context

As persons, we are what we might call our own "continuing sensor" over time. We learnt about this from the moment of our birth. We carry memories, we have new sensations, we evolve hopes for the future. As we make each move through life, we represent our own continuity to ourselves in our context (Figure 6.2).

To the newborn infant, it is reasonable to assume that there is no differentiation between the person and the context: all is simply "me", so I feel unboundedly "real". "Me" goes on for ever. I perceive

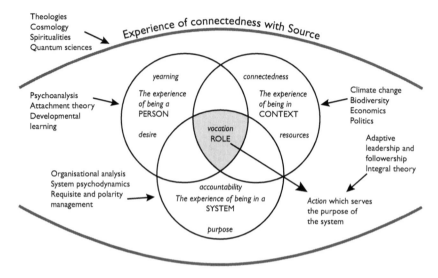

Figure 6.1. Transforming experience into authentic action through role (TEF.

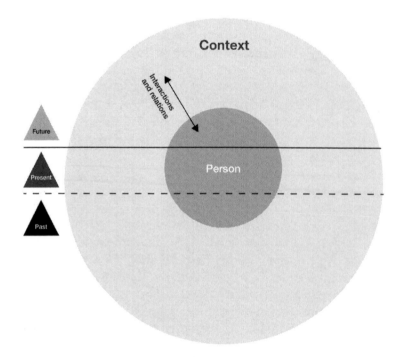

Figure 6.2. Person in context.

everything solely from within, thus, in the diagram, person and context are all "me". As time goes on, awareness develops that I am not all there is: there is something beyond "me". At first, that which is beyond me gives me pleasure, comfort, satisfaction, and increasing awareness of "me" being real: mother, father, siblings are experienced as being extensions of "me" but "more of me but different". So my sense of my reality is extended, becoming richer in the process. In doing this, I am beginning to think inwards from outside my skin to the inner "me". While that experience is satisfying, all is well with my world. But there are times when those extensions frustrate, disappoint, hurt, and anger me. When that happens, they are clearly sensed as *not-me*. Here, I am thinking from "inside" to "outside" and discovering the boundaries between us. Without having the words, I am beginning to think in terms of a system. The system I am subconsciously creating in my developing mind is "family". Miller and Rice (1967, pp. 6–7) define a system as "activities with a boundary which differentiates those activities from their context".

At first, thinking in terms solely of an "inside-out" perspective, I am tempted to behave as if the systems were only there to be used as simple extensions of "me"; only existing to meet my needs and my demands. When they fail to do this, they are "not-me". They represent opposing forces that exist primarily to frustrate, oppose, and overcome me.

As memory develops, the developing me becomes aware of a past, populated by things some of which satisfied me and some that upset me. Then things arrive which I have never encountered before, so I develop a sense of a future from which new things come into my experience. Since, for most of us, the overall experience is a satisfying one, this first "institution" is a place of hope for us.

Learning about role through experience

As time goes by within the family system, I begin to discover that the relationships that I have shape my sense of the "real" me. I learn to call them "Mummy" and "Daddy" and, thus, to integrate person and system through named roles. At first, I saw myself solely as a person, but I am discovering that in reality I am more than that: I am part of that system—the "family"—and I am a "son" or "daughter", maybe with a "brother" or a "sister". In this collection of relatedness, I sense that being "in role" (though I never use that term or even want to use a word for it) helps me to understand what is happening to me: what starts with me, what starts elsewhere, how the pieces of the system fit together. We can usefully call this process learning that I am a *person-in-role*, engaging with others who are also in roles. So, I am beginning to think from outside to inside, as well as from inside to outside.

Figure 6.3 illustrates this in simple terms. I am still thinking from inside to outside, so a large part of person and context are still experienced as "me", but as I became aware of the family system of which I am a part, being "me" feels different. The circle with the words "son/daughter" represents something that is part of me and also more of me. As I mature, the family overlap becomes more and more an affective part of me and I become more an affective part of it. I bring more and more past experience into play in how I engage with the family, while relatives will put questions to me about my future—in school, further education, and employment. I am beginning to

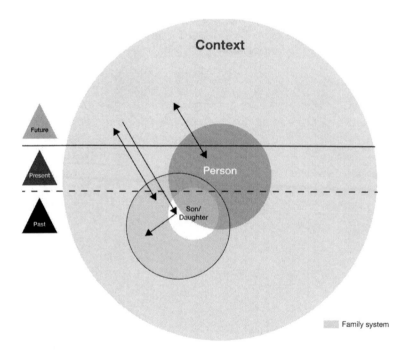

Figure 6.3.   Person-in-role in the family.

develop crude skills for analysing an organisation and finding my place in it.

As I go beyond the persons of the family, I discover that I am treated by "outsiders" as part of the family system, that I have a family name. I am no longer just "John"; I am "John Smith". I am treated by others from outside it as an extension of my family system and I experience how that system is seen by others who are not part of it. As I experience the relatedness which we share, a wider sense of the "real me" becomes apparent, which includes other members of that family. Going to school heightens this way of understanding the world I am in (Figure 6.4).

I now begin to learn to belong to more than one system and take roles in each of them. I discover that I can be a "son" in one system and a "pupil" in the other. While, at the age of five, I might have some-times called my teacher "Mummy", it did not take long for me to find that was a mistake: it did not elicit the responses I hoped for. In a

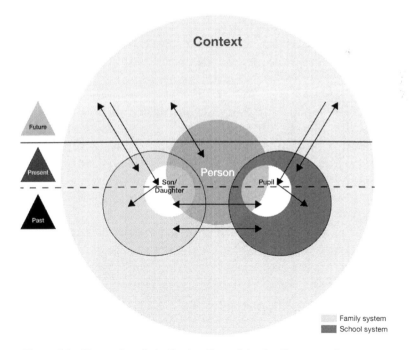

Figure 6.4.   Person-in-role in the family and the family system in context: am I a "son" or a "pupil", or both?

recent BBC radio programme, a distinguished man who was at board-
ing school from the age of seven until eighteen, found himself always
calling his father "Sir" on his return home for holidays. Each role has
its own cluster of expectations and relatedness, and, as I come to
understand them, I discover more about what it is for me to feel real
in different ways when in different systems. I begin to develop new
patterns of interactions between myself and the other persons in their
roles within different systems.

New patterns of behaviour also developed between the different
systems and their differing purposes. My parents and my teachers
developed relations through which the purposes of each system
engaged with one another, supporting me to a greater or lesser extent.
Parent–teacher meetings had implications for how I was treated as
"son" or as "pupil". To have thought solely from an inside-out perspective could lead to confusion and aggression. The challenge was to
think both inside-out and outside-in.

A dynamic experienced as being between roles is emerging, which
is, in reality, a function of two systems. Given that the great majority
of families are places where love and affection are natural features of
how people engage with one another, my experience as a child was
that my family was a reservoir of hope, both for the present and also
for the future.

Given how impressionable one is during one's early school years,
the mental templates that are laid down at this time provide the
"master plan" for all future ideas about role-taking and the interactions between systems, right into adulthood.

The challenge of working in multiple roles in multiple systems is now
coming into view. Below the level of full consciousness, children are
being prepared for the adult world with both its richness and its difficulties.

In school, focus is on other things: academic work, records, formal
organisational structures, boundary management, assessments,
implicit and explicit contracts, leadership and management are significant factors in the schooling system. At school, one learns to work in
an organised way, which is more relevant to the adult world. The child
now has to learn skills of self-management and role-taking which
differ depending upon which system they find themselves in. A class
is not the same as a tutor group. A French lesson is not the same as a
Design and Technology lesson. It is unlikely that much thought will

go into either system about how to enable the child to develop much understanding about learning to belong and role-taking. In a secondary school, taking multiple roles is a central fact of life, but careful attention to learn from that experience is rare. It takes place through trial and error. Secondary schools are probably the most complex organisation that the majority of people will encounter throughout their whole lives.

We have written elsewhere about the social significance of learning how to engage with schools through understanding how to find, make, and take roles (Bazalgette, 1978; Bazalgette et al., 2006). We have made the point there that this fundamental area of learning about role taking is seldom adequately worked at through schooling. This leaves emerging generations ill-equipped to handle the complexity of adult organisational life. The question relevant to this chapter is how far schools are experienced as reservoirs of hope. To the extent that they are, they provide a basic level of social learning that will enable other institutions to be approached as potential reservoirs of hope. Where they fall short, the challenges of handling relations in multiple systems through multiple roles are likely to be substantial.

Applying what one has learnt about role to adult life

Adult life in modern society is one in which each person experiences a host of different systems. Consequently, one is never *not* in role. Figure 6.5 illustrates this.

Family experience of role taking is the most likely core resource in learning to engage with working organisations. School life adds to it, but inevitably in haphazard ways. The diagram suggests a few roles an adult might take, each with contrasting considerations about how to use power and authority, how to locate boundaries and manage them. We have continued to draw the family as a potent factor in working out how to behave with and towards others.

The implications for handling oneself in multiple systems, calling for multiple roles

Organizational size is an example of one influence on discovering and enacting of the multiple roles required in an organization. A larger

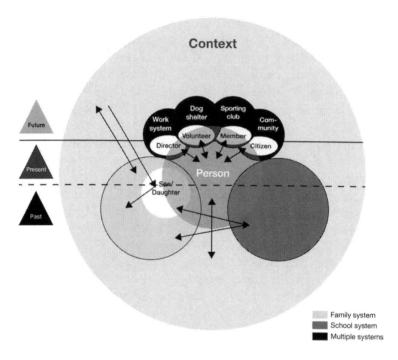

Figure 6.5. Emerging implications for organisational life and leadership.

multinational might have boundaries clearly in place in relation to borders/geography, departments or division of labour and its structure or hierarchy. How these boundaries inhibit or enable the finding of roles will be organization, person and role specific. A smaller organization will have its own challenges related to resourcing, division of labour and infrastructure etc. There have been some attempts to do away with boundaries in organizations in attempts to create freedom. This desire needs to be treated with caution. (Hirschhorn & Gilmore, 1992)

The person working in a small or medium-sized organisation, especially one with its origins in a family based business that works in a community with an egalitarian culture (context), is going to experience different dynamics at play from a person in a large multinational (system) operating across up to five continents with origins in a collective culture (context). How many differing roles they each are required to find in their organisational systems, while interacting with other organisational systems, will be dependent on factors both inherent within the organisations and the contexts these two organisations operate within.

Over the past couple of years, we have worked with many leaders to reveal the multiple roles that they are finding, making, and taking in their organizational systems and contexts. Initially, this can be experienced as challenging current assumptions or paradigms, given that people can articulate broadly why the organisation pays them. Once the exploration deepens, however, multiple roles emerge and can be utilised as a resource.

We now offer some examples from our own work with different organisations, linking each of them with implications for practice.

Multiple roles and family business

A graphic design company was set up some fifteen years ago. The owners were a married couple, one of whom was a gifted graphic designer while the wife was an experienced businesswoman. Five years after their foundation, the staffing needed to expand considerably, so they appointed a man whom they named as Chief Executive to lead their major projects in the UK and the USA. They also gave their eldest son, who had been working in a multi-national company, a roving brief. He had gifts as a project manager and also in terms of general administration, so he was a suitable person. By the time we were engaged to provide role consultancy to the son, the firm had some fifty full-time employees plus freelance designers who were hired as they were needed. There was no strategy formulated, and neither was there a shared idea about what the company was for. Internal structures were haphazard and frequently circumvented in the name of efficiency.

Since the owners seldom met to develop overall strategies, or even medium-term plans, the company culture was one of separateness, autonomy, and ill-co-ordinated work. This was exacerbated because the kind of clients who use the services of graphic design companies tend to behave in highly arbitrary ways, change their minds at short notice, and tend to demand deadlines that are frequently impossible to meet. Anyone representing this company to clients had to expect external working relations that were typically stressful. However, what was clear was that the work the company attracted was particularly exciting and the salaries were above the norm in the field. So, despite the stresses, people tended to stay on or, if they left, many of them looked for opportunities to come back. The family business culture in this enterprise had much to recommend it, despite its drawbacks.

Implications for practice

This was a company where multiple systems created multiple role relations, with the owners' son as the heart of it all. By not attending to the internal functioning of the organisation guided by purpose, each staff member was working on an instinctive sense of what was being called forth from them; consequently, staff members were working below their capacity. Family and organisational roles were increasingly confusing for the staff in the organisation. Through the consultation work, the CEO began to work with the organisation, including the founding family, on these questions related to purpose, roles, structure, and succession in order to face the emerging future that was not at all like the past.

Multiple roles in a large services firm

A leading national services firm had the leader of a practice area taking up six roles that were formally in view in the organisational system and external systems. The roles were: team leader, professional lead, part owner role, key committee member, geographical representative, and sector representative. The culture of the organisation was fast paced and demanding. Productivity was tracked and there was a strong focus on growth and, subsequently, performance. People talked about feeling busy, stressed, and at times overwhelmed. At the outset of our work, this person was not fully utilising all resources available in these roles as they were not held in his mind as "roles" in systems, but, rather, they were part of "why he was at the organisation" and were more about trying to manage time and keep things moving along or people happy with certain tasks. Closer examination of the purpose of these sub-systems and roles, explored in relation to the purpose of the organisation highlighted some shifts that could be taken in each of the six roles that would provide better outcomes for the organisation and relieve internal stress.

The dialogue we commenced with was the holder of the roles talking about "wearing different hats" in the organisation. While at first pass this seemed liked a useful metaphor, it was too superficial, seemingly easy to put a hat on and change it at will. If the hat was being worn, were other members of the organisation able to see the hats? Were they able to understand why the way this person operated in the leader role in its overall system might need to be different at times than in a sector role in one of its sub-system? That belonging in this system as a hole was influenced by subtle and unconscious ways of working that could often be in conflict with what was actually being called forth from all of the six roles and systems in regard to organisational purpose. The hat represented a desire to be able to "put it on" at will. However, the disciplined attention to the six roles took more effort.

Implications for practice

The key insight from this case is the criticality of being able to name the multiple roles that are required from people within the system/s they are part of. Work can then be done on discerning what is required from each of those sub-systems and the roles, *vs*. assuming a "one size fits all" is adequate. This also allows people to analyse which system they are working in, and the roles they are privileging in their own behaviour, based on their experience and personal preferences. The organisational system can also preference roles based on internal pressures and needs that can sometimes be short-sighted or reactionary. Through exploring the multiple systems and roles at play, conscious choices can then be made that are purposeful for the organisation and allow the person to feel authentic.

Purpose enabling multiple roles

In a recent example in organisational life, a group of directors asked us to work with them as they were experiencing dreadful conflict that was having impacts on them and the organisational system. We rapidly began to see that they had no shared purpose for the organisation and no sense of the multiple roles required to effectively lead

the organisation. Instead, they stayed stuck in interpersonal entangle-
ments and blame. Their intention was to affect the planet in very
useful ways, but this was not being realised. Rather than begin work
on the "dynamic", we began by living into the question of "Why does
this organisation exist at this moment of time in the context?" "What
is being called forth from it?" We were then able to begin the process
of truly finding the director system and roles, and the various roles
that are required to bring the purpose to life in the world. The conflict
was understood as emerging from a lack of purpose and, therefore, a
lack of functional boundaries that enabled a structure and processes
to support the work of the organisation.

Implications for practice

If multiple roles are not worked or understood in the light of purpose,
conflicts can emerge and be experienced as "interpersonal". This can
be navigated if there is shared understanding, in an ongoing way, of
the purpose and how roles are taken up and understood in the light
of purpose. Determining what system and its roles are foregrounded
and which are not taken up at all can reveal resources and opportunity for the organisation.

The influence of biographical roles and now

One leader unsure about the purpose of the organisation, her team,
and role, when faced with having to give a clear direction or make a
decision, consistently found herself taking up a familiar role from her
past experiences in her school system. This role was the "don't make
trouble" role. This biographical "psychological" role was experienced
by her colleagues as unproductive in the organisation. It manifested
in behaviour where decisions were not being made. It was at odds
with the "sociological" role they projected on her, reinforcing her
desire "not to make trouble", which actually had the opposite effect.
By thinking in terms of functional boundaries, that is, purpose, roles,
tasks in the organisation, the leader was able to initiate optimum
conditions for work and discover vital roles for herself and others,
where psychological roles and sociological roles could mesh creatively
rather than be conflicted.

Implications for practice

Understanding key default roles from our role biographies assists us to see where the opportunity or challenges might lie when taking up organisational roles. This can be transformed by working with the functional boundaries in organisational systems. The functional boundaries can offer a compass for action in role. Foundational boundaries are: organisational purpose, team purpose, and role purpose. These boundaries can provide a hypothesis for the role taker to live into: that is, Why is this role being called into existence in this organisation at this time? What does my behaviour need to be in order to take up this role? Is this understanding shared with other members of the organisation whose roles will be affected by this one?

Multiple team roles and shared purpose

In working with an internal specialist team, they held a shared belief that one role they had in the system that was to provide "internal consulting support" to leaders of the organisation. Initially, this seemed relevant and correct from the organisation's perspective. However, we discovered through exploring the team's purpose in relation to roles, how team members were actually taking up their roles. They were required to take up multiple roles within the organisation: however, they were taking up only one or two roles consciously. We encountered team members who felt they could only take up the roles in a very "soft" helper way in order that the team would not come under scrutiny by the organisation and be disbanded. The people in the team were from a specialist background and spoke of "loving" the work they did in the system. They were consciously and unconsciously protecting the team rather than serving the purpose of the organisation. "Belonging" and "survival" in the organisation became an unconscious purpose of the team and greatly limited the multiple roles available to, and required by, the team members.

Implications for practice

Teams exist to serve purpose in the organisation and can collectively hold multiple roles within organisations. Specialist teams or discipline areas require an ongoing review of the purposes they serve and what is the intersection or not with the professional discipline's purpose or picture in the mind purpose. The span of impact can become reactive based on the history of the profession in society and, in order to utilise resources and respond to purpose, the ongoing orientation to organisational purpose is required. How do the technical knowledge and skills need to be taken up in this organisation in this context?

Multiple systems and interconnectedness

In our current situations the world over, there is much that is being called forth from all of us in how we live, contribute, and offer our abilities in both organisational systems and the context. The global environmental landscape is an example of where critical, urgent decisions are required beyond our "known" ways of working. It might seem that we can no longer manage ecosystems *per se*, but, rather, we must learn to manage our interactions with our ecological context. This view, which incorporates notions of multiple, interacting, nested hierarchies, feedback loops across space and time, and radical uncertainty with regard to prediction of system behaviour, requires rethinking. This is being done. In one company we know of that works globally, within a few months the newly appointed Head of Environmental Efficiency identified a host of ecologically sensitive initiatives, some of them very simple, which were both environmentally efficient and actually contributed to conventional "bottom line" performance. The creation and resourcing of a new sub-system with a global reach shifted the perceptions which had been conventionally "lazy" in terms of waste disposal, energy use, and more.

Successful discovery of common purpose beyond personal, organisational identities and boundaries is a critical challenge faced all over the world. President Obama is known to believe that institutions of all sizes were originally set up to bring hope and wellbeing to communities, that their founders' views were that real needs existed in their contexts to which they wished to respond creatively. Each institution came into being to give substance to some form of hope, both for the founder and for those in the community their institution was intended to serve.

The evidence we have is that institutions which offer hope are ones in which those in positions of leadership understand the subtlety and complexity of taking multiple roles in them.

There is growing evidence to suggest that when we are able to work beyond a purpose for ourselves, sustainability becomes possible. Determining what systems we are part of, their purpose, the impact of purpose, and the roles we take up to serve the purpose is critical for both making progress and navigating the global tipping point we find ourselves on the edge of. In short, there is a need for institutions that are run competently in the interest of the communities they were created to serve. Of such are strong institutions made which provide reservoirs of hope to those communities.

Discerning and discovering our multiple roles can allow us to be "more real" and utilise parts of ourselves that enable us to manifest our light, intentions and connectedness. We can continue to work from the "inside out" and reveal what it means also to work from the "outside in" with a sense of freedom and creative energy, discerning what is being called forth from the system purpose we are able to serve and, in that process, finding a capacity to go to our learning edges in our multiple roles, not once but many times.. When explored with others whom we work with, momentum emerges and, watching closely, we notice that anything is possible. We are speaking of a level of consciousness required to work from the "outside in", an awareness that allows us to manage our valencies in order to hold the course on behalf of the whole in discovering our roles.

This challenges us to wrestle with the practice of developing our awareness and our skill of identifying systems, their boundaries, and purposes, whatever way they might relate to one another. Having mapped them, we can then work out which is to be prioritised at any one moment and then to do the work necessary to find, make, and take one's role in service of the purpose of that system. This allows us to use our conscious awareness to contribute to ongoing institutional strength and effectiveness, in whatever system we might find ourselves.

Where sufficient people can do that, institutions can cease to be used inappropriately, but can become the reservoirs of hope that we need. We can also let the family carry appropriate expectations rather than be misused with idealised projections and expectations.

References

Bazalgette, J. L. (1978). *School Life and Work Life in the Inner City*. London: Hutchinson.

Bazalgette, J. L., Irvine, G. B., & Quine, C. (2009). The purpose of meaning and the meaning of purpose: a container for our atomized yet globalised world. Paper presented to the Annual Conference of the International Society for the Psychoanalytic Study of Organizations 2009, Toledo, Spain.

Bazalgette, J. L., Reed, B. D., Kehoe, I., & Reed, J. M. (2006). *Leading Schools from Failure to Success*. Cambridge: UIT.

Beck, D. E., & Cowan, C. (1996). *Spiral Dynamics, Mastering Values, Leadership and Change*. Oxford: Blackwell.

Clinton, R. H. (2014). *Hard Choices: A Memoir*. London: Simon and Schuster.

Gallagher, M. P. (2010). *Faith Maps: Ten Religious Explorers from Newman to Ratzinger*. London: Darton, Longman and Todd.

Hirschhorn, L., & Gilmore, T. (1992). The new boundaries of the "boundaryless" company. *Harvard Business Review, May–June*: 104–115.

Laloux, F. (2014). *Reinventing Organizations: A Guide to Creating Organizations Inspired by the Next Stage of Human Consciousness*. Belgium: Nelson Parker.

Macmurray, J. (1935). *Reason and Emotion*. London: Faber and Faber.

Miller, E. J., & Rice, K. (1967). *Systems of Organization*. London: Tavistock.

Obama, B. (2006). *The Audacity of Hope: Thoughts on Reclaiming the American Dream*. Crown: Three Rivers Press.

CHAPTER SEVEN

Finding, making, and taking role: a case study from the complexity of inter-agency dynamics

Aarti Kapoor

Background

F inding, making, and taking my role (Quine & Hutton, 1992), in service of purpose in the systems where I work, have been dramatic, eventful and emotional. This chapter will provide but a glimpse of my journey, using a particular working role as a team leader of a donor-funded, NGO child protection project. It is my hope that this writing will reflect, as a fractal, much of what was occurring on both an intricate and macro level (Wheatley, 2006).

While in hospital recovering from my second spontaneous pneumothorax (commonly known as a collapsed lung), I signed up to the Grubb School's global Master's programme in order to learn a methodology and train in a skill that would enable me to understand why I had found myself in the current state and situation.

I was at the threshold of a new chapter of life where I was to understand why working across numerous inter-agency systems had the potential for immense stress, anxiety, and confusion. At the first course seminar, the Master's programme director, Rebekah O'Rourke, shared her hypothesis that I was fighting *barriers* instead of negotiating across *boundaries*. My initial reaction to this was defiance. I believed that I was up against externally erected barriers—not boundaries. Boundaries differentiate and are permeable (so I thought), whereas barriers divide and are impermeable. In retrospect, I had not realised what she was pointing to. A few months later, I dreamt of Rebekah O'Rourke wearing a sari while taking up her professional role. In wondering how she had learnt to "choose, fit and wear a sari" while in her everyday working role, a co-participant made an association with "finding, making, and taking up role". My unconscious told me I had already started my path towards insights.

The situation

In order to illustrate my path in finding, making, and taking my role, I present an intertwined parallel narrative of two arenas of experience where I worked as a team leader. The first covers my management of the team, within and across the organisation (Organisation Y), and the second exhibits my engagement with a governmental donor agency. The identification, use, and perception of system boundaries have been of the most fundamental importance in this journey.

To aid in this narrative it is worth outlining the players:

Organisation Y: an international not-for-profit aid organisation.
Donor agency: The governmental donor agency that contracted with Organisation Y's International Office (Organisation YIO) to implement the child protection project in an Asian country.
Organisation YIO: The international fundraising office of Organisation Y based in a developed country.
Organisation YNO: the national office of Organisation Y based in a developing country in Asia.
CP project: A child protection project run by Organisation Y, under contract by donor agency, in a developing country in Asia.
CP Team: Central CP project team of the CP project within Organisation Y:
Regional CP Teams: Regional teams of the CP project based in different regions of the country.

The CP team had been experiencing significant challenges in relation to its health, morale, and capacity. It was composed of four staff: team leader, technical adviser, communications officer, and administrative officer. This team's remit covered the management of, and support to, the regional CP teams across four regions of the country.

Early in the year, the CP team was directed to physically move out of the Organisation YNO premises due to their lack of capacity and perceived responsibility to provide the management and oversight to the CP project. Their view was that the CP Project was an "external grant project" which had been directly contracted between Organisation YIO and the donor agency. It was, therefore, not within the remit of the Organisation YNO to oversee it.

During the run up to the move out of Organisation YNO's premises, and immediately thereafter, the CP team members experienced a bizarre set of serious sicknesses and health complications necessitating surgeries, hospitalisations, medication, energy healing, and spiritual cleansing rituals. The sicknesses included two pneumothoraxes, a fully torn knee ligament, severe psychosomatic behaviours and two root canals with recurrences and further complications experienced in each person. At least one member was sick at any given time over this five-month period. On some days the newly rented office was not even opened for business. It felt as if the CP team had been decimated by a disaster and was disappearing.

In my position as team leader, I was reporting to Organisation YIO and in regular direct liaison with the donor agency's in-country team. At the contextual level, the relationship between the donor agency and the CP project was challenging, harshly hierarchical, and process-driven from almost the beginning of its implementation. Over this time, the donor agency had conducted a number of unilateral reviews and evaluations of the programme, largely based on incomplete data, overly narrow considerations, and inaccurate information. Furthermore, they had taken a strictly "contracting-out" view of the relationship rather than one of partnership, and had rarely sought to understand the approach, circumstances, and realities on the ground. Furthermore, the directions given by the donor agency over the three preceding years were inconsistent, and, at times, contradictory, causing confusion and a high level of tension with rare acknowledgement from their side of these inconsistencies.

A new team had recently taken over at the donor agency's in-country office, which the CP team experienced as even more heavy-handed, judgemental, and hierarchical. Since the advent of the donor agency's new team, a strict communication protocol was put into place outlining how the project should communicate with the agency's Asia-based office—that is, only through certain role holders by email or in writing. This had, in effect, put into place a new structural arrangement whereby I, as team leader could not directly contact the head of the donor agency's team. Instead, I was allocated a focal person in her team. On two occasions, when the head of the donor agency's team head sought to raise issues with the project, she communicated them directly with the senior leaders within organisation YIO, rather than with me, as team leader of the project. I was left feeling silenced and infantilised.

Overall, my experiences of dealing with the donor agency were of anxiety, stress, frustration, and panic, and it was the most challenging aspect of taking up my role as team leader. Together with the clearly urgent situation of the state of the CP team at the time, I set about exploring the metaphors and meaning of what I saw as symptomatic of something. I was seeing the patterns and now I needed to decipher what they were pointing me to.

Roles, boundaries, and systems

A work system can be defined as a group of people working together on a task within a boundary. The existence of a system depends on a boundary. Such a boundary is in the mind (Hirschhorn & Gilmore, 1992) as much as it is in physical existence. Within the boundary, the events, actions, and behaviours take on a *systemic* aspect. This is to say that the system works through a collective, combined consciousness so that the feelings, behaviours, and actions of any one person within the group is regulated by the system as a whole, rather than belonging only to that person (Bion, 1961). This has particularly important implications in the system's unconscious, which, similar to the personal unconscious, is the ground where repressed emotions and feelings are relegated. Therefore, systemic unconscious feelings, thoughts, and emotions continue to influence the way groups behave, even where they are unaware of it (Bion, 1961). The experience of discovering the "systems perspective" has been like discovering the fourth dimension!

Role can be seen as "the outward and visible behaviour of an inward discipline of knowledge, thoughts, feelings and will". It is "a formed idea-in-the-mind leading to action" (Reed & Armstrong, 1972, p. 6). In organisational analysis, the idea of role is dynamic rather than static; a conscious engagement in adaptive navigation rather than the strict adherence to a formulaic job description. It enables one to meaningfully pause and consider where one is in the here and now. In group relations work, the "role" is taken as "a regulating principle inside oneself which enables one, as a person, to manage what one does in relation to the requirements of the situation one is in" (Reed & Armstrong, 1972, p. 6).

I have found the following three-step process of finding, making, and taking the role helpful. In *finding* role, one is searching for the role through identifying the system and its boundaries and owning the purpose the system it is serving. In *making* one's role, one observes and develops an understanding of the forces, influences, processes, and expectations at play within, and on, the system, as well as identifying one's own abilities and capacities to serve purpose. Finally, in *taking* up role, one is discerning the best cause of *authentic action* to take, having considered all the forces and influencing factors, in service of the purpose of the organisation.

Reed and Armstrong propose that "being in role is a ceaseless disciplined process because once taken, it is easier to find; once found it is easier to make; and once made it is easier to take an upward spiral of knowledge" (Reed & Armstrong, 1972, p. 5). Therefore *role* is a tool for enabling learning.

Once taken, easier to find

The idea of learning from experience as developmental, and using "role" as a tool for managing this learning, has enormously elucidated the way I have approached finding, making, and taking role. The time pressure and constant scrutinising I was experiencing from the donor agency had created a toxic atmosphere of a hatred of learning and development (Armstrong, 2002; Bion, 1961). This was expressed through the illness and withdrawal of staff. This added to my own valency (tendency) towards being fearful of failure. Armstrong writes that the work group is an expression of the push to develop and actively *learn from experience*, while "basic assumptions" in groups is the regressive pull (Armstrong, 2002).

Understanding the idea that *learning through experience* was a positive symptom of a work group led to an opening and enabling "environment-in-the-mind" where all my actions-in-role became sensibly geared towards both learning and ever-increasing effectiveness in my leadership, as two sides of a confluent journey. This understanding brought an immense relief to my approach, freeing tension and enabling me to better divert my energies towards a spirit of enquiry.

At a CP Project team meeting (including regional team members as well as the central team), I conducted an activity to discover how people experienced the team. This was called an "organisation-in-the-mind" exercise and involved people in drawing their impressions of their team. It was immensely valuable. It felt like a pulse check of the entire project team (Ostroff, 2006). Among my findings, I gained an appreciation of the internal boundaries and role-relatedness of the central team and the regional teams within the programme. I had not consciously considered this before, and realised the differences in underlying assumptions about how the central team was supporting the regional teams, as well as the different expectations the regional teams had of the central team. Some regional teams were heavily reliant on the central team, while others seemed more indifferent. Interestingly, but perhaps not surprisingly, some of the junior staff revealed infantile, dependent perspectives. Following this exercise, my resulting working hypothesis was that: the central CP team is treading a perilous journey. The regional teams are dependent on the central team while the central team (which lacked fundamental organisational support), in turn, is buckling under the burden, relatively unsupported and untethered.

Having begun to identify more clearly the systems and boundaries within the wider team and my role within them, as well as other systems and the context beyond, I experienced a shifting of perspective to systems-based thinking. My valency had been to take on too much personal responsibility for events and interactions. This was not only harmful for me, but was also limiting the opportunity for other resources to be revealed, particularly from regional teams. My "organisation-in-the-mind" drawing was the only one displaying "groundedness", in the form of a sprouted seed through which the whole project emerges, poignantly (and perhaps deceivingly) symbolised through a broken heart, or, indeed, a hole in my lung representing a loss of hope and irretrievable energy. Clearly, I was creating dependency as a leader and trying to do all the work. I had been unaware of how this was ignoring the group dynamic at play in any given situation (Bion, 1961). I had previously been aware only of the domains of person and source, and was blurring all the other dynamic boundaries between system and context (Bazalgette & Roberts, 2006).

I set about contemplating how I needed to engage with the context and re-evaluate the system boundaries in furthering the purpose of the programme.

Once found, easier to make

The Master's programme includes the participants undertaking role analysis with a faculty member. Through working with metaphors to make meaning in my first role consultation, I came to the somewhat distressing realisation that I was acting out the experience of an abused and neglected child in relation to the donor agency. Linking this with both the purpose of the project to protect abused children, I became rather overwhelmed. Ostroff discusses how holding on too tightly to one metaphor rather another can feel like a prison rather than a prism for exploring meaning (Ostroff, 2006). Cognisant of my own valency for these feelings and for settling on this metaphor rather than another, I developed my first working hypothesis in regard to the relationship with the donor agency. This was that the CP project and the donor agency are behaving and communicating "as if" the CP project is within the donor agency system rather than the Organisation Y system (see Figure 7.1). This system is reflecting one of a dysfunctional family whereby the project was borne by the donor agency but is being neglected and treated as an unwanted child. The donor agency's perceived neglect and abuse of the project emanates from a sense of envy for not being able to do the things that the project can.

An unconscious process of envy within an organisation can provoke attacks on what is perceived to be good and desirable (Stein, 2000). Where this becomes endemic, even newer recruits can, consciously or unconsciously, become enrolled in new envious attacks on others (Stein, 2000). With the donor agency, this had not only occurred with the new team, but also with independent consultants tasked with evaluating the CP project.

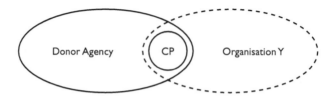

Figure 7.1. How the CP project and the donor agency were communicating.

Through reflecting on the above working hypothesis, I concluded that although it is correct that the donor agency had "contracted out" this programme to be implemented by Organisation YIO, the realities of the situation were that it was being implemented within the organisational boundaries of Organisation Y (both IO and NO), even if *on behalf* of another organisation. Therefore, the direct access and management function that the donor agency was exercising over the programme was incongruent with the realities of working within a large organisation such as Organisation Y. As I had been managing this contract, I was the one acting at the boundary "as if" I represented Organisation YIO. This clearly was not serving the purpose of the project and it was time to bring in the other parent, or, indeed, the *adoptive* parent: Organisation YIO.

In taking up my role I decided that I needed to focus on the boundary region between the donor agency and the CP project (Miller, 1989; Ostroff, 2006). Clearly, this boundary needed strengthening (and untangling) from a number of angles. The main actions I took in role were to re-establish the relationship with, and rooting of the central CP team within, Organisation YNO, and to bring the Organisation's YIO's senior management team to the boundary between the CP project and the donor agency. Identifying Organisation YIO's senior managers as the contract and boundary holders, I started more readily to involve them in the discussions, emails, and meetings.

Once made, easier to take

Meanwhile, within Organisation YNO, I prioritised the rebuilding of systemic relatedness and relationships between my central CP team and the staff of Organisation YNO as a way of healing the "sentience" or conscious connections in service of the broader purpose of the organisation. The relationships had taken quite a bruising due to gossip and misunderstanding about why we had moved out. The reasons for our moving out were not formally announced initially to Organisation YNO's staff outside my team. In turn, they had felt a sense of loss which was expressed through sadness, guilt, anger, and "pushing away". I proactively took all opportunities to visit them and made a point of attending and participating in weekly-held "town hall" meetings. I saw these gatherings as a chance to commune with both the leadership and the staff in general through our shared connectedness to purpose. In turn, this resulted in fewer complaints about the "bad feeling" and significantly motivated the CP team in re-entering the sentient system with Organisation YNO (Miller & Rice, 1967; Reed & Armtrong, 1972).

On noticing that the CP project was not formally included in any structural "organograms" within Organisation YNO, I actively sought introductory meetings with the two newly appointed senior directors to the office and successfully advocated for a matrix-management line within Organisation YNO through which I could report to them. Within a few months, the central CP team were back on the map. There were ongoing challenges in the alignment process, which raised new issues. Nevertheless, the central CP team became better established in Organisation YNO, albeit in separate accommodation, providing the team with the broader support and containment they needed in their daily work while, in turn, supporting the regional teams.

The shift of focus from the personal to person–system–context–source, through using the TEF, had already started to release phenomenal resources for me. Previously, I felt limited by the relationships I had established with my colleagues and stakeholders, due to the expectations I felt, as well as because I wanted to be well regarded. However, through understanding role, I started interacting with the same persons through role-relatedness (Reed & Armstrong, 1972). I realise now that the role I was taking up was not just a reflection of me as an individual, but also a considered and more conscientious choice of action in serving the purpose of the organisation within its systemic life. Previously, I would be worried about the impact on my reputation, my standing, my spiritual path, and so forth. I was not able to disaggregate the parts from the whole. I was, therefore, struggling, and often vacillating between representing myself and doing what I strongly felt was expected of me (Reed & Armstrong, 1972).

In further exploring the engagement with the donor agency and confronted with my own sense of giving up perceived control of the relationship negotiations with them (to Organisation YIO), I started to explore the distinctions between what was being expected of me *vs.* what I felt was the right thing to do. I had begun to rediscover my role as team leader of the CP project, rather than as *the* Organisation YIO representative. I was able to see that a significant cause of the stress and anxiety had been my confusion about *which* purpose I was supposed to be working towards: the CP project's or Organisation YIO's? The purpose of Organisation YIO is to raise funds, whereas the CP project's purpose was to promote the protection of children. I was previously experiencing the two purposes as distinct and somewhat mutually exclusive. I have reached a new appreciation and understanding as to how these purposes fit together. In bringing the Organisation YIO to the table in almost all my engagements with the donor agency, I have been better able to discern my system boundary, its purpose, and what my authentic-action-in-role is. The involvement of Organisation YIO has resulted in me being better able to work to the specific purpose of the CP project as team leader in the boundary engagement.

Once taken, easier to find

In being able to take up my role as team leader, I was able to have further insight into the relationship between the donor agency and Organisation YIO, further illuminating why I was feeling the pressures and expectations that I had. I drew up the following working hypothesis: the donor agency and Organisation YIO are behaving as if in a parasitic, master–slave relationship with each other. The donor agency is mirroring the culture and climate of working within a government department under threat. Organisation YIO is behaving like this through its "supporter centric" culture.

This hypothesis further focused on the issues around envy and also portended further attacks on the CP project as the donor agency moved towards certain "death" under a new government (they were to be reorganised into its foreign affairs ministry). Following the recognition of my feelings of powerlessness leading to the above work-ing hypothesis, I began to explore power and authority dynamics. Focusing on my position as team leader of the CP project, I rediscovered that now I was, in fact, freer to fully and more authentically act-in-role to the project's purpose. For example: in response to a longstanding proposal made by the CP project for a five-month, no-cost extension, a meeting was held, whereby the donor agency informed Organisation YIO and the CP project that the no-cost extension would not be given and, furthermore, the project needed to be completed two months before the planned end date. The project also needed to narrow the scope of its activities with immediate effect. I felt as if the CP project was being unnecessarily amputated, and was able diplomatically but passionately to express my anxiety as team leader in the face of such decisions (Ostroff, 2006). Although this expression did not result in any tangible changes for the project, the management of the process by both the donor agency and Organisation YIO over the CP project has been handled with a greater degree of delicacy. Meanwhile, in reclaiming my authority-in-role, I have instigated a twenty-four-hour time lag before responding to any emails to the donor agency as well as negotiating further time, task, and territorial boundaries with Organisation YIO.

The lived experience

The above narrative provides one vehicle for exploring how I was finding, making, and taking role in my working system at the time. For the purpose of illustration, Table 7.1 highlights a snapshot of the behavioural changes I have recorded since understanding the fundamental concepts and theories of systems thinking, group dynamics, and unconscious processes and using these in finding, making, and taking roles. This table should not be seen as a "before and after" but, rather, a snapshot of a continuous process.

The donor agency's engagement continued to be experienced as destructive, perhaps mirroring their experience within the broader government restructuring that was taking place. Notwithstanding, I continued to support Organisation YIO in negotiating an alternative means of "narrowing the scope of the project" that the donor agency insisted upon, even as the project wound down for completion in its final four months.

After bringing in these changes, I received a number of confirmations from Organisation YNO that we were "part of the office". The

Table 7.1. Snapshot of behavioural changes.

From . . .	To . . .
Focusing on me	Focusing on all
Taking personal responsibility for everything	Understanding my accountability, the part I am playing
Feeling burdened with guilt and self- doubt	Observing my feelings of anxiety with a spirit of enquiry
Feeling fragmented	Taking back my parts and giving back other's parts
Conflictive and frustrated	Conflictive and courageous
Unable to express myself	A new language to express myself
Feelings of powerlessness	Realising the authority I have
Resistance	Negotiation
Blurring boundaries and seeing barriers	Identifying boundaries and curious about where I see barriers
Confusion	Meaning making
Open and honest	Transparency with purpose
Lack of trust in choices and decisions made by boundary holders	Curiosity and partial acceptance of decisions of boundary holders
Feeling trapped	Finding spaces
Fear of failure and making mistakes	Committed to learning from experience
No time	Making bits of time
Not sure which is the real me	Trying to choose the "me" I need to be right now
Stuck in dilemmas	Waiting and testing
Unsure and vulnerable	Gathering my confidence even though vulnerable
Communicating directly	Communicating in new ways
Somewhat blind	Seeing through new eyes
Attacking myself	Confronting myself

health and wellbeing of the central CP team vastly improved, resulting in only two sick days in a subsequent period four months and no further pneumothorax experienced as of writing this chapter. The strengthened establishment of the CP team within Organisation YNO facilitated a smoother consultation process for planning a second phase of the project.

As I finish this chapter now and look back on the journey, I am able to see with more clarity how confusing (and crippling) the situation became with the expectations, influences, and agendas of all the different systems playing out. It is common to see and understand these dynamics from a personal perspective, but the reality is that this is only half the picture (at most). Once we are able to see beyond the personal views of feelings, events, and behaviours around us, and reframe from a systemic perspective, we begin to see things from a completely new light. As I mentioned earlier, it is like adding another dimension of understanding to the complexity of all the dynamics we find ourselves in. From this vantage point, we are more informed and empowered to make better decisions. The Grubb's "transforming experience through authentic action in role", in order to find, make, and take role, is a dynamic discipline which can help gain such clarity in an incremental and ongoing way. The key is to simply start from where you are.

References

Armstrong, D. (2002). The work group revisited: reflections on the practice and relevance of group relations. In: *Organization in the Mind: Psychoanalysis, Group Relations, and Organizational Consultancy* (pp. 139–150). London: Karnac.

Bazalgette, J., & Roberts, V. (2006). *Daring to Desire: Ambition, Competition and Role-transformation in 'Idealistic' Organisations*. London: Grubb Institute.

Bion, W. R. (1961). *Experiences in Groups*. London: Tavistock.

Hirschhorn, L., & Gilmore, T. (1992). The new boundaries of the boundaryless company. *Harvard Business Review*, May–June, pp. 104–115.

Miller, E. J. (1989). The "Leicester" model: experiential study of group and organizational processes. *Occasional Papers, 10*. London: Tavistock.

Miller, E. J., & Rice, A. K. (1967). *Systems of Organizations*. London: Tavistock.

Ostroff, S. (2006). Whispers of the whole: tending to the system by the system for the system. In: *Dare to Think the Unthought Known?* (pp. 51–88). Tampere, Finland: Aivoairut.

Quine, C., & Hutton, J. (1992). Finding, making and taking the role of head. London: Grubb Institute Working Notes.

Reed, B., & Armstrong, D. (1972). *Notes on Professional Management.* London: Grubb Institute.

Stein, M. (2000). After Eden: envy and the defences against anxiety paradigm. *Human Relations, 53*(2): 193–211.

Wheatley, M. J. (2006). *Leadership and the New Sciences; Discovering Order in a Chaotic World* (3rd edn). San Francisco, CA: Berret-Koehler.

CHAPTER EIGHT

Transitioning tasks in an impossible context through use of drawings: a case example

Rose Redding Mersky

T his chapter describes a consulting intervention, only later seen, in the light of the TEF theory in this book, as a way of helping a group make the transition from its original impossible task to a more reasonable and fulfilling one. Unable to find an authorised consulting role during an important meeting, I began to draw in order to understand the situation as revealed in the discussion around the table. This personal drawing transitioned into a group drawing and ultimately served as a transitional object for them all to reframe their purpose and goals for a very important roll-out of a new product.

The organisation

The organisation is an international pharmaceutical corporation, whose headquarters were located in New Jersey, USA.

The roles

The group was convened by the corporate vice president of marketing for the non-USA and western European market, an organisation within the larger corporation, whose president sat on the corporate board. Attending were the heads of the separate regions that were in this system, all of whom reported to its president. These regions were East Europe, Japan, Southeast Asia, Russia, and South America. The convenor, along with colleagues in finance, human resources, information technology, and sales, was part of the staff support group for this region. As the executive coach of the VP, I was asked to help facilitate the process.

The persons

All participants were men. I was the only woman. My client and I are USA citizens. Two of the regional presidents were also from the USA, but the others had other nationalities.

The task

The task of this day-long meeting, held at corporate headquarters, as conceived by the convenor, was to develop a strategy and an action plan for rolling out a new drug, which was already rolled out in the rest of the organisation.

The context

Tensions between corporate control and regional autonomy were always a major issue in any such meetings. From the corporate side, it was essential that strategies and plans be co-ordinated. From the regional side, directors often felt that corporate did not understand the particular issues and compromising influences that they had to cope with.

In addition, the corporate VP was a staff position, and the regional heads were in line positions, which gave them more status in the system at large and a direct reporting relationship to the president. I, as an unknown female, had even less status than my client. And, despite my effort, I was not able sufficiently to clarify from him exactly what my task was. I had to authorise myself.

How the meeting started

Despite cordiality and even a bit of effusive hugging on seeing one another again, once the meeting was officially called to order, the tone changed. While my client had carefully planned the agenda and shared it in advance with the participants (my idea), there were almost immediately objections and requests for other issues to be placed on the agenda. Clarifications of the seemingly obvious were needed. One latecomer finally arrived; another noted that he must leave early.

For reasons perhaps known only to my unconscious, I found myself at this point needing to orientate myself to this disparate group. I was sitting at the table, but at a corner, diagonally opposite from my client. I began to make some doodles on a piece of paper, more to orientate myself than to offer anything to the others. At one point, I asked for a small point of clarification, which called the attention of the group to what I was doing. Eager, I believe, for any distraction, I was asked to share my drawing.

Propelled by I know not what, I stood and took my drawing to the whiteboard and explained what I had noted. People began making corrections to the drawing and finally, with it so marked up that it was hopeless to follow, I took the initiative of enlarging it on a whiteboard. Everyone waited patiently while I attempted to make a copy. I do not know what my client was thinking, but the group was engaged.

The drawing I was attempting to make was a picture of the group that included pressures mentioned previously, past historical events (a failed roll-out), and other dates of major events. As the task began to overwhelm me, one of the regional directors, noting the need for corrections, took over. We had more than one colour, so before you knew it, others were contributing. During the first coffee break, the discussion was lively and people would return separately and in pairs to review and alter its contents. It seemed to have sparked quite an interest.

The drawing

In retrospect, I can see now that the drawing to which they were contributing was becoming the new task for the group. Whether intentionally wishing to undermine my client's agenda or truly wanting to clarify (I am sure the motives were mixed), what began to emerge was a much clearer picture to all of what the issues and conflicts were in relation to the task at hand. One stark example was the bureaucratic impingements facing the regional head from Japan, who was not authorised in his region in the same way as were the others. In a sense, these regional heads, in the pursuit (or non-pursuit) of a particular corporate, were actually undertaking a new task, which was learning more about one another's role dilemmas and task challenges.

This process was engaging. I loosened up and started asking the right questions. I knew we would not get anywhere rehashing old conflicts, so I kept asking questions relating to role, task, and context for each of them. Ignoring me, they spoke with respect to one another. They seemed to need a "nobody" to guide them.

Meanwhile, my client, with whom I had had a long working relationship, began to comment. Gradually, it became clear to him that the original task was completely unrealistic and that part of his future role would be to explain that clearly to the corporate powers that be.

The new task emerges

It was not long before it became clear that the concept of a corporate-led roll-out strategy and action plan was unrealistic. Not least were the resentments about previous failed efforts. It appeared that each of the regional presidents understood the importance of the roll-out and took it as a matter of pride that their parts of the organisation should accomplish this as successfully as their more profitable parts. In an ironic sense, this disparate (and often competitive) group seemed (temporarily at least, or at least in terms of this task) to surmount their differences and think together.

The roll-out would take place, but each regional president would be authorised, within certain general parameters as outlined by my VP client, to manage his own roll-out strategy and timeline. Critical to this process would be the support of the VP for managing various obstacles, many of which were clearly articulated at this meeting and were reflected in the drawing.

The role of my client VP would change from a strategic master to a co-ordinator of information and, most importantly, a source of resources and support to the different regions. And again, it was his role to be a buffer between this group and his masters, who would be demanding a full report of the meeting.

The source?

Using Susan Long's phrase "framework of connectedness", one could perhaps say that, particularly through the work with the drawing, a certain framework became realised that, at least for the purpose of this task and organisational challenge, led to a successful outcome. As Long puts it in Chapter One of this book: "Often, the source must be discovered through a process of enquiry and connection", which somehow took place in this most unlikely context. It is interesting to speculate on how drawing as an activity also mobilised my own source and brought me more in contact with myself, my identity, and what I had to offer, all of this taking place unconsciously. At the same time, it was helpful to me in managing my own anxiety in role.

Summary

It was no great strategic moment. It was no great consulting master plan. I was just in this situation, powerless, more or less friendless, but fascinated, as one always is, when one finally sits face to face with role-holders one has only heard described by one's coaching client. Perhaps my fascination became a bit contagious. Perhaps the available colours made a difference. Certainly, my client's trust for me was a big help. I think also my being able to accept my low status and my igno-rance of the reality lent a kind of modest tone to a meeting of many big egos with great accomplishments behind and in front of them.

CHAPTER NINE

Connectedness with source: our collective reality

John Bazalgette (in conversation with Bruce Irvine)

Introduction: searching for a framework for understanding the experience that each can own for themselves

This is a chapter about connectedness in all its forms—positive and negative—and how wrestling with seeing the world in terms of "both–and" leads us to the third consideration of "also", which enfolds the "both–and", enabling us to reveal to ourselves our personal and collective accountability for the local and global state that we have co-created.

I do not set out to argue a single position, but invite the reader to look at a range of evidence that I assemble and invite you to make your own connections for yourself, so as to arrive at your own understanding of "connectedness with source"—however you define it for yourself.

One connectedness that will be important is between the reader and this text. I invite you to ask yourself how your existing understanding of connectedness with source engages with what you are reading. From what you reveal to yourself, I anticipate that you will understand more about what might be informing your own decisions and actions, especially when these are made in collaboration with others. I write from my own personal perspective as a Christian, but have set out to indicate it in general terms of human experience: I hope that those thinking from other perspectives can see potential links with what I describe in their own experiences. I assume that no one is without some faith—the capacity to trust—in life: faith in the competence of airline pilots to get us to our destinations safely, in the diligence of builders who construct buildings that will stand up, in other car drivers that their vehicles have been serviced and are safe on the road at the same time as ours.

The background of the narrative

I open this chapter with recent examples of very different public and private behaviour. Drawing on the framework used by the Grubb School of Organisational Analysis to interpret lived experience, I go on to explore some themes that link them. I follow that by outlining an approach to human development, drawing especially on the work of Donald Winnicott about transitional objects and illusion as a necessary part of our maturation and connectedness. That leads me to make links with the thinking of Bruce Reed and Bruce Irvine, which has been put into practice through the Grubb Institute's work on analysing behaviour in organisations and their contexts for over fifty years. This focuses, in particular, on the way faith/no faith, belief/unbelief and spirituality/lack of spirituality provide potent practical resources for addressing the challenges of accountable living in today's interconnected world, and, indeed, universe. In this way, I hope to surface meaning from these examples. I close with a final example drawn from the current thinking of a colleague that leads into some short observations about finding, making and taking a role.

Focusing on experience

The Grubb's "framework for transforming experience into authentic action through role" invites people, especially those in leadership positions—where "leadership" is an essential component of systems, not a personal quality—to regard their lived experience in the here-and-now as one of their most important resources in managing themselves as persons-in-role who take decisions and action in organisations, offering consolation and inspiration to others. Human experience is explored using four different lenses: person, context, system, and connectedness with source, which combine to enable one to interpret one's own behaviour in role. The first three lenses are usually quickly grasped conceptually and have been written up in depth elsewhere in this collection of papers. I also particularly refer the reader to Bruce Irvine's paper in this collection on the Grubb Institute's three pillars and six principles, and ask you to bear those in mind as you engage with this chapter (see Chapter Two of this book).

The chapter is written to explore and clarify the domain least easy to grasp: connectedness with source. The hypothesis, which is, of course, open to testing, is that what makes source different from the other three domains is that it continuously permeates and influences all the others, whether we know it or not. To open this exploration, I describe four twenty-first century examples: the first is of a well-known politician.

I then offer three more that have had less publicity, which I interpret. One links source with context, one with system, and the third with person. These three provide illustrations of people whose thinking and actions show a willingness to lead by connecting with the "other", exemplifying behaviour that seeks to reach out to connect with, rather than demonise, the absent "other". This leads me to describe some conceptual questions about human development. After that I will address source in more depth, drawing out some considerations for practical issues of making decisions and taking action together in leadership and life.

Demonising the "other"

At the end of January 2015, Boris Johnson, the elected Mayor of London, entered the debate about young British Muslims becoming jihadis and going to Syria to join the ISIS forces fighting there. In his usual colourful way, he labelled them "wankers . . . porn watchers . . . failures . . . tortured . . . lacking forms of spiritual comfort". He went on to say that they were "in desperate need of self-esteem . . . lacking a mission in life . . . This makes them seem strong, like winners" (found on Twitter, 31 January 2015). Those men and women he is talking about see Mayor Johnson's outburst in exactly opposite terms. Those he was branding speak of feeling disgusted by the culture that he represents, which they see as oppressing Muslims and Islam across the world. They see themselves as setting out to take action to bring about something radically opposed to the society and culture that elects people like Mayor Johnson. Far from lacking a mission in life, they describe themselves as being prepared to risk their lives—to be martyrs—in service of a cause that they believe is more worthy than the cause that life in today's Britain offers them.

I choose this incident as a starting point for this chapter because it sharply illustrates a profound dynamic that characterises human life at every level in societies, be it from one-to-one personal engagements, intergroup and organisational engagements, up to encounters between the nations and religious/cultural groups of our global society. This dynamic is evident in the predisposition to exaggerate differences between us, attributing to our own self-image what we feel good about ourselves, while projecting on those who are different from us those characteristics that most trouble us consciously and unconsciously. They become for us the "other", in psychological terms, the "not-me" that I feel free to demonise.

In the introduction to his book *The Quest for Meaning: Developing a Philosophy of Pluralism*, Tariq Ramadan, Professor of Contemporary Islamic Studies at Oxford, puts the issue with great clarity:

> We are lacking in confidence . . . fear, doubt and distrust are imperceptibly colonising our heart and minds. And so the other becomes our negative mirror and the other's difference enables us to define ourselves, to "identify" ourselves and, basically gives us reassurance. (Ramadan, 2010, p. ix)

On the whole, most adults are mature enough find sufficient truth in our personal and close social relationships to conduct our differences in a reasonably cordial manner. We have developed the self-management capacity and grasp of reality that is called for in such circumstances. Most of us can say with confidence that, on the whole, we have learnt to rub along together without our frictions bursting into flames. However, once we get into our wider social, economic, religious, and political lives, finding agreements with the "other" about what is "true" becomes much more demanding. Shared meaning is harder to find; what is normally handled with reason (perhaps with some warmth) breaks out into bush and forest fires, especially where the threat of scarcity lurks in the undergrowth of our subconscious minds.

The desire to turn one's currently held meaning into an absolute quickly takes hold, leading to fundamentalism, clashes, and, at worst, to violence. In this dynamic, the Mayor of London is at least as much a fundamentalist as the jihadis. He is in his fundamentalist mode, and those who applaud his "directness" need the "jihadist" other in order to "identify" themselves through contrast. Four key interlinked questions this chapter sets out to explore are:

- What is it about we human beings that makes us instinctively polarise between "good" and "evil" and to take sides so virulently?
- Is this the whole story about our instinctive behaviours? Do we have other, more profound, instincts that could lead us to behave in another way?
- Must we accept that one of our human limitations is that we need "illusions" for us to live creatively and imaginatively?
- Does the "illusion" of connectedness with source provide a practical function in enabling us to make a difference in the healing and repair of the world: the duty of *Tikkun olam*[1] put upon Jews in the Mishnah?

I do not propose to write a linear response to these questions, but to weave paths between them, around them, above and below them. The reader is invited to embark on a journey in which you are your own navigator, choosing to leap forward and backwards, accepting that to come to your own understanding you need to find that and make it your own: do not be convinced by entering entirely into mine.

Death's ferryman: connectedness with source through context

In its edition of 5 January 2015, *The New York Times* reported a story from southern Afghanistan about Malik Abdul Hakim, whom the journalist described as "death's ferryman". A ferryman works at the crossing point on a river that divides two pieces of land from one another. In this vignette, drawn from today's Afghanistan, Hakim creates a bridge between the government's forces and the Taliban, making his unique contribution to creating a more compassionate and humane context in his war-torn country. He delivers the bodies of Afghan soldiers and of insurgents to their relatives for dignified burials. His work has included finding and administering the last rites to the remains of two of his own sons. *The New York Times* described what he does:

> Hakim collects the bodies of soldiers and police officers killed in areas of Taliban dominance, and takes them home. From government centers, he carries slain insurgents back to their families, negotiating roads laced with roadside bombs.
>
> Mr. Hakim, a slender 66-year-old with a white beard that hangs to his chest, laughs when asked what drives him. He never envisioned he would have this life, crossing front lines for strangers. But he finds meaning in his work, delivering a measure of dignity to families scarred by war.
>
> Still, he prays that one day he will be out of a job.
>
> "Every time I see a body, I pray there will not be another," he says in a soft and oddly youthful voice. "I will be thankful when there is peace and stability, and I no longer have work."

Malik Abdul Hakim is following the *Quran*, which instructs Muslims: "Believers, obey God and the Apostle when he calls you to that which gives you life. Know that God stands between man and his heart, and that in His presence you shall all be assembled" (*The Koran*, 1916, p. 128).

A CEO initiates a challenge to his leadership team: connectedness with source through system

The leadership edge and connectedness in this next story is between a large organisation and its context, where the organisation was originally set up to meet human and spiritual need, paying special attention to those living in conditions of poverty.

During late 2013, the recently appointed Chief Executive Officer (CEO) of one of the world's largest Christian non-government organisations (NGOs) published a review of the context in which their organisation worked. The review explored some of the major challenges faced by that NGO in the world today and how these impact upon its purpose. In a section devoted to the context and how that links to connectedness with source in terms of serving God, the review made the following core points.

> In our time humanity is experiencing a turning point in its history as we can see from the advances being made in so many fields. We can only praise the steps being taken to improve people's welfare in areas such as healthcare, education and communications. At the same time we have to remember that the majority of our contemporaries are barely living from day to day, with dire consequences. (Bergolio, 2013, p. 32)

The review (Bergolio, 2013, pp. 31–57) described people living lives "gripped by fear" even in "so-called rich countries". It made the point "The joy of living frequently fades, lack of respect for others and violence are on the rise and inequality is increasingly evident". It went on, "We are in an age of knowledge and information, which has led to new and often anonymous kinds of power". To drive the point home, the review listed seven major challenges to its work as an NGO. These included: "the economy of exclusion, the new idolatry of money, a financial system which rules rather than serves, inequality that spawns violence . . . and the challenges of urban cultures". The review then listed the temptations that can divert those who seek to address those challenges from working to purpose, noting in particular "poor levels of spirituality, spiritual worldliness, and warring amongst ourselves".

In his 2014 Christmas message to his gathered Chief Executive Council, the CEO drew on that review (Bergolio, 2013) and delivered what the press called a "blistering message" to them. He accused his colleague council members of grabbing power and wealth, of living "hypocritical" double lives, of sustaining a back-stabbing culture, a "terrorism of gossip" that could "kill the reputation of our colleagues in cold blood". He criticised the way cliques can "enslave their members and become a cancer that threatens the harmony of the body" and eventually kill it off by "friendly fire". He pointed out how some of his colleagues suffer from "spiritual Alzheimer's", which causes them to forget what drew them to the work in the first place.

He set out to call them back to their original vocation—which he shared with them—so that the system of which they are all a part might be healed and repaired, returning to fulfil its original calling to serve the needs of the world, not to provide a career ladder for self-interested people (Winfield, 2014).

Meditation and prayer: connectedness with source through person

In this narrative, we read about that inner edge, where the narrator's work on his own personal, internal wilderness is engaged with making connection with the cutting edge of the thought of another person with whom he is in strong disagreement; in this case, the faith of a distinguished religious thinker and leader.

This is a selection of passages from one man's daily prayer journal.[2] He writes this document as follows: having read a passage, sometimes from scripture, sometimes other material, he then devotes time to recording an imagined conversation/correspondence with Jesus of Nazareth about what that passage says to him. The writer had been reading and meditating on the book *Faith Maps*, a collection by Michael Paul Gallagher SJ (Gallagher, 2010) of the work of ten "religious explorers" drawn from the past 100 years. His notes, drawing on his experience as an Anglican, were stimulated by reading about the faith of Joseph Ratzinger, who had been Prefect of the Congregation for Doctrine and Faith and who became Pope Benedict VI.

> I was taken aback as I read Gallagher's précis of Ratzinger's thinking. My image of him was of a rigid thinker, devoted to protecting the inhuman defences of Roman Catholic dogma: celibate male clergy; opposition to contraception and abortion; rejection of homosexuality; unable to respond sensitively to the abuses of children by clergy and religious orders . . . I felt a deep revulsion towards him, separating myself from him and everything he stood for . . . I saw him as an opponent of all I hold dear: my practice, based on the centrality of experience reflected on as the path to understanding of God, was open to attack as "woolly thinking"; my fierce resistance to being "ruled" by indefensible dogma seemed to be seen as disobedience; while most of my life has been built on my willingness to live with uncertainty, he seemed to stretch out for ways to banish it . . . my sense of a call to be

open to other faith positions ... was portrayed as betrayal ... he wished to take us back to a hierarchical society, bulwarked *against* the emerging realities of the 20th and 21st centuries; his Church was set on defending itself against greater freedom and change ... I saw his vision of God as manifested in his leadership of the Roman Church had no connection with mine.

That he saw the history of humankind as "a love story with God" is a surprise to me. His concern for the search for unfolding truth, rather than his seeing truth as something already established, is new and of interest to me ...

As I see it you (Jesus) were not seeking to set yourself apart from human beings, but to identify with us completely. Your earthly life was fully human, not the appearance of humanity. Your invitation to us was that we should have the courage to seek to take the Christ role ourselves ... In our turn, in our own flawed persons, we could live out the capacity to be the co-creators of God's Kingdom, not waiting for orders or following rules without thought. Thus we would know and be able to show others how to be "God-with-us" today and "to have a love affair with God" and show that to the world as you did. (From Personal Journal, entry 22 December 2014)

"A source of a new experience" ... I immediately thought how far going to church on a Sunday is a "source of new experience" ... As Ratzinger puts it, the new experience springs from being loved, being the recipient of the initiative of an Other. In the case of experiencing your love I am laid open to experiencing the love which is manifested both in the whole of creation and in the microcosm of daily life. That challenges me to respond to anyone and anything that I might encounter ... So to "teach"—to give expression to the experience of love—is to manifest my understanding of truth. (From Personal Journal, entry 23 December 2014)

... But the issue for Ratzinger is one of love and the importance of not watering that down ... As I contemplate Ratzinger I find myself feeling compassion for him. He was locked into a position in a specific system with the Congregation of the Doctrine of Dogma and Faith from which he was expected to look outwards in criticism of other positions, but without the latitude to consider in what ways they might be right. I value what he wrote about experience and that the work of the Church is to enable new experiences to emerge. (From Personal Journal, entry 24 December 2014)

Linking themes

Each of these three stories share key themes about connectedness: *the sense of a call from something greater than themselves.*

Hakim began his work apparently by chance. A Taliban commander in his district in Afghanistan had been killed and the insurgents wanted his body back from the police. Hakim was a volunteer with the Afghan Red Crescent at the time and neighbours suggested to the Taliban that they ask Hakim to present their request to the police. When he spoke to the local police, asking for documentation to help him to find bodies, they asked why he was not offering to do the same for government forces who wanted the remains of their colleagues back from the Taliban. From that, he discovered himself doing something he had never thought of doing before. Over seven years, he has now retrieved 713 bodies for both sides, including those of his own two sons.

The CEO of the NGO had been working in South America as a local leader. He was known especially for his dedication to the poor. Before joining the NGO, he had worked as a chemical technician and a nightclub bouncer. After experiencing a call to join the NGO, he became a teacher in faith-based schools, especially in slum areas. When he was promoted to organisational management jobs, he led the substantial expansion of the NGO's work into those deprived areas. His appointment to the CEO post, based in Europe, was unexpected. His career was not one that he had planned, but one built around his response to discernment of the will of God working in a system at the "edge", connecting it to service the poor. His review of God's call to the organisation from this context shaped the challenge he put before his senior colleagues and was designed to inspire them to a reinvigorated approach to the organisation's founding purpose based on its essential connectedness with the context. He saw this sense of connectedness as needing to be reflected in their own personal lives and their behaviour with one another. Only by living connectedness themselves would they be fit to respond to God's call in the present world context.

After graduating, the journal writer we have quoted turned away from promising openings in favoured occupations and experienced a call to teach in an experimental state school. After five years, he received a new call to leave teaching and to take up work as a youth worker in a city area that had the highest murder rate in Europe in the year he started. His task was to work with the street gangs of the area to build a club, led by the gang leaders themselves. What he learnt from that experience led him into organisational research, adult education, and a series of projects leading up to today. His search is still to discern the next step through which he is called to serve the world. As is evident from his journal, he finds himself naturally intolerant of attitudes that differ from his own liberal convictions, but wrestles to find connectedness with those with whom he has differences.

Working from the heart in the now

None of these three had planned a career leading to what they have finished up doing. They had not sought promotion or high reward: that did not constitute the purposes to which they felt called to work. They followed their hearts. They found that they had a path of connectedness that opened up in front of them, not a ladder. Those paths were signposted by heartfelt convictions that they were being drawn to find meaning in their lives from what they did in the immediate present. In each case, the edges they found themselves working at, and the heartfelt connections they were called to make, were surprising to them and often to those around them. The direction unfolded before them in the moment, rather than being a conventional thought-through process.

Connectedness with source[3]

All three connect to a monotheistic God. As the *Quran* says, "God is One, the Eternal God. He begot none, nor was He begotten. None is equal to Him" (*The Koran*, 1916, p. 434). The first of the Ten Words, as the Jews name them, or the Ten Commandments, as the Christians name the same passage from the book of Exodus, is "I am Yahweh your God . . . You shall have no gods to rival me" (Exodus 20.2–3). All three Abrahamic faiths are built upon the oneness of God, his implicit connectedness with human beings and his[4] imminence in the world's affairs at the greater and the lesser levels.

As men of faith, all three linked their call as coming from God or Allah. As the child Samuel, later a respected priest and prophet, learnt from his mentor Eli, they each effectively said "Speak Lord, for thy servant is listening" (1 Samuel 3.10). They interpret their experience of relatedness with others as being triadic between humans and God or Allah.

Inspired by the unity of humankind

For all three, the edge they worked and led from was that between humanity and God. They have based their lives on seeking to advance the oneness of humankind, sometimes at the cost of being misunderstood and open to ill-informed criticism. Hakim placed his own life in danger and risked his wife's failure to understand his work. The CEO risked his relatedness to his team of colleagues. The challenge to the journal writer is to expose his experience of his conversations with Jesus to others, who might treat his experience as an example of personal delusion, rather than a deeper sense of discovering the unity of humankind.

Not knowing where they were going

All three come from the Abrahamic faiths and followed that prophet's example: "By faith Abraham, when called to go to a place he would later receive as his inheritance, obeyed and went, even though he did not know where he was going" (Hebrews 11. 8–9). Abraham lived and moved at the edge of the familiar. In the *Quran*, it is written of Abraham that he was "An upright man, one who surrendered himself to God" (al-Imran 36.7).

What is "connectedness with source"?

My first question at the beginning of this chapter was, "What is it about us human beings that makes us instinctively polarise between 'good' and 'evil' and to take sides so virulently?" This question is based on a hypothesis that human beings act like this, so it is time to close in on that question to test the hypothesis.

Every major human civilisation has evolved a shared way of handling the intuitive awareness that human beings are part of something vaster than themselves, a context that is beyond their control, yet that affects their daily lives. Without something to guide that shared intuition into a compassionate and bountiful state of being, what is dreaded is to be engulfed in chaos. The fear is that the loss of familiar, trusted boundaries will threaten to unleash savage, malevolent forces that will destroy everything and everyone. Not to have a faith shared with our associates in something that exists beyond ordinary optimistic understanding runs the risk of being replaced by nihilism:

- the desire for freedom, replaced by servitude;
- hope, replaced by despair;
- love, replaced by hatred.

For Buddhists, to achieve the state of enlightenment is to have released oneself from the attachments that engulf the unenlightened in fear.

Every civilisation has developed narratives and myths about good and evil that give shape to what has been identified intuitively across a population. These are used to bind the people together, shaping their sense of identity and of belonging. Normally, these myths form around an image of some kind of deity or divine being, generating cultures that usually relate to rules of life and work. The shape and form of that divinity (or divinities) have varied depending on cultural, geographical, and other factors, giving rise to significant achievements. Sogyal Rinpoche, the Buddhist master, put it, "At the heart of all religions is the certainty that there is a fundamental truth, and that this life is a sacred opportunity to evolve and realize it" (Rinpoche, 1992, p. 47). Jews, Christians, and Sikhs speak of God; Hindus of Shiva, Brahman, and Vishnu; Muslims of Allah; Buddhists the Buddha nature. These narratives enrich the civilisation's culture. In ancient Greece and Rome, the nature of their gods and goddesses provided the seedbed from which sprang the legends of the Oresteia, the thinking of Archimedes, Aristotle, and Plato, the drama of Aristophanes, the legal frameworks of the Roman Empire and its government, along with its engineering achievements, many of which are still with us today in its architecture and physical infrastructure of roads, forums, and bridges.

The narratives that rely on benevolent divinities commonly also have myths about malevolent spirits and beings—the Tempter, Lucifer, Satan, Beelzebub, and the Devil. Myths about the Evil One convey in vivid language or pictures what awaits those who transgress or actively oppose the deity of the prevailing narrative; for example, in the poetry of Milton's *Paradise Lost*, Goethe's play *Faust*, and Dante's *Inferno*, or the paintings of Hieronymus Bosch. Thus, good and evil are split and separated socially, just as they are kept apart in individual psychology.

Both the positive and the negative narratives illustrate the personal, contingent nature of human beings: our need for food, air, water, the company of others, continuity, and so on. They recognise the difficulties posed by having to depend on one's fellow creatures who are fickle and unreliable. They build on an intuitive yearning for a much greater, completely dependable entity beyond oneself, which (or who) gives deeper meaning to life and emanates from beyond the single human being. This yearning is particularly strong at times of a birth or a death, but is present also at those times when rites of passage are called into play: naming ceremonies, transitions to adulthood, such as bar and bat mitzvah, marriage, and retirement. In this way, the sense of personal uniqueness in daily life is celebrated, as well as being connected with this sense of being entwined in a wider being.

Myths serve important purposes. They give courage and resilience to face challenges and setbacks, providing a rationale for opposing "evil" and choosing the side of the "good". Modern narratives vary in their forms from the older religions and philosophies, but the characteristic human search for truth continues in all of them. Implicit belief systems underpin the principles and practice of governance, justice, social relations, education, economies, and defence, providing the narratives that shape and link how human beings engage with one another at the personal, tribal, and wider levels.

Some of the major narratives link the "one" with the "many". The monotheistic religions posit a single deity where the one, the many, and the One are integrated (Johnson, 1961). In Buddhism, the teaching does not depend on an opposing figure, but focuses back on the person. Tariq Ramadan describes the life and work of the neo-Confucian Wang Yang-Ming (1457–1529), who taught of the need to understand the activity of the human mind rather than externalise good and evil into outside beings; he invites us to wrestle with our own ego and desire within oneself (Ramadan, 2010).

In an important sense, all these imagined structures are illusions. They are tacit agreements to treat as real what is intangible and ephemeral, not currently accessible to conventional empirical proof. Yet, these illusions are essential to experiencing a predictable life where we rely upon one another in order to live together harmoniously. In a sense, these myths are, in practice, shared working hypotheses that enable us to put the narratives of good and evil to the test, less to prove them, but to enable us to take the next step in our personal and corporate lives (Ramadan, 2010, p. 96).

Bhaumik (2008), in his thought-provoking book *Code Name God*, points out that as human experience has evolved, we have increasingly discovered empirical support for much of what was, until then, intuitive. This evidence, by posing new, more sophisticated and evidentially informed questions, increases the grounds for developing the narratives of our desire to be connected with that which is both larger than ourselves and is, at the same time, rooted in each one of us.

Because these narratives give shape to understanding about where people came from, how they live now, and where they might be going in the long run, we call this human experience "connectedness with source". Every action and decision taken is, in practice, the moment-to-moment working out of a tacit testing of hypotheses about the relatedness of our actions to the narratives we live by. This includes our understanding of the sciences that tell the story of the evolution of the species and of the universe, which, as we now know, is far from fixed, but is itself in a process of evolution.

While each person may take what appear to be personal decisions, the fact that we are inextricably enmeshed in our societies, cultures, economies, and politics means that the direction of the unfolding overall movement conditions the nature of the impact of those decisions, as certainly as gravity has affected every aspect of human physical lives since long before the apple dropped on Isaac Newton's head. Since the time of Icarus, we have wished to fly, but to do so demands that we accept the laws of physics, while not being trapped in accepting a fixed understanding of them. We can now fly to the moon and send rockets to land instruments on Mars, and even on a moving comet.

We are now called to put our experience of living and working together to similar scientific rigour in order to analyse the organisations we design to achieve our shared purposes. This is what the writer of the Foreword to the *Mandukya Upanishad* points out when he says that the philosophy of the Upanishads "employs the scientific method more rigorously than modern science does" (Swami Nikhilananda, 2000, p. vi).

The progress of civilisation has been made possible by the spirit of enquiry of people who lived, thought, worked, and travelled at the edges of the known, working with the realities they felt called to grapple with and seeking their connectedness with other realities. This process includes such organisational systems as the evolution of democracy through the expansion of suffrage, the joint stock company, which expanded the concept of ownership, the system of banking, which opened up wider access to finance and the introduction of universal education. Offering leadership at the edge is, therefore, to place oneself at the heart of understanding how to be alert to the evolutionary processes at work around and within us, which shape our connectedness.

It is not enough just to talk and write about these matters. Leadership comes from those willing to experience living at the edge and offering others connected thought, decision, and action from that position. In doing this, each person is the potentially live wireless link, whose experience of connectedness involves simultaneously receiving the messages from a range of different wavebands. Each person tunes themselves to be alert to some of those messages, interpreting and conveying their interpretation to others, but each one is—by choice or by ignorance—also deaf to the frequencies that they are not tuned into. How one is tuned fundamentally affects one's capacity to connect and to be connected with.

The interpretations that each person relies upon lie on a spectrum. At one end, there are the most familiar and trusted stories, based on, and confirmed by, their conformity to the past. For some, the sun has always risen in the morning, so it is bound to do so tomorrow, so let's not think any more about the sun. At the other end are the natural scientists, whose curiosity leads them to want to understand the continuous unfolding of the universe, the meaning of time and space, and to predict what will happen to us in due course. Just as in quantum theory, where what happens to every particle affects what happens to every other particle in the universe, each of us is at our edge, and as we work at what is being called forth from us, we affect what happens to everyone else.

The concept of "connectedness with source" in the TEF offers a lens that enables an objective exploration of this domain of all our connected and lived experience, which enhances our understanding of the profundity of our human nature. This chapter offers some insights as tools to further that exploration in analysing organisations. In particular, it takes the question "why?" very seriously and also connects it with "how"?

Relevant insights into our psychological processes

We can now bring into view a more developed understanding of our own functioning as human beings. If you are familiar with psycho-analytic approaches to understanding maturational processes, you might wish to skip the next two passages, picking up again when we begin to explore illusion.

The human condition is a constant process of seeking to reveal to ourselves our own uniqueness in the contexts in which we experience ourselves. As one six-year-old asked of his parents, "What does it mean to be me?" So, we can think here in terms of "me" as being at the "edge" of the person. The fact that the boy needed to ask his parents this question is evidence of his instinctive sense of the connectedness of his "me" nature to the context in which he found himself. Thus, this process is interrelated in due course with discovering what it means to be "us". Rooted in one of the normal maturational processes, getting a grasp on this question enables us to function in what we call the "real" world.

Splitting and projection[5]

Conventional psychology and psychoanalysis describe these processes as the maturing infant's discovery of the experience of the relatedness between "me" and "not-me". In the child's developing mind, those objects that confirm their personal goodness, lovableness, and emerging conception of humanness, are attributed to the self and experienced as "me". Conversely, those objects that cause pain and distress, threatening destruction, are experienced as "not-me". Faced with the confusing experience of having both "goodness" and "badness" within what one yearns to be a coherent whole "me", the infant splits the "good" from the "bad" and projects the unwanted "bad" outwards, to the being who is presumed to wish one pain and trouble and must, therefore, be malevolent. The "good" me is protected and defended against the "bad" me, who is, of course, "not-me". This process does not feed a state of disconnectedness; it feeds a state of negative connectedness—persons welded together by hate. It is to be hoped that a manageable sense of differentiation between inside and outside is defined, consciously and unconsciously, and, in due course, transactions begin to be managed (Klein, 1959).

Boundaries and systems[6]

A boundary has been defined by Eric Miller and Ken Rice (1967) as a semi-permeable membrane across which transactions pass inwards and outwards. It marks what might be thought of as the skin of the organisational entity and its semi-permeable nature is critically important (Miller & Rice 1967). Below the level of consciousness, each child learns to draw a mental boundary, which provides a sense of the edge between the self and the rest of the world. This boundary provides the basis of the emergent sense of personal identity, distinguished from the context. For each child, this provides him with the initial paradigm of what he assumes to be human—one's own self—built on this conscious and unconscious splitting. While, in the person, one's skin marks the boundary, in everyday connected life, boundaries might be marked by walls, fences, ditches, and so on, with gates and bridges to enable connections to take place. It is important to recognise that the psychological differentiations that are being marked are about something that is, in its essence, imagined, and subsequently treated as if it were real.

Splitting and projection are not the whole story. As time goes on, the child experiences his connectedness with others in the family: other people are experienced as belonging together with "me". Reciprocal smiles and cuddles, gifting, shared joy and happiness, all foster the sense of being "more-of-me-but-different". From this, the capacity to desire good things both for oneself and for others (more-of-me) emerges, and experiences of belonging, empathy, generosity, altruism, and compassion all expand. Thus, the paradigm of what it is to be human expands as the boundary of "self" becomes more and more inclusive, the edge moves outwards, thus "me" morphs into the awareness of being "us". In this way, "me" becomes connected within the boundary of the larger "us". The sense of connectedness is organisationally significant, as we shall see later.

Thus, new edges and a new connectedness begin to become evident. These are systemic edges and systemic connectednesses, since the edge of the new entities have no natural, tangible "skin", but one that exists primarily in the mind. Of course, markers may be devised to make the boundary appear to be physical: languages, uniforms, or procedures. In due course, the capacity for compassion that began in the family system can widen and be extended to other systems. We now get the boundary of "more-of-us-but-different" becoming more and more inclusive as experiences in schools, clubs, and other groupings extends. These developments lay the foundations for experiencing positive connectedness both personally and systemically, which contrast where the connectedness is seen negatively— "not-me" and "not-us" (DeWaal, 2009; Smith, 1759).[7] Within groups and systems, "good" figures, especially those associated with the success and future of the group, now begin to be exaggeratedly good and idealised, endowed with powers and wisdom beyond reality. With the "good" figures, the permeability of the boundary is increased.

Conversely, the leaders of the "other" become demonised; consider the Mayor of London. Just as in the person, in groups and systems holding the "good" alongside the "bad" is an emotional challenge, so, conversely, negative attribution is also true systemically. Those things that cause pain and distress are projected outside the group and are experienced as "not-me". These now feed an opposite conception of exaggerated non-humanness. This group-related non-humanness lays the foundation for later seeing "not-me" as a demonised "other", imputing to that "other" all ills and evils. These threatening "others", whatever their origins and however irrational, must be hated and either attacked to destruction or fled from. The edge becomes harsher, the negativity loses sight of the individual human beings on the other side of the boundary and the whole group is lumped together. While for most people the attribution of non-humanness is manageable in childhood, and its consequences are usually recoverable, this can grow to terrifying proportions in adulthood. In a BBC television documentary programme titled *Angry, White and Proud* (Roberts, 2014), broadcast on 14 January 2015, one of the subjects, a former nightclub DJ, declared,

> I'm extremely racist against Muslims. I hate them, fucking hate them with a fucking passion, more than I hate West Ham football club and that's saying something because I hate them bastards, but yeah, I hate them, with a whole lot of hate. (Wollaston, 2015)

Such hatred between an individual who regards those identified as the "others" as his enemies is difficult enough, but when his hatred is shared by groups, systems, nations, and other large bodies and who rely on the connectedness shared through hatred, mobilising and directing it against others, disaster might not be far away. The "whole" within which the battle lines are drawn requires the negative exchange to exist to sustain the protected fragmented "us". The videos by ISIS as they carry out their beheading and mutilation of their prisoners are designed to arouse visceral rejection, which feeds the chasm and the desired self-image. Under these circumstances, martyrdom is seen as honourable. The treatment of Muslim prisoners by US guards in Guantanamo Camp performs a similar function for both sides that is only marginally less gruesome (see, e.g., Ould Slahi, 2015).

It can be argued that examples such as these demonstrate that human beings never cease splitting and projecting, using groups and institutions to draw the boundaries that differentiate "us" from "not-us". This provides the "not-us"—the other—by which we can define our own "approved" identity. On this differentiation, groups are negatively connected through such emotions as envy, fear, rivalry, and betrayal. The "seven deadly sins" give their energy and drive through the channels of connectedness.

Illusion and its part in adult and organisational life

This takes us to exploring boundaries as "illusions". First, I need to be clear about how I want to suggest that the word "illusion" is understood. The *New Oxford Dictionary of English* (1998) defines "illusion" as "a false idea or belief". I am offering a departure from the conventional negative connotation of the word and suggest a different, creative way to use it. The etymological definition of the word "illusion" says that one of its roots is the Etruscan word "ludere"—to play. I am suggesting that we think of "illusions" as ways to play with the idea of illusion. I can now seek to develop an image in my mind that goes beyond the tangible: this is an illusion. In this way, we might find that playing with illusions could provide us with new "illuminations".

The child psychoanalyst Donald Winnicott explores the importance of illusion in human development. He describes how the nursing mother enables the suckling infant to live happily with the illusion that the breast is an extension of "me". As the infant is weaned, the idea of "me" including the breast—an illusion—still exists within the infant, even when she is no longer given contact with the breast, so she intuitively seeks a way of reminding herself of the comforting sense of that extended "me". In meeting the need for a physical representation of the breast, the child discovers a physical object that can be treated as if it were a breast. This might be embodied in a piece of cloth, a soft toy, or whatever. Thus, she finds what Winnicott called a "transitional object" but, as her awareness grows, her sense is that not only has she found the needed object, but she, through her own actions, created it. Because she "made" it, she can attribute feelings to the apparently inanimate object. Asked if her teddy bear loved her, my daughter, aged four, said, "Of course he loves me." Similarly, when frustrated or upset by him, she would attribute malign intentions to him and punish him.

Winnicott defines illusion like this:

> We can share a respect for "illusory experience", and if we wish we may collect together and form a group on the basis of the similarity of our illusory experiences. This is a natural root of grouping among human beings. (Winnicott, 1958, p. 231)

As we associate with others, we form images of what holds us together. A family is not a tangible thing like a breast, but it generates comparable experiences. The idea of "family" is held broadly in common by those who feel they belong together. Further than that, those outside the family perceive that "family" in ways which recognise that belonging and probably behave towards the family in ways that confirm it. The "family" is, in these terms, an illusion.

Similarly with organisations and institutions: persons gather around and engage with them, take actions, have expectations of them, gain satisfaction and frustration from them. For example, if I wish to fly to Australia, I might look up an airline and their lists of prices, timetables, the types of aircraft they use, reviews of efficiency, and the experience of others flying with them. The whole institution might be called "British Airways" but there is, in tangible reality, no such "thing" similar to my mother's breast that I can directly engage with. British Airways is, in these terms, an illusion. It has its discrete parts, but my assumption about their connectedness and the totality is, in effect, an illusion in that it is a mental creation that has sufficiently widespread agreement for a large number of people to behave it into existence. Just as British Airways is, in these terms, an illusion, so are all institutions, nations, and even the cosmos. There are things that can be measured, timed, and felt, but when we aggregate them we make an assumption about the connectedness of things.

The anthropologist and management consultant Gouranga Chattopadhyay has explored the links between the consequences of splitting and projection in organisational behaviour. In his paper, "A fresh look at authority and organization: towards a spiritual approach for managing illusion" (Chattopadhyay 1999), he argues that the consequence of failure to manage the human proclivity to split and project—which we never grow out of—feeds organisational dysfunction of all kinds. His point is that in working organisations, boundaries are constantly created both consciously and unconsciously. Even where boundaries are consciously drawn to facilitate tasks, the residual memories from infancy mean that hierarchies are imposed that turn task-related boundaries from resources into threats (Hirschhorn & Gilmore 1992). He links this to the memories of dependence upon the mother, which inherently reactivates the hierarchy between the helpless infant and the omnipotent mother.

His proposal is that management education needs to begin to develop spirituality, which he describes as being "about discovering connectedness and managing perceived differences". He goes on, "It is spirituality that questions the very existence of boundaries of various kinds and can pave the way for reviewing and exploring boundaries for greater task effectiveness in organizations" (Chattopadhyay, 1999, pp. 124–125). A similar argument is developed by Hirschhorn and Gilmore in their paper, "The new boundaries of the 'boundary-less' company" (1992).

This takes us on to a significant new step: into the realm of meaning-making, theology, and philosophy. The idea of the importance of illusion in this sense is present in other cultures: for example, the *Mandukya Upanishad* (Swami Nikhilananda, 2000). There, in exploring the three states of human experience, waking, dreaming, and deep sleep, the *Upanishad* proposes that all aspects of life are illusory, yet they still provide the basis for ways of living in the "real world". Chapter III explores the use of illusion in the following terms:

> In dream, also, what is imagined within by the mind is illusory and what is cognized outside (by the mind) appears to be real. But (in truth) both these are known to be unreal. Similarly, in the waking state, also, what is imagined within by the mind is illusory: and what is experienced outside (by the mind) appears to be real. But in fact both should be rationally treated as unreal. (Swami Nikhilananda, 2000, 9th and 10th Karikas (verses))

This process of using shared illusions is present and influential as human beings develop the sense of belonging together in institutions. Lawrence (2000) makes this clear in work he did with orders of priests and nuns. Their shared "illusion" of God as described in scripture was clearly manifested in their relationships with one another and with himself as an authority figure. From this, he came to the working hypothesis that when human beings assemble for a shared purpose, they co-create an illusion which provides principles on which to manage their behaviour around what he called their "imago of the cosmos". He went further and hypothesised

> That it is the imago of the cosmos that structures relationships on the planet. To be sure, there will be variations because all humankind does not have a common picture in the mind of the cosmos. The imago maybe a non-imago, the shadow—that is chaos. (Lawrence, 2000, pp. 79–80)

He offered examples from organisations with which he had worked over the years to support this hypothesis.

Working in a similar terrain, Bruce Reed, the founder of the Grubb Institute, developed his theory of oscillation (Reed, 1978). In this, he linked Winnicott's concept of regression to dependence to the need to function autonomously in the "real" world. He hypothesised that just as the small child moves naturally between exploring his surroundings but reaches a stage at which he feels things are getting too much for him, at which point he runs back to mother, so, in adult life, men and women function autonomously, but also need to gather together to integrate what they are in terms of their larger whole. This is not a "practical", conventional activity, but it fulfils emotional and spiritual needs as well, enabling the values and purpose of the organisation to be revisited, refurbished, and, thus, sustained. These things matter.

Reed called the upper point in the oscillation "realisation", where the "real" task of the organisation in its context is attended to through differentiated roles and activities; the lower point, he names "identification", where the experience of human connectedness among the people is re-established (Reed, 2013). In the sense of how I am using the term "illusion", identification is around the shared illusions—the myths and narratives, the values and beliefs—held in the organisation about its purpose in context. These shape the way its culture, decisions, and achievements are understood and maintained.

Effective organisational structures build in ways to facilitate this oscillatory process. As an Anglican priest researching the task of the church in society, Reed described in detail the way the church in England handles regression to dependence. He included in his writing close analyses of Anglican liturgy as providing a structure that facilitates regression to dependence, the experience of identification with the Creator and one's fellow creatures, and then transformation to realisation in the "real" world. The great ceremonial occasions in societies, such as presidential inaugurations and the funerals of national heroes, express oscillation representationally for whole populations. The extraordinary national behaviour of the British at the funeral of Princess Diana is one major example. The weekly services in gudwaras, mosques, synagogues, and churches based in local communities provide conditions for individuals to manage oscillation on their own behalf, but also to do it representatively on behalf of their community. When working in a hotel in Bangkok, it was moving to watch representatives of the hotel staff perform a weekly fifteen-minute ceremony at the Buddhist shrine beside the hotel's main entrance.

It is key to Reed's thinking that connectedness with source is understood as being present in both realisation and in identification modes. His point was that having sustained the challenges of being authentic in relation to organisational values and beliefs, and to be effective in realisation behaviour, organisations need opportunities to regress to dependence in identification. They need to do this in order to regain, refurbish, and reinterpret the values and beliefs and spirituality that are expressed in practice in realisation, but come under pressure in that behaviour. Retreats, "away days", and similar occasions provide opportunities for this necessary oscillation to take place.

In this thinking, Reed was following Bion's idea about institutions fulfilling unconscious purposes for society. Thinking of basic assumption processes in groups, Bion hypothesised that religious institutions in the UK have a specialised function handling *dependence* on behalf of a society. He also suggested that the armed forces in Britain handle *fight/flight* and the aristocracy handle *pairing* and *hope* (which Reed and Palmer rename *expectancy*) on behalf of British society (Bion, 1967).

This body of thinking raises the question of what we have called "purpose". To the extent that institutions and organisations in communities and societies conceive of themselves as inevitably entwined in these unconscious processes and influenced by them, they become sensitised to what is being called forth from them by active forces and factors at work in their contexts (Bazalgette et al., 2014).

Our hypothesis is that connectedness with source is always present to the extent that when it is taken into account the full range of available resources becomes evident, especially in terms of human imagination, inventiveness, resourcefulness, and resilience. Where this potential collective resource is ignored or suppressed, the result is that organisations and institutions become fragile, brittle, and under-perform. They are at risk.

It gives us a way of producing more imaginative and potentially radical hypotheses about human behaviour in organisations. First, by adopting a stance of curiosity or spirit of enquiry, we can seek out objective ways of describing evidenced examples of the behaviours. Then we can hypothesise the possible nature of the connectedness between them and the patterns they express. We can follow that by identifying what new evidence might support that kind of connectedness and seek that evidence through posing questions to reveal how far one's hypothesis stands up. While not making the connectedness any more tangible than electricity or gravity, we can begin to predict the dynamics of what is taking place and might take place next. In the TEF, "purpose" is regarded as a way of understanding the patterns of behaviour of a human system responding to the triple influences of persons (through their desires and yearnings), the context with which it is connected and which provides it with resources, and its connectedness with source in terms of the underlying integrating force that links back to the origins of the universe and the unfolding history of all living species, including humankind. This relates to the science of evolution.

We can offer two brief examples from our work over the years.

In a power distribution company, a major resource available to the company to fulfil its desire to be a paradigm of sustainable functioning was the experience of senior engineers. This experience was regularly subordinated to the presumed prior demands of the legal, financial, and human resources departments, who could mobilise "facts" and "figures" on spreadsheets to make their case. Consequently, the genuine understanding of how to be a global example of what the planet was actually calling for, which the engineers understood as a result of their training and formation, was relegated to a lower order than satisfying the demands set by the banks and the shareholders.[8] The creation of wealth, on which strategic decisions were made, was based on what could be read from the two dimensions of a spreadsheet, rather than the more difficult to read multi-dimensional realities of efficient and safe delivery of power from generation to the end user. Of course, energy obtained from oil and gas is itself geologically connected with source, while solar energy is connected to source in its own way.

In a global manufacturing company, all employees were offered up to ten hours of personal coaching a year. As in many places, the coaching tended to become focused on "work–life" balance. Those providing the coaching were markedly cynical about the work of the company. They tended to work in isolation from one another, seeking to "reduce stress" by encouraging clients to defend themselves against the inevitable and natural stresses of the work of a large and complex organisation. As part of his own professional development, the manager with responsibility for the supervision and development of the coaches was advised to visit the company's website. He was asked to explore how, if the coaching were consciously related to the vision of the executive team's explanation of the company's existence (to make a major contribution to health and wellbeing on the planet), coaches might find systemic meaning in the ebb and flow of the work in the company. By linking their day-to-day work with the purpose to which the company was being called, greater satisfaction and hope would become more accessible to men and women who were looking for it from their own work. Again, connectedness with source, seen as the ongoing call to heal, repair, and transform the world and its peoples, would be met both internally and externally.

Leading for the whole

We need to return to the opening passages of this chapter: the quotations from the Mayor of London and our three vignettes. Let us place them in the setting of connectedness with source and the call to "play" with the idea of illusion. We have conceived of connectedness with source as a way of providing an open way of thinking objectively about why human beings are on this planet and what the universe is calling forth from us. Thinking of the universe from the perspective of physics, quantum dynamics, and evolution, it is clear that we exist in the middle of forces we only partially understand. We are participants in an unfolding mystery. The sane approach, therefore, is to recognise that we need to work with hypotheses that we can test. Hypotheses are articulated illusions formulated so that they can be put to the test. This calls us to learn to manage our splitting and projection in our desire for certainty and security. In particular, we are invited to avoid using our fellow human beings as objects to carry our projections that caricature and demonise them while portraying ourselves as angels.

To return to the Mayor of London and our three vignettes: the Mayor appears to need what Muslim jihadists represent to him and those who agree with him in order not to acknowledge his own behaviour, values, and beliefs, but to see them as "not-me", rather than "more-of-me-but-different". The evidence in the public domain of his personal life and relationships give some support to this hypothesis. Here, the connectedness is not with source.

Malik Abdul Hakim sees the need for a dignified burial for all those fathers, sons, and brothers, so he returns their remains to their sorrowing families. Pope Francis—for he is the CEO of the NGO—seeks to call his fellow members of the Curia back to their vocation from God in terms of meeting the needs of the poor, the sick, and the oppressed through offering them unconditional love. For him, connectedness is with the Creator God, who calls on those created in his image to live up to the call to be part of the work of healing, repair, and the wellbeing of the world.

The journal writer finds that by processing his experience of reading about great men of faith through an imagined conversation with Jesus, this enables him to integrate his judgements about someone with whom he felt he was in deep disagreement. In this way, by acknowledging their connectedness with the same God, he finds new and illuminating connections with someone towards whom he had felt almost viscerally opposed, as well as discovering new ways of experiencing relatedness to that God.

All three, and the others I have described here, find that the iterative process of working with one's internal processes, the overarching call from source, and the collective realities that reveals, leads to the emergence of capacities to love and to find their lovable selves, even when this seemed impossible initially. For them, the whole of humankind provides the overarching system to which they pledge themselves. Another example of the same dedication to the whole of humankind is in Sikhism. The last Guru, Gobhind Singh, founded the Khalsa, the body of Sikhs dedicated to defend Sikhism *and* all faiths, 300 years ago. Indeed, their festival of Vaisakhi is dedicated to that position and falls at the same time as Orthodox Christians celebrate Easter.

Illusion revisited

It is time now to complete Winnicott's description of illusion: "It is a hallmark of madness when an adult puts too powerful a claim on the credulity of others, forcing them to acknowledge a sharing that is not their own" (Winnicott, 1958, p. 231).

We can all recall instances where forcing others has been used as a way to avoid the hard work necessary to integrate with ourselves the plurality of the world in which we are participants; a world that gains or loses from our lived behaviour, not simply as persons, but as persons-in-role shaping the universal system of which, in truth, we are real parts. The inclusive concept of connectedness with source offers an approach to thinking about our experience in context, in systems, and as persons that enables our behaviour in role to integrate the gallimaufry which is our lived experience and to live a life of which we can be proud.

A closing example from organisational analysis

A colleague who knew I was writing this chapter offered me her own story, which provides a further perspective, particularly related to organisational analysis. She describes an epiphany that she had in her understanding of connectedness with source in a role consultation. She writes from her memoir as if to the consultant she was working with:

> Ever since my grandfather died (maternal step-grandfather), I assumed that G-d clearly did not exist, otherwise why would G-d leave us so alone? And then one afternoon, sitting with you in a role consultation in one of the consulting rooms at Cloudesley Street, I had the sudden realisation that I did know G-d after all. We had been talking about conflict, and why it seems to always take place right on the boundary between people. I was volunteering as a community mediator at Camden Mediation Service at the time, and thinking about how conflicts take place with neighbours, with neighbouring gardens, or neighbouring country borders. Suddenly it just came to me that G-d exists in the gaps, in the difference, in the conflict. I said that to you at the time, and you replied "well yes, of course, that's right". I thought it was hilarious that such a revelation to me seemed so ordinary and obvious to you! If only we could "know" what and who was right next to us, our sibling, neighbour, or next-door countrymen, then we could observe both our difference and our connectedness—and even how our difference can connect us in the shared experience of it.

> What I realised is that Source does not exist "out there". Source is our experience of inherent connectedness. So G-d could not possibly leave us alone. Because we're not alone—we are connected. And that connectedness, that gel, the stuff in between that both distinguishes us from others whilst at the same time holding us firmly together, that is Source: sticky, connecting, holding, Source.

> In the seminar I worked with you and ******, on Organisations and Institutions, I built a picture-in-mind that reflects this. The picture was

of the Earth, representing human beings and all of life and existence, as opposed to the geographical Earth. Every mound, bump, or large mountain range is a different expression of life on the globe of human experience, emerging out of the same amorphous living organism. Our experience of connectedness to Source is about our ability to identify ourselves as the particular mound or mountain rising up out of this bundle of being. Where are we in relation to the whole, what is our form and character, how do we occur or seem to ourselves and others, what is our unique nature that defines our shape and being, where are others in relation to us, and can we look to the centre of the globe and locate the point at which we connect with others, with the whole? Expressions of life, sitting just next to us, can seem so far away ... how do we locate the aspects that join us together, and the aspects that sit apart, like Siamese twins?

And so, how do we account for what we share and what distinguishes our natures, and how do we work and lead purposefully in organisational systems, with one another, with this in mind? Honouring and utilising our differences as well as our understanding of our connectedness?

More recently, in a discussion with another colleague in the field, we were talking about how they rarely bring in the concept of Source when working with clients and using the Transforming Experience Framework. A lot of people tell me they just don't know how to talk about connectedness to Source in the framework, and so choose to leave it out. I had a few thoughts about this:

- Source is not a distinct domain, it is connected and runs throughout. We are never not working with Source, but we may not be working with it and seeking to make sense of it purposefully and consciously (this is thought I shared at the time with the colleague).

- Source is about connectedness, and resides throughout the TEF, throughout our experiences of role, as if it wasn't for our connectedness, experience, and knowing, how would we have any data on the systems in which we reside in order to be able to take action? We would be taking a stab in the dark every time, and be filled up with (even more) anxiety and not-knowing. So instead of asking "what" is Source, we might instead ask "what is the nature of connectedness?" That will tell us what we need to know about our experience of connectedness to Source, which is ultimately driving it.

- And so ... what is the Source of my experiences—what are the deeply shared and connected values and beliefs that is keeping the current experience/"show on the road"? What are the experiences of authority, faith, belief, loving and lovable-ness, and values through the experiences of being a person, in a system, in a context, that is driving the here-and-now occurrence? These are the deeper questions we can ask, as close to the Source of experience of human being-ness as we can take ourselves. Bruce Irvine talked about how we constantly test in systems whether we are capable of loving or being loved—that is at the Source, the deepest depths, of what's really going on around here, on this "mortal coil" of human experience.

- When we are able to consciously work with our nature of connectedness to Source, we find immense resources for transformation, as we are working with the literal root or creative Source of the experiences and occurrences. In that sense, we are truly re-sourcing ourselves.

I'm not sure where you are in the writing of your chapter, but hope that sharing the progress I have made in my own thinking is in some way purposeful! I'm still learning and making sense of what all of this means and building on my understanding ...

And so am I.

Role and vocation

In the opening passage of this chapter, I commented on the importance of connectedness with source in the framework being related to its presence, consciously or unconsciously attended to, in every other domain. Because we are inhabitants of this planet in its place in the cosmos, source provides the collective reality which embraces us all, however little we attend to it or give it thought. The TEF, in its Venn diagram form, expresses the overlap area of the domains of person, context, and system as the domain of role defined as "Action that serves the purpose of the system". This indicates that connectedness with source is present in any action that is taken both as a person and on behalf of a system. The system that embraces us all is the universe in which we are located. Here, what can so easily become an intellectual debate between philosophies, theologies, spiritualities, and even sciences, is brought down to earth and practicality through being embodied in action. Every action I take expresses a level of commitment and motivation to some form of truth. In this way, the extent to which it is for me to be authentic can be judged, and to the extent that I take my internal dynamics seriously, I can judge myself.

The overlap area of role also includes the word "vocation". It is this word that indicates that through behaviour in role is perceived the amalgam of the beliefs, faith, and spirituality of those on whose behalf action is taken. This is explored in the chapter on taking multiple roles in multiple systems (see Chapter Six). However conscious one is about it, every time one takes any action one is in role in a system and expressing representatively the values, beliefs, faith, and spirituality of that system. In the real connected world, while the perceived values and beliefs expressed by a representative who works across boundaries might not wholly accord with all those held by every person in their system, what is represented to other systems is what the system stands for as a whole. Policies and strategies are evolved so that they are enacted through the actions of the representatives of systems, whose authority might range along the spectrum from an "observer" who collects information, a delegate with restricted powers, to a plenipotentiary who has full power to act within a policy framework. No policy framework exists without embodying, in some way or other, the values and values shared between those who make that policy, whatever their personal position.

It is important to recognise that the overlap of role between the three circles of the Venn diagram is not fixed. It is mobile and variable under different circumstances. In principle, a Venn diagram is composed of three "slices" of a single "column" that have been fanned out. Source would be at its most potent when the column has been reconstructed into its whole. What that state means will differ from faith position to faith position: for Christians like me, that is thought of as the Day of Judgement when the Kingdom of God is completed. Other beliefs think of that moment differently and have their own way of naming it.

The principle on which roles are taken by us all is, in the now, to make our next contribution to the day.

Notes

1. *Tikkun olam* is a Hebrew phrase that means "repairing the world" (or "healing the world") that suggests humanity's shared responsibility to heal, repair, and transform the world.

2. Quoted with the author's permission. The passages have not been changed in any way, except to delete pieces that are not relevant to this argument.

3. I hope those who follow other traditions and teachings, which involve a number of gods or none, can be patient with me and not yet feel disconnected with the overall argument. Those who profess a philosophy rather than a divine being might find that the argument includes them if, where the theists find a personal god, they relate to the philosophy from which life derives meaning for them.

4. For convenience, the male pronoun is used and the writers beg forgiveness from those to whom it causes offence.

5. The theory described here is broadly based on the work of Melanie Klein, the psychoanalyst, and others who followed her initial insights and writing, especially at the Tavistock Institute.

6. The concepts and theory about systems, their boundaries, and management I draw on here are the work of A. K. Rice and E. J. Miller.

7. There is also a growing body of evidence from the neurosciences that provides empirical support for human connectedness which influences human behaviour below the level of consciousness.

8. In some power distribution companies (not this one) the loss of power between its generation and delivery to the end user is as great as 90%; that is to say, only 10% of the power generated is actually available for real use.

References

Bazalgette, J. L., Irvine, G. B., & Quine, C. (2014). The purpose of meaning and the meaning of purpose. In: *The Grubb Reader: Freedom to Make a Difference: A Collection of Papers* (pp. 350–368). London: Grubb Institute.

Bergolio, J. (2013). *The Joy of the Gospel*. London: Incorporated Catholic Truth Society.

Bhaumik, M. (2008). *Code Name God: The Spiritual Odyssey of a Man of Science*. New York: Crossroad.

Bion, W. R. (1967). *Systems of Organization: The Control of Task and Sentient Boundaries*. London: Tavistock.

Chattopadhyay, G.P. (1999). A fresh look at authority and organization: towards a spiritual approach for managing illusion. In: R. French & R. Vince (Eds.), *Group Relations, Management and Organization* (pp. 112–126). Oxford: Oxford University Press.

DeWaal, F. (2009). *The Age of Empathy: Nature"s Lessons for a Kinder Society*. New York: Harmony Books.

Gallagher, M. P. (2010). *Faith Maps: Ten Religious Explorers from Newman to Ratzinger*. London: Darton.

Hirschhorn, L., & Gilmore, T. (1992). The new boundaries of the "boundaryless" company. *Harvard Business Review*, May–June: 104–115.

Johnson, A. R. (1961). *The One and the Many in the Israelite Conception of God*. Cardiff: University of Wales Press.

Johnson, B. (2015). Twitter, 31 January 2015.

Klein, M. (1959). *Our Adult World and its Roots in Infancy*. London: Hogarth Press.

Lawrence, W. G. (2000). *Tongued With Fire: Groups in Experience*. London: Karnac.

Miller, E., & Rice, A. K . (1967). *Systems of Organizations*. London: Tavistock.

Ould Slahi, M. (2015). *Guantanamo Diary*. London: Canongate.

Personal Journal Entries (2014). 22, 23, 24 December.

Ramadan, T. (2010). *The Quest for Meaning: Developing a Philosophy of Pluralism*, Harmondsworth: Penguin.

Reed, B. D. (1978). *The Dynamics of Religion: Process and Movement in Christian Churches*. London: Darton, Longman & Todd.

Reed, B. D. (2013). The psychodynamics of life and worship. In: *The Grubb Reader* (pp. 206–240). London: Grubb Institute.

Rinpoche, S. (1992). *The Tibetan Book of Living and Dying*. San Francisco, CA: Harper-Collins.

Roberts, J. (2014). *Angry, White and Proud*. BBC television documentary, 14 January 2015.

Smith, A. (1759). *The Theory of Moral Sentiments*. Minneapolis, MN: Filiquarian.

Swami Nikhilananda (2000). *The Manukyopanishad with Gaudapapa's Karika and Sankara's Commentary*. Calcutta: Adavaita Ashram.

The Koran (1916). N. J. Dawood (Trans.). London: Penguin.

The New Oxford Dictionary of English (1998). Oxford: Oxford University Press.

Winfield, N. (2014). www.huffingtonpost.com/2014/12/22/pope-francis-vatican-curia_n_6366752.html

Winnicott, D. W. (1958). Transitional objects and transitional phenomena. In: *Collected Papers: Through Paediatrics to Psychoanalysis* (pp. 229–242). London: Tavistock.

Wollaston, S. (2015). TV Review. *Guardian* G2, 15 January, p. 21.

CHAPTER TEN

The experience of connectedness with source: how does one's understanding of connectedness with source contribute to thinking about accountability in role?

Marjoleine Hulshof

Introduction

The conception of this chapter involved a wonderful reflection of struggling with the concept of "connectedness with source", one of the domains of the Grubb's "framework for transforming experience into authentic action through role" (TEF, Bazalgette et al., 2006). Understanding and admitting to the discomfort with, and hesitation over, this idea created the curiosity for choosing it as focus for a paper initially written in 2009 as part of my candidature for the Grubb/UEL Masters programme, Freedom to Make a Difference. Connectedness with source, for me, implied exploring how this idea, rightly or wrongly, links to the concept of religion, a concept heavily influenced by a Christian upbringing I thought I had left behind after my adolescent years. Since then, I chose the thinking of existentialist philosopher and atheist Jean-Paul Sartre to influence my understanding on life, living, values, and sense-making of the world. The following words extracted from his works have always deeply resonated:

> There is no destiny for man. Man must create his existence himself. It is in these acts that man exists. He is nothing before existing, as it

were, before making his life himself. He is but the sum of his acts. Man can make/do or not make/do, this or the other thing. It is by continuously making his choice that he builds his existence. The man who does not choose any more, who does not act any more, does not exist any more: he died. (Sartre, 1989, author's notes from Satre's lecture)

My interpretation of these words as an adolescent and held as a mantra for my life is that of taking responsibility for one's own life and the choices one makes, and not to become a victim of circumstances. When creating one's life through the choices one is making, one should accept the outcomes as one's own responsibility, without blame or looking back in regret. In other words, we exist through our choices, which manifest in our (non-)actions from which we can understand the accountability for who we are. This understanding of accountability and its relation to connectedness with source is what I am curious about exploring in this chapter. As Sartre says, *l'existence précède l'essence* (1943, p. 6): the core of existentialism which he, in his approach, applied to humanity and not as a universal principle.

This chapter takes as its starting point my experiences of religion, analysing in what way those experiences facilitate an understanding of source, from which I consider whether religion is only one of many ways to relate to source in my understanding of what source represents. This then opens up the question of how experience of connectedness with source can be accessed from the perspective of the development of human consciousness and what the implications might be for accountability in role(s), following the Grubb's thinking about "role".

The question that came up while writing this chapter was inspired by the paper, "The absolute in the present" (Bazalgette et al., 2006). It is that if "authority" provides a frame to assess how a person uses his power and to whom he is accountable as a person taking a role in the world, then to whom is one accountable when making one's existence through choices and actions in role, especially if one does not believe in the authority of institutionalised religion or "God"? Does a person's experience of connectedness with source indeed provide a frame for that?

From very early on I experienced the concept of accountability and religion as two mutually exclusive perspectives. In my experience, "being religious" was identified with joining an institution, where people tend to hand over personal responsibility and their capacity to critique and question to the institution. I felt that followers of religion submit themselves to the rules of the church, or a particular grouping that claims to know how to interpret and apply the will of God as laid out in the Bible: assuming a powerful authority to determine what is wrong or right, to separate the decent from the doomed, and good from bad. I recognise that these quite un-nuanced experiences are derived from a childhood in a mainly western Christian context; other faiths or religious options were further removed. Today, while I can see more nuances and differences, there are still many examples confirming those initial experiences, especially considering the current rise in fundamentalism and extremism in the name of various religious traditions. On a smaller scale, there has been the experience in my work as consultant, especially when working with leaders in the Caribbean and Latin America who found it hard to acknowledge their actions, as if their destiny, that is, the decisions and actions they made, were only able to be attributed to what God had told them "last night", yet behaving quite incongruently with the accountability that their leadership roles involved.

I could not connect my sense of responsibility, as inspired by Sartre, with the submission to an institution that was created by other human beings and/or to an abstract voice telling one what to do. Too often, I found the church and God used as the easy way out for transferring the responsibility outside oneself, even to a point of passive awaiting or victimising. Strong feelings of resentment developed into a hypothesis that my struggle with, and anxiety around, the heaviness of a deeply engrained sense of responsibility is rooted in the Calvinist upbringing and a personal narrative based on an assumption that "if I act/take charge of, I am worthy". It seemed also a reflection of my anger and distress about the harmful and aggressive actions that take place under religious flags, at a micro-level between human beings as well as at a macro-level between nations or ethnic groups across the world. I was experiencing a sense of inadequacy, loss of words and power as an individual towards the realities of society.

Wells (2006) was one of the authors from a Christian faith-base that I read. I had little tolerance for the certainty of his description about the institution of Church, the almost prescriptive practices he lists, and the emphasis on dependence through standards. While I connected to some of the messages referred to as gifts, like the gift of humility and the beautiful way in which he describes friendship as companionship: "for the essence of friendship is to be a companion – a person with whom one shares bread" (Wells, 2006, p. 93), I could not see these thoughts as exclusive to Christian or other religious interpretations, but as a deep human expression of generosity.

At an intellectual level, I appreciated Wells' view on the value of the greater goals and the role of the church body that

> if high standards get in the way of members expressing needs, joy, hurts and thanks, then those standards have gone beyond their usefulness. God's gift to Christian community is divine, but the divine gift is a gift that makes the community human. (Wells, 2006, p. 88)

That seems an invitation to soften the rigidity of any (religious) institution and create more openness and forgiveness.

Reading Wells' writing about religion and the containing role of the church enabled a next step for me in the exploration of connectedness to source, opening a door beyond that of religion. When Sartre speaks of the choices one makes to create one's destiny, it leaves it open as to how one makes those choices; what might be guiding a person that might reveal something about a connectedness to a source?

A concept that was helpful to understand how source can be accessed in a different way is Theory U (Scharmer, 2009). This social technology model describes transformation through a movement that follows a U, where, at the bottom of the U, we can connect to source and experience a oneness between self and source, an experience of connectedness, where our usual human need to create a separateness between what is me and what is not-me (Armstrong, 1992) is left behind: a "letting-go", in Theory U terminology. At the bottom of the U, the core questions emerging are "Who is self?" and "What is my work?" This is a place of potential and of being present with what is being called forth, that is, purpose (Figure 10.1).

In summary, the U shows that the movement along it is one of reframing, inviting us in "seeing" with fresh eyes, opening the mind, and suspending the voice of judgement, the near-enemy of the open mind. This is followed by "sensing" and entering the dialogue with self and our environment, which enables deeper assumptions to surface, at the open heart-level, so we can accept self as part of the

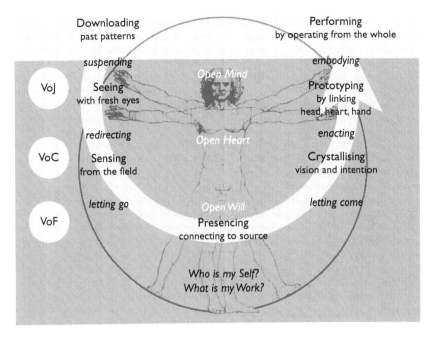

Figure 10.1. Depiction of 'Theory U'.

systems we co-create, suspending the voice of cynicism, with which one wants to disengage and move to "presencing", in a place of stillness to access our authentic purpose and self, where we can let go and let new possibilities emerge, which is suggested to be the manifestation of open will, suspending the voice of fear.

While pictured as a flow, the U is an iterative process, because "Instead you dance with what surrounds you and with what emerges from within all the time. You dance all three movements of the U simultaneously, not sequentially" (Scharmer, 2009, p.45). The question is with what attention and intention we choose to move? If source is in us, or, rather, is us, then it is part of everything and everything is in me. This is similar to what is described in "The absolute in the present; ". . . within me and without me are the same" (Saraswati, 1992, p. 9, cited in Bazalgette et al., 2006, p. 7)

At the time, there were two different events where I experienced the sense of connectedness and oneness described above. The first was when I listened to Queen Beatrix of the Netherlands as she expressed her despair and deep sadness for the drama on 30 April 2009, Queen's

Day, when seven people were killed by a car deliberately driven into the celebrating public. Thousands of miles away from my home country, and several hours later through the time difference, sitting in front of a laptop, I felt tears rolling down, in what was quite a raw connectedness with a deeper universal sense of grief and loss expressed by her as a (grand)mother, a stateswoman, and a usually strong and composed woman.

The other moment was when facilitating a debrief session at a retreat with public sector managers in Trinidad, in which Theory U had guided the design, where, at a key moment, each person shared a story about their role, passion, and concerns. It was a rare moment of flow, where a universal level of connection emerged that was deeper than each one of us and there were no boundaries between them or between them and me as a foreign facilitator, a stranger. The oneness I felt was an embracing sense of gratitude, generosity, and acceptance, which, in hindsight, felt like a significant spiritual "here and now" experience. It was in a spirit of enquiry and wonder that I could let go of fears of acceptance and of the cynicism that opened a self to access deeper experiences of connectedness with source.

That understanding of connectedness as "within and without" seems to become synonymous with a cosmic oneness, not as the basic assumption oneness behaviour described by Turquet (1985), but as a place of generative purpose and creativity that transcends a religious interpretation of source as objectified God. How effectively can we access a level of consciousness that enables that connectedness to source in our hectic day-to-day lives and what does the awareness of connectedness then reveal about the choices we continuously make to create our destiny and our accountability for what we create?

I was wondering what link could be made between one's ability to access source at the bottom of the U, presencing in the call to self and purpose with the concepts of consciousness development (Barrett, 2006) and stages of adult development (Cook-Greuter, 2004; Kegan, 1994). The working hypothesis around this is that many of these concepts focus at the level of person and personal development, which could be taken further to the person-in-role, taken up in a system.

Barrett (2006) uses a model, based on Maslow's hierarchy of needs, to describe the development of consciousness at seven levels. In that model, the bottom three levels focus on self-interest and meeting the needs of ego, the top three focus on spiritual needs, connectedness, and common good—using such terms as "to find meaning, make a difference and be of service" (see Figure 10.2). The transitional space between bottom and top is positioned as a circle; it is level four, the space where one faces the fears and human ego needs of survival, belonging, and status to enable the development of a connection with the soul, one's own and that of systems to the context and world to which one belongs.

Development of consciousness is suggested to be development of the full spectrum, not a hierarchical process, and this speaks to the fact that it is not about developing as a human being from an inferior level one to the ultimate level seven, but to be able to master level by level and being able to hold those levels of consciousness together.

This model helps me to develop compassion towards my own development and to understand that in a journey of transformation one moves through level four, while still acknowledging the struggle that happens at lower levels and acknowledging the journey ahead.

At level four, I can start to access "the bottom of the U" and connect to source, but also understand why there are still many ques-

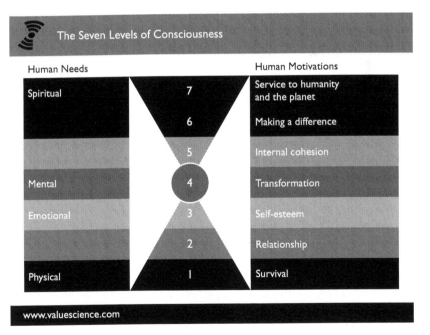

Figure 10.2. The seven levels of consciousness model (Barrett, 2006).

tions unanswered and why I am often dancing around desire and purpose, almost scared to touch the unconscious "un-thought known" (Bollas, 1989).

The other concept that helps to link consciousness development with the experience of connectedness with source is Kegan's description of the stages of adult development (1994) (Figure 10.3), and the further development of his idea by Wilbur in his integral approach (2001).

As with my understanding of Barrett's concept, it is at stage five (Kegan starts his model with stage 2), the "integral self", as depicted in Figure 10.3, where the individual has developed the inner cohesion to acknowledge and hold the light and darker sides of self, is able to recognise and accept them in others, and greet them and self with compassion. At this stage, I can see self as us, accepting the connectedness, and sense the oneness with the whole, with source, or with what others might call creation.

This sense of oneness links me also to the South African spirit of the word "*Ubuntu*"—I am because we are (Bazalgette & Reed, 2004), a word that has stayed with me since reading De Liefde's (2002) book on African tribal leadership and the references in Bazalgette and Reed (2004). It emphasises the connectedness of the person with its community; it points me to my personal desire to belong, and it links me now

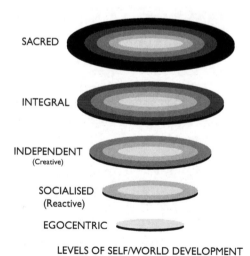

SACRED

INTEGRAL

INDEPENDENT
(Creative)

SOCIALISED
(Reactive)

EGOCENTRIC

LEVELS OF SELF/WORLD DEVELOPMENT

Figure 10.3.   Five stages of development (Kegan, in Anderson, 2005).

more explicitly to the notion of accountability because if "I am because we are" instead of the individualist Cartesian perspective of "I am because I think", then that helps me to accept that there is a sound basis for the accountability that I sense I have as a human being to the collective of humanity, which goes beyond the perspective of religion, to the sense of connectedness and oneness described earlier.

At this point, I came across an intriguing question asked by Ken Wilbur (2001) after he describes in his integral approach how individuals and society evolve through waves of human existence, or spiral dynamics, using the research done by Beck and Cowan (2005). The question he explores is whether we (still) need religion if we move up in our levels of consciousness as a society and as individuals? It is a hypothesis I could be working with, which allows me to step away from the resentment, tension, and impatience expressed earlier about the role of religion and maybe accepting religion and religious institutions as part of human development, not as ends in themselves.

Now, in what way is the spiritual journey described above opening up further understanding of accountability? The key question raised in Bazalgette and colleagues (2006, p. 8, quoting Irvine, 2005, p. 3) is "How can we individually and corporately take responsibility for the world we have contributed to create as it is and make decisions that lead to actions to heal and transform the world?" I sense the deep-felt accountability; the one at an emotional and spiritual level, emerging at the moment we access "the bottom of the U", when we connect self to source and the boundaries between me and not-me disappear. If we can access our sense of purpose in life at that moment, we access an "unthought known", that scary part of us that we are currently dancing around without really touching it. What I became aware of through this writing is that the moment I can touch that and dance with it as a guiding partner, it is that moment where I cannot escape the felt accountability for my actions, which is what is giving them meaning.

Here, I can give new meaning to Sartre's accountability, mentioned earlier, to what moves me in "The absolute in the present"; when we make choices and take actions we become alive and determine our destiny and if we understand that "the way we connect our actions to a deeper form of connectedness with source, with purpose, with creation, "then we are aware that they have more meaning than our conscious intentions and that we are accountable for the outcomes of what we do" (Bazalgette et al., 2006, p. 7).

Conclusion

My personal question when writing this was inspired by the question: if "authority provides a frame to assess how a person uses his power and to whom he is accountable as a person taking a role in the world we live in, then to whom am I accountable (for my own purpose and role taking) if I do not believe in institutionalised religion or 'God'?" (Bazalgette et al., 2006, p. 45). It seems that the answer to this question lies in self, meaning that if one can suspend judgement, cynicism, and fear and let go to connect with source and connect to that which lies within and what is outside me at the same time, in these rare moments of silence or deeper human connection, one can feel all as one and all in me, with an instant invitation to take accountability for what one creates. Even if one feels limited in one's capacity to change the world, once one can access the inner source of purpose and connectedness, one becomes accountable to self and, thus, to the world we are co-creating.

Writing this chapter has contributed to a glimpse of the purpose and the true source of energy and passion deeper inside; it confirms my vocational desire for facilitating and contributing to the development and transformation of fellow human beings and, through their learning, opening up new learning for self as well, not at the macro scale of an entire nation or population, but at the small scale of one-by-one transformation.

This implies also my accountability to be aware of my own stage of development and how that might be both enabler as well as obstacle when working with others. For instance, if, as organisational analyst, my task is to facilitate a learning space for others, I have to be aware of how and when my own anxieties and ego needs become part of the working relationship and how to use them. If, unconsciously, there is a desire to seek approval or recognition, there is a risk of losing the integrity of the working relationship, that is, by holding back or playing "nice". Or, if I am not aware of a higher developmental question and awareness coming from a client because I am operating from a lower stage of development, then his/her question might scare me or make me feel inadequate and generate defensive or basic assumption activity (Bion, 1961). However, through moments of stillness, through extra-vision and journaling, as a practitioner I can follow my own U process and learn to see with fresh eyes, to sense what is happening within that I need to let go of, in order to "let come" new and different sources of working material for the situation and its purpose.

The reality is that healing happens between people, the wound in me evokes the healer in you, and the wound in you evokes the healer in me, and then the two healers collaborate. (Rachel Naomi Remen, quoted by Anderson, 2005, p. 14)

In retrospect

Writing this chapter was itself a spiritual activity, a reflection of the struggle of letting go to let deeper connection with self emerge, which, at times, brought tears and frustration. Very much a person-in-role journey, sharing the thoughts and questions with others made the separateness fade away, creating a sense of relief and moments of stillness, opening doors to a higher sense of consciousness and a feeling of oneness with the world where connectedness with source was possible.

This is the reflection of a journey, my journey of about six years ago. It will be different for others. It would be differently described and analysed if done on a clean slate today. It is with gentle curiosity that I review the then end now, trying to honour the organisational analyst in becoming that I am as well as the experience of myself as the organisational analyst today.

References

Anderson, R. (2005). The spirit of leadership, is change possible? Position Paper www.theleadershipcircle.com.

Armstrong, D. (1992). The need for strangers: introduction to Dialogue at Social Dreaming for Management of Transformations, London, Grubb Institute.

Barrett, R. (2006). *Building a Values Driven Organisation: A Whole System Approach to Cultural Change*. Oxford: Butterworth-Heinemann.

Bazalgette, J., & Reed, B. (2004). *Reframing Reality in Human Experience*. London: The Grubb Institute.

Bazalgette, J., Irvine, B., & Quine, C. (2006). The absolute in the present: role, the hopeful road to transformation. In: A. N. Matur (Ed.), *Dare to Think the Unthought Known?* (pp. 89–119). Tempere, Finland: Aivoairut.

Beck, D. E., & Cowan, C. (2005). *Spiral Dynamics: Mastering Values, Leadership and Change*. Chichester: Wiley Blackwell.

Bion, W. R. (1961). *Experiences in Groups*. London: Tavistock.

Bollas, C. (1989). *The Shadow of the Object: Psychoanalysis of the Unthought Known*. New York: Columbia University Press.

Cook-Greuter, S. R. (2004). Making the case for a developmental perspective. *Industrial and Commercial Training, 36*(7): 1–10.

Irvine, G. B. (2005). Being meaning engaging: resistance and transformation in systems. Presented to the International Group Relations Conference, The Grubb Institute, London.

Kegan, R. (1994). *In Over our Heads: The Mental Demands of Modern Life*. Cambridge, MA: Harvard University Press.

Liefde, W. H. J. (2002). *African Tribal Leadership for Managers—From Dialogue to Decision*. Netherlands: Kluwer [in Dutch].

Sartre, J.-P. (1956). *Being and Nothingness: An Essay on Phenomenology*. London: Routledge. Original publication in French (1943): *L'Etre et le néant: Essai d'ontologie phénoménologique*. Paris: Gallimard.

Sartre, J.-P. (1989). Existentialism is a humanism, P. Mairet (Trans.). In: W. Kaufman (Ed.), *Existentialism from Dostoyevsky to Sartre* (pp. 345–368). Santa Barbara, CA: Meridian.

Scharmer, C. O. (2009). *Theory U: Learning from the Future as it Emerges*. San Francisco, CA: Berrett-Koehler.

Turquet, P. M. (1985). Leadership: the individual and the group. In: A. D. Colman & M. H. Geller (Eds.), *Group Relations Reader 2* (pp. 71–87). Springfield, VA: A. K. Rice Institute.

Wells, S. (2006). *God's Companions: Reimagining Christian Ethics*. Oxford: Blackwell.

Wilbur, K. (2001). *A Theory of Everything: An Integral Vision for Business, Politics, Science and Spirituality*. Boston, MA: Shambhala.

INDEX

abuse, 51, 139, 181
  of children, 156, 181, 202
Adorno, T. W., 46, 82
Age of the Sage.com, 45
Alagiah, G., 123
Anderson, R., 238, 241
anxiety, 8, 21, 39, 41, 49, 55, 63, 67, 70,
      81–82, 85, 107–109, 118–120, 125,
      140, 143, 152, 175, 178, 184–186,
      193, 224, 233, 240
  annihilation, 64
  normal, 70
  of survival, 21
  protean, 116
  provoking, 49, 141
  secondary, 70
  social, 64
  unconscious(ness), 140–141
Aram, E., 71
Aristotle, 36, 207
Armstrong, D., 8, 11, 70, 81, 85, 145,
      179, 183, 234
Aurelio, M. S. G., 40
autonomy, 1, 86, 119, 137, 141, 157,
      167, 190, 218

Bain, A., 65–66, 121
Bakan, J., 95
Barrett, R., 236–238
Baxter, R., 71
Baynes, H. G., 53
Bazalgette, J. L., xx, 10, 12, 116, 125,
      143, 149, 158, 165, 181, 219,
      231–232, 235, 238–240

Beck, D. E., 157, 239
behaviour(al)
  analysing, 196
  assumption, 27, 67
  chains of, 70
  changes, 185–186
  corporate, 132
  disciplined, 146
  emotionally linked, 95
  evocative, 56
  exemplifying, 197
  group, 67
  human, 110, 219, 227
  individual, 95
  instinctive, 199
  lived, 222
  manipulative, 116
  moral, 95
  national, 218
  organisational, 216
  outward, 124
  private, 196
  psychology, 45
  psychosomatic, 177
  public, 196
  reaction, 94
  realisation, 219
  system, 172
  transformed, 125
  unconscious(ness), 110
Benedek, L., 56
Benjamin, J., 66–67
Bennis, W. G., 81
Bergolio, J., 201

Berlin, H., 95
Bhaumik, M., 209
Bion, W. R., 21–22, 40, 58, 61–71, 75,
    111, 127, 132, 219
    cited works, 6, 8, 10, 40, 52, 61–63,
        65, 68–69, 73, 91, 126, 149,
        178–179, 181, 219, 240
    O, 62, 87, 149
Boccara, B., 70, 84–87
Bohm, D., 90
Bollas, C., 64, 74, 238
Bott Spillius, E., 55, 62
Brewster, B., 82
Briskin, A., 129
Brochure, 115
Brown, N. O., 26, 46
Brunner, L., 71

case studies
    Lina, 136–141, 146–148, 150
    Malik Abdul Hakim, 200–201, 204,
        206, 221
Chalquist, C., 53
Chattopadhyay, G., 79, 129, 149, 216
Chiasson, P., 91
Chiesa, M., 73
Clarke, S., 61–62
Clinton, B., 110, 126–128, 131–132
Clinton, R. H., 155
conscious(ness) see also:
    unconscious(ness)
    aspirations, 140
    associations, 59
    awareness, 95, 137, 173
    choices, 169
    collective, 52
    connections, 182
    desires, 7
    development(al), 236, 238
    domination, 82
    ego, 50
    engagement, 179
    experience, 6–7
    false, 82–83
    focus, 63
    human, 232

indebtedness, 141
intentions, 239
knowledge, 62
level, 130, 173, 212
motivator, 140
pre-, 50, 79
purposive idea, 49
reasoning, 50
reflections, 94
repression, 87, 93
self-, 36–38, 48, 88
splitting, 212
sub-, 199
thinking, 61, 95
translation, 49
will, 94
Cook-Greuter, S. R., 236
Couve, C., 55, 62
Cowan, C., 157, 239
Culler, J. D., 43
cultures, xv, 7–8, 13, 53, 76, 93, 95,
        207, 209, 217 see also: phantasy
    contemporary, 123
    human, 93
    organisational, 8
    urban, 201
    western, 1, 123

Das, S. B., 38
Davin, A., 91
De Coster, P. L., 53
Descartes, R., 36–37, 42, 52
development(al) see also:
    conscious(ness)
    adult, 24, 236, 238–239
    child, 80
    conceptual, 119
    edge, 17
    epistemological, 39
    germ theory, 43
    group, 81
    human, xxi, 17, 196–197, 215
        personality, 39
    leadership, 135
    of group relations, 20
    of intellect, 6

of personhood, 6
personal, 7, 79, 124, 236
physical, 6
professional, 220
psychology, 6
roots, 51
DeWaal, F., 213
Dictionary.com, 55
Donne, J., 127

ego, 7, 39–40, 48–51, 57, 59, 62, 80–82,
    87, 92, 193, 209, 236, 240 *see also*:
    conscious(ness)
  boundaries, 60
  -centric, 5
  forces, 48
  human, 237
  ideal, 50, 67, 81, 140–141
  individual, 9, 12
  psychology, 58
  super-, 48–50, 62, 67
Ehrenzweig, A., 63, 91
Eisold, K., 94
Elam, K., 43
Elfrida Rathbone Society, 19
Encyclopedia Brittanica, 55
envy, 69, 72, 126, 137–138, 141, 146,
    151–152, 181, 184, 214 *see also*:
    unconscious(ness)
European Graduate School (EGS),
    43

fantasy, 8, 86, 115, 124, 148
Fazioni, N., 59, 78
Ferenczi, S., 56
Fertuck, E. A., 95
Feynman, R., 16
Ffytche, M., 37, 46
Fisch, R., 88
Flowers, B., 145
Foucault, M., 42–43
Foulkes, S. H., 75–77
Fraher, A. L., 71
free association, xx, 47, 63–64, 89–90,
    92
  collective, 90

French, R., 68, 131
Frenkel Brunswick, E., 46, 82
Freud, S., xx, 17, 36–37, 39–41, 44–59,
    61–65, 67, 73, 77–78, 80–82, 85,
    89–92, 96
  cited works, 32, 39, 44, 47, 49–51,
    56, 61, 67, 78, 88
  Dora, 56
  Wolf Man, 51
Fromm, E., 75–77

Gallagher, M. P., 157, 202
Gardner, M., 41
Garvey, P., 55, 62
Gilmore, T., 166, 178, 216–217
Ginzberg, C., 91
Girard, R., 77–78, 81
Glover, N., 40
Goffman, E., 12
Gomes, M. E., 17
Gould, L., 65–66, 68, 80
Greene, J. D., 94–95
Grotstein, J., 40–63, 69
Grubb, 24, 26, 113, 117–118, 121, 187,
    196, 231–232
  foundation, 20
  Guild, xx, 15, 71
  Institute, xv–xvii, xx–xxi, 4, 20, 71,
    108, 111, 114–116, 118–119,
    121, 125, 127–128, 130, 132,
    135, 142, 149–150, 196–197, 217
  International Conference, 117
  Masters programme, xx, 15, 175, 231
  School of Organisational Analysis,
    xvi, 196
guilt, 81, 130, 141, 150, 183, 186
  see also: unconscious(ness)
Gutmann, D., 117, 127, 141

Habermas, J., 82
Hammer, A., 54
Harney, M., 31, 33, 45, 89–91, 94
Harre, R., 88
Heidegger, M., 36
Herder, J. G., 43–44, 68
Hinshelwood, R., 70, 73

Hirschhorn, L., 66, 70, 166, 178, 216–217
Hochschild, A., 84
Hoggett, P., 52, 83–84, 87
Hopper, E., 76–77
Humbert, D., 81
Hutton, J., 148, 175

id, 48–50, 55, 62, 93
  instinctual, 40
illusion, xxi, 25, 89, 196, 199, 209, 211, 214–218, 221–222
  articulated, 221
  collective, 84
  dis-, 155
  shared, 218
  space, 84
instinct, 47, 49, 52 *see also*: unconscious(ness)
  death, 61
  drives, 44, 55
  forces, 49–50
  id, 40
  inherited, 48
  irrational, 59
  life, 61
  representations, 44, 49
  representatives, 50
  satisfaction, 55
intervention, xxi, 4, 35, 71, 75, 109, 189
Irvine, G. B., xv–xvii, 15, 125, 143, 149, 158, 165, 196–197, 219, 225, 239–240

Jameson, F., 83
Janis, I. L., 65
Jaques, E., 50, 70, 81
Jaworski, J., 145
Johnson, A. R., 113, 208
Johnson, B., 197–198
Jung, C. G., 40–41, 52–55, 88–89, 92

Kaes, R., 74
Kahn, S. R., 56
Kahneman, D., 94
Kanner, A. D., 17

Kant, I., 36, 44
Kegan, R., 236, 238
Kehoe, I., 231–232, 235
Kernberg, O., 57
Kets de Vries, M., 8
Khaleelee, O., 79
Klein, M., 56–58, 61–62, 64, 110–111, 212, 227
Krantz, J., 70
Kris, E., 48, 63

Lacan, J., 40, 52, 57–60, 64–65, 78, 80, 83, 86
  Imaginary, 58–60
  Real, 58–60
  Symbolic, 58–60
Laloux, F., 158
Lawrence, W. G., 64–65, 89, 111, 117, 121, 127, 149, 217
Lehman, P. R., 47
Lerner, M., 139
Levinson, D., 46, 82
Liefde, W. H. J., 238
Little, D., 82
Long, S. D., xix, 8, 10, 17, 31, 33, 35, 46, 52, 64–66, 70, 72, 83, 88–91, 95, 115, 142, 193
Love, J., 38

Macmurray, J., 10, 158
Malan, D., 50
Malhotra, A., 79
Mandela, N., xv, 123
Mant, A., 115
Marcuse, H., 46, 82
Marshall, I., 129
matrix, 68, 91 *see also*: unconscious(ness)
  dreaming, 89, 127
  -management, 183
  mental, 68, 70, 75
Matthews, B., 37
McAfee, N., 83, 87
McCaulley, M. H., 54
McGrath, S. J., 37–40, 46, 48
Menzies Lyth, I. E. P., 8, 21, 50, 70, 81

Miller, D., 8
Miller, E. J., 71, 111, 144, 161, 182–183, 212, 227
Milton, J., 55, 62
Mitchell, J., 80
Morgan-Jones, R., 68
Mullainathan, S., 17
Murray, H., 66
Murtagh, D., 25
Myers, I. B., 54
Myers-Briggs Inventory (MBTI), 54

narcissism, 39, 47, 64, 71–72, 80, 141, 149
National Health Service (NHS), 144
Neri, C., 89
New World Encyclopedia, 41
Newton, I., 209
Newton, J., 115
Nutkevitch, A., 71

Obama, B., 155–156, 172
Obholzer, A., 66
object(ive), 32, 36–37, 42–46, 51, 59, 62–63, 69, 81, 87, 89–90, 93, 119, 128, 131, 141, 211–212, 221
  element, 67
  endeavour, 46
  epistemological, 43
  evocative, 74
  exploration, 211
  external, 55–56
  inanimate, 215
  internal, 55–57
    psychic, 55
  lost, 59
  needed, 215
  of identification, 81
  of knowledge, 43
  partial, 51, 55
  physical, 215
  relations, 44, 51, 55–55, 67, 71
  study, 46
  subject–, 42, 46, 66
  transitional, xxi, 189, 196, 215

ways, 219
whole, 19
objectivity, 42, 76, 148
Ostroff, S., 129, 149, 180–182, 185
Ould Slahi, M., 214

Palmer, B., 20, 115, 132, 219
Pannikar, R., 149
personhood, 4, 6–7
phantasy, 51, 55, 57, 61, 84 *see also*: unconscious(ness)
  cultures, 67
  inner, 67
  internal, 57
  intrapersonal, 61
  introjective, 57
  projective, 56
Pistiner de Cortinas, L., 40
Plato, 44, 207
projection, 44, 55–56, 61, 109, 111, 122, 128, 135, 139, 198, 212, 214, 216, 221
  idealised, 173
  positive, 108
projective identification, 56–57, 61, 73
Puget, J., 57, 74

Quenk, N., 54
Quine, C., 143, 149, 158, 165, 175, 219, 239, 240

Rabstejnek, C. V., 36, 47
Ramadan, T., 198, 208–209
Redl, F., 81
Reed, B. D., xv–xvii, xx, 19–21, 111–121, 125–128, 130, 132, 179, 183, 217–219, 231–232, 235, 238
Reed, J. M., 231–232, 235
Reiff, P., 46, 80–81
repression, 32, 36–37, 48–50, 52–53, 60, 63–64, 80, 82–83, 95–96, 141 *see also*: unconscious(ness)
  action, 48
  ambition, 140
  desire, 87

emotions, 178
forces, 49, 51
idea, 49–50, 52
images, 52
material, 51
mechanisms, 83
motivations, 41
political, 82
process of, 47–48
representative, 49
social, 82, 87, 89–90
surplus, 82
trauma, 52
theory of, 47–48
thoughts, 49–51
Restivo, G., 52, 60
Rice, A. K., 20, 71, 111, 113–114, 118, 121, 127, 132, 144, 161, 183, 212, 227
Richmond Fellowship, 19
Rinpoche, S., 207
Rioch, M., 68, 113
Roberts, J., 214
Roberts, V. Z., xx, 66, 139–140, 181
Roszak, T., 17
Rustin, M., 8, 70, 81
Ryle, G., 45

Sanford, N., 46, 82
Sartre, J.-P., 231–234, 239
Scharmer, C. O., 145, 234–235
Schelling, F. W. J., xx, 33, 37–41, 43, 45, 47–48, 53–54, 63, 69, 79–80, 82, 87–88, 92
Schmidt, J., 38
Schopenhauer, A., 44–45
Schwartz, H., 80
self, 7–8, 36, 39, 55–56, 67, 128, 211–213, 234–236, 238–241
see also: conscious(ness)
-analysis, 36
-authorisation, 17
autonomous, 157
-critical, 131
-discipline, 124

-doubt, 186
-esteem, 197, 237
-evident, 10
greater, 113
-image, 198, 214
inner, 36
integral, 238
-interest, 202, 236
-made, 1, 24
-management, 164, 198
noumenal, 36
-realisation, 54, 143, 156
-recognition, 48
-regulation, 95
representations of, 57
-revelation, 37
-sacrifice, 78
sense of, 6
-serving, 139–141
shadow, 52
Senge, P., 145
Shafir, E., 17
Shakespeare, W., 2, 51
Hamlet, 2
Shapiro, E., 145
Sharov, A., 94
Sharpe, M., 83
Shepard, H. A., 81
Sher, M., 71, 131
Sievers, B., 8, 35, 66, 70, 72, 74, 115
Simpson, P., 68, 131
Skogstad, W., 70
Slater, P. E., 46
Smith, A., 213
social see also: anxiety, repression, unconscious(ness)
activism, 86
animals, 10
arenas, 83
arrangements, 76
breakdown, 80
care, 135
character, 75, 82
concept, 60
connectedness, 8
construction, 33

context, 3–4, 6, 9, 11, 47, 74–75, 93, 111, 117
contracts, 8
defences, 21, 50, 70, 81, 85
dreaming, 89, 91, 127
dynamics, 71, 77–78
effects, 83
establishment, 68–69
experiences, 83
factors, 7
forces, 48
groups, 7
history, 48, 89
ideas, 8, 68
inequalities, 7
institution, 43, 76
interactions, 75
issues, 76
justice, 77, 138, 147
knowledge, 89
learning, 165
level, 63, 67, 87, 95
life, 87
manufacture, 84
media, 86–87
memory, 74
mores, 51
movements, 86–87
nature, 68
networking, 87
perspectives, 76
position, 2
processes, 33, 72, 74, 77
products, 11
psycho-, 47, 86–87, 93
psychological space, 76
rebellion, 69
relations, 82, 93, 198, 208
relevance, 111
scientists, 33, 66
service, 112
structure, 1, 93, 110
systems, 2–4, 7–9, 11, 46, 70–71, 74, 77, 79, 89, 93
technology, 234
theory, 46, 66, 78, 88

transformation, 120
unawareness, 76–77
understanding, 46
worker, 11
spirituality, xvi, xxi, 22, 25–26, 120, 125, 129, 149, 151, 196, 201, 216, 219, 226
splitting, 37, 56, 65, 81, 111, 122, 128, 131, 135, 138–140, 146, 208, 212, 214, 216, 221 see also: conscious(ness), unconscious(ness)
Cartesian, 17
internal, 132
Stapley, L., 66
Stein, M., 66, 181
Steiner, C., 55, 62
Swami Nikhilananda, 217
Symington, J., 62
Symington, N., 62

Tavistock
group relations method, 113
Institute, 20, 33, 71, 110–111, 117, 227
tradition, 33
Ternier-David, J., 141
The Koran, 200, 205
The New Oxford Dictionary of English, 9, 214
Thompson, S., 84
Torres, N., 68
transference, 56–57, 73, 76, 131, 233
see also: unconscious(ness)
counter-, 57, 131
dynamics, 57, 75
transforming experience framework (TEF), xix–xxi, 2, 4–5, 7–9, 15, 21–22, 33–35, 47, 52, 65, 71, 74, 87, 92, 142–143, 145–146, 149–151, 159–160, 183, 189, 211, 220, 224–225, 231
trauma, 28, 52, 63, 70, 83–85
Trist, E., 66
Turquet, P., 20, 65, 111, 113–114, 132, 236

unconscious(ness) *see also*: anxiety,
    behaviour(al), conscious(ness)
  activity, 41
  associative, 31, 56, 88–93
  assumptions, 65, 73
  cognitive, 94
  collective, 52–53, 89
  collusion, 84
  complexes, 53
  connections, 13, 89
  creative, 92
  deeply, 10
  defences, 12
  desires, 7
  drives, 55
  dynamics, 46, 67, 71, 73, 77–78, 84,
      87
  emotional, 94
  enacted, 26
  envy, 141
  feelings, 178
  guilt, 140, 147
  ground, 38
  group, 74
  ideas, 51
  infinite, 65, 69, 73, 88
  instinct, 80
  interpretive, 59
  issues, 76
  level, 8, 54, 78, 130
  linguistic, 78
  material, 49
  matrix, 75
  network, 68, 89
  obstacles, 115
  personal, 52–53, 178
  perversion, 72
  phantasy, 56–57
  political, 83
  primordial, 48
  processes, xx, 32, 34–36, 41, 46–47,
      57–58, 61–65, 70–74, 76, 82,
      87–88, 92, 95–96, 115, 121, 123,
      127, 181, 185, 219
  purposes, 219
  reaction, 93
  real, 59
  replication, 76
  representations, 53
  repression, 55, 70, 82, 87–89, 92–93
  scanning, 63
  signifiers, 59
  social, 75–76, 82
  spirit, 37
  splitting, 212
  structuring, 59
  system, 44, 47, 51
  task, 21
  thoughts, 32, 90, 92, 95
  transference, 59–60
  unity, 36

Verrier, C., 141
violence, 77–78, 109, 199, 201
Volkan, V. D., 76, 84

Waska, R., 57
Watzlawick, P., 88
Weakland, J., 88
Wells, S., 233–234
Western, S., 86–87
Wheatley, M. J., 175
White, A., 40
White, K., 79
Whitehead, A. N., 131
Whyte, L., 41–42, 46, 63
Wicks, R., 44
Wilbur, K., 238–239
Williams, R., 108
Winfield, N., 202
Winnicott, D. W., xxi, 6, 58, 62, 148,
    196, 215, 218, 222
Wollaston, S., 214
Woodard, B., 40, 88

yearning, 5, 7, 28, 80, 143, 150, 160,
    208, 220

Žižek, S., 83
Zohar, D., 129